Transforming Despair to Hope

Transforming Despair to Hope: Reflections on the Psychotherapeutic Process with Severely Neglected and Traumatised Children offers a thorough overview of the problems and rewards of trying to help severely neglected and traumatised children. Drawing on over 40 years of clinical experience, Monica Lanyado provides a historical and social perspective on this challenging population, as well as helpful theoretical frameworks and thoughtful support for all professionals and clinicians working with these children.

This book brings together selected past writings and new chapters from Lanyado. In it she describes the consequences of severe neglect and trauma on a child's emotional development, and then goes on to examine what it is that brings about positive change. By using vivid clinical examples of therapeutic practice with these children, she elucidates the difficulties associated with this population, as well as for those who care for them in families and in residential settings.

Transforming Despair to Hope is a valuable resource for child and adolescent mental health professionals and trainee clinicians, as well as those in related fields working with children in need.

Monica Lanyado is a child and adolescent psychotherapist who has worked with severely neglected and traumatised children for 40 years. She is a training supervisor at the British Psychotherapy Foundation. Her publications include *The Presence of the Therapist: Treating Childhood Trauma* (2004) and, co-edited with Ann Horne, *The Handbook of Child and Adolescent Psychotherapy: Psychoanalytic Approaches* (1999, 2009) and the Independent Psychoanalytic Approaches with Children and Adolescents series.

Independent Psychoanalytic Approaches with Children and Adolescents Series

Series Editors: Ann Horne and Monica Lanyado

Transforming Despair to Hope

Reflections on the Psychotherapeutic
Process with Severely Neglected
and Traumatised Children

Monica Lanyado

Routledge
Taylor & Francis Group

LONDON AND NEW YORK

First published 2018
by Routledge
2 Park Square, Milton Park, Abingdon, Oxon OX14 4RN

and by Routledge
711 Third Avenue, New York, NY 10017

Routledge is an imprint of the Taylor & Francis Group, an informa business

British Library Cataloguing-in-Publication Data
A catalogue record for this book is available from the British Library

Library of Congress Cataloging-in-Publication Data
A catalog record for this book has been requested

ISBN: 978-1-138-06471-3 (hbk)
ISBN: 978-1-138-06472-0 (pbk)
ISBN: 978-1-315-16026-9 (ebk)

Typeset in Times New Roman
by Florence Production Ltd, Stoodleigh, Devon, UK

Contents

Foreword

Peter Wilson

Children behave in all manner of ways. At different times and in different circumstances, they can impress, bewilder, shock, infuriate, delight, charm or alarm us and all else besides. Some, the majority, enter the world with a kind of readiness and curiosity that is so joyously creative that they delight and endear themselves to us. They are of course never perfect, hardly saints but they have been loved by devoted parents and their spirited mood and eagerness to learn heralds good things to come. But sadly, there are many other children whose lives are not so blessed, not so lucky in the way life has treated them. They encounter what happens to them with caution, mistrust and fear. They are on guard, forever looking over their shoulders for things that might threaten, things that are likely to disappoint, hurt or terrify them. And so much of this is expressed through attitudes that are wary and defiant and behaviours that are often angrily destructive, whether of themselves or others. Sadly, more often than not, they do not endear themselves to us.

The adult world – the parents, the carers, the teachers and the general public – greets the majority, for the most part, with pleasure and generosity. But for the others, they react in bafflement and outrage and are quick to condemn or disown. Some despair and turn a blind eye, resorting to vague notions of evil or untreatability. Others want to discipline or 'treat', punish or medicate. But surprisingly few, whether it be in the professional field or not, seem at all inclined to ask seriously what it is that could have possibly happened in the early lives of these young human beings to have brought about behaviour, so difficult, so hostile and at times so violent.

The overriding value of this book is that it steadfastly gets down to attempting to answer that question and a whole host of others, just as puzzling and perplexing. What, for example, are the meanings and consequences for children of being stuck at the butt end of the various maltreatments meted out to them by the very adults upon who they depend so much? And, to quote from the book, 'How much recovery is really possible in such damaged internal and external lives?' What is the most productive way of helping these children in the therapy room? This book, in other words, faces the appalling travesties that so many children with behavioural problems have endured and, despite all the indignities that have followed, reaches some clarity and resolve in finding new and more constructive paths in helping these children move forward.

Monica Lanyado has brought together a collection of both her new and past writings that focus on the sheer psychotherapeutic challenge of understanding the disturbed behaviour of the children she has known in her clinical work, and heard about through seminars and supervisions – behaviour that simply defies clear orderly explanation. She shows an unfailing preparedness to lend her imagination and thought to finding ways into the child's experience and inner psychic world. As always, she does so with compassion and courage. And, throughout the book, she gives a range of case examples that so movingly and vividly illustrate the awfulness of some children's lives and the sheer fortitude and determination of those child psychotherapists who have set out to make these children's lives more bearable.

At the center of her heart and mind is something so fundamental that the short word used to describe it may sound insufficient to do justice to its severity. The word is 'neglect' and its importance can only be underlined enough through magnifying its meaning. Essentially, neglect, if nothing else, is a profound failure on the part of parents and carers to respect and meet the physical and emotional needs of the child – for nurturance, for comfort, for protection, for stimulation and for affirmation. At worse, this failure may be malicious. But more often, it is a reflection of the tragic circumstances that many families have suffered which have interfered with parents' natural ability and willingness to do what they know to be right or good enough. The horror of the story of neglect is that in its wake, anything goes, whether it be abuse of the physical, sexual and/or emotional kind. Care is simply not forthcoming or held; there are no bounds.

Inherent in neglect is despair, a hopeless abandonment of any sense of possibility that life could be enlivening and enriching. Parents for one reason or another have given up, lost connection or any hint of attachment – some heartlessly, some helplessly and others with guilt and sadness. And as a result, children are left in isolation, alone, untrusting and in jeopardy. They are basically rendered terrified, angry and unwilling or unable to comply, to 'behave'. Too often, they give up, hide themselves away in some kind of narcissistic retreat; or protest, fight and, as Winnicott once put it, 'stake their "claim"' on that which has been withheld or taken away. These children have had to find ways of somehow holding themselves together in their fray, to make use of whatever defensive manoeuvre they might find within themselves to block out feeling, harden against intimacy and forestall being hit and hurt. It can be of no surprise to anyone reading this book why some children behave so aggressively, disruptively and offensively.

This is the work of a highly accomplished child psychotherapist who, like her colleagues and students whom she teaches, is prepared to venture into the psychic turmoil of the child, and whose understanding has been, and is, informed and inspired by psychoanalysis, developmental psychology and neuroscience. Children who are showing the greatest difficulties in their behaviour and attitude need desperately this kind of child psychotherapeutic involvement. Other forms of therapy, based on more cognitive, 'objective' and rational approaches, simply fall far short of providing anything near to what is needed. None of this work is at all easy; it places enormous emotional demands on the child psychotherapists who attempt to carry it out. Nor is it, of course, a quick fix. It is unrealistic to expect that the future lives of the children described in this book will be free of the scars and impairments inflicted upon them as a legacy of their rocky foundations. Favourable outcomes will not be immediate, nor always clear – at best, 'small islands' of change in personality may occur together with some diminution in aggressive behaviour and a greater capacity and energy to find and accept the true nature of their selves.

But what this book shows above all is the sheer humanity of vulnerable and young people – those 'seriously neglected and traumatised' – for whom due attention must be properly paid. What is so uplifting in this book is Monica Lanyado's message of hope – not one of treacly unrealistic sentimentality, but one that has evolved out of the hard facing of hard truths and an implicit faith in young human beings' search for something better in their lives, despite the odds against them. Her therapeutic work shows the value of the therapist's sustained attention and perseverance against the force of inevitable resistance. It also shows her belief in the value of play, the very serious business of personal exploration and discovery.

This is not only an important message for psychotherapists and others seeking to help, but also for those commissioners and politicians who have the power to determine and prioritise the funding of child and adolescent mental health services. Commissioners may of course find themselves having to cut such funding under the prevailing conditions of economic austerity. However, so long as they decide to curtail the kind of work described in this book, whether it be because of funding or, maybe much more to the point, through an unwillingness to bear looking at the misfortunes of these children, they shall forever sell these children short of the help they need, much to the cost of the emotional, social, intellectual and spiritual lives of these children, their families and ultimately to the cost of us all.

Acknowledgements

Beginning with my father, I have been very fortunate to have been blessed with many teachers in my life, each of whom have guided and inspired me in their own unique ways. This book is the result of what they, my patients, colleagues, supervisees and seminar members have taught me. It gives me great pleasure to have the opportunity to acknowledge all I have learnt from them and to express the gratitude I feel towards them.

Over many years of working together, my thanks go to Ann Horne for patiently reading, commenting on and encouraging me with many drafts of the chapters and the paper reprinted in this book. Jill Wilson, Peter Wilson and John Simmonds all gave generously of their time when I was researching some aspects of this book, as did my supervisees and their colleagues in commenting on my accounts of their clinical work in the context of individual chapters. As confidentiality is so important in psychotherapy, there are many people I cannot mention by name, however I can directly thank Coralie Lasvergnas, Elspeth Pluckrose, Jo Bent-Hazelwood, Robert Fleming, Kasia Zych, Lynne Conway and Kate Mills for the stimulation of the work we have done together. Colleagues in my organisational home, Independent Psychoanalytic Child and Adolescent Psychotherapy Association (IPCAPA) at the British Psychotherapy Foundation (BPF), and particularly Janine Sternberg, have been a source of great encouragement and support as well as friendship. I am very grateful for this. Many thanks also go to Joanne Forshaw at Routledge who has been the editor of the books I have written or co-edited with Ann Horne. It is very good to have her and Routledge's expertise in bringing beautifully produced books to fruition.

The two patients referred to by the names of 'Sammy' and 'Gail' were seen many years ago and, although I have tried to contact them again in the preparation of this book, it was not possible. I have clearly learnt a tremendous amount from thinking and writing about their therapy and I hope that if they or their families should by any chance come across my writings, they will appreciate the debt that I owe to them.

Sadly, many of my important teachers are no longer alive, but their influence and the memory of all I learnt from them remain strongly with me. Firstly, my father Kurt Feldman who was a loving and gentle maths teacher who drew what were then called 'backward' and troubled children to him, and somehow managed to teach them some maths. Years later they would still greet him on the street with affection. As a teenager, I was extremely fortunate to be a part of a discussion group with Rabbi Lionel Blue at the start of his rabbinical career and he remained a lifelong friend. His influence on my ethical, moral and spiritual development paved the way for my interest in meditation, so that when in my thirties I met Margaret Sampson, a member of Irina Tweedie's Sufi group, I immediately recognised that she was the meditation teacher I needed to help me to develop this side of my Self. Through many years of learning from her wisdom, I gained a very broad perspective on life which remains as powerful as ever. The integration of ideas from psychoanalysis and meditation practice that are referred to in this book all started with what I learnt from Margaret Sampson.

Having had many stimulating psychoanalytic teachers, I was particularly fortunate to have years of supervision which grew into friendship with Frances Tustin and Isabel Menzies Lyth. The focus of my work became different from theirs over time, but it grew out of the to-and-fro of our conversations. I learnt a great deal from their intellectual integrity and ability to think freely about their clinical and professional observations, as well as their compassion and humanity. In addition, I am especially grateful to Rosemary Davis who enabled me to finally become myself in ways I would never have thought possible.

Much of what I have written over the years has been read by my dear friend, and at times fiercest critic, Tammy Fransman. I have learnt an enormous amount from her psychoanalytic knowledge, duly interspersed with shared observations of everyday family life in all its richness and diversity. This is a rare and creative combination.

And finally, my thanks go to Sam Rodin, who has given me the love, support and peace of mind to be able to immerse myself in writing. Through our life and conversations together, and his interests and deep knowledge, he has enabled me to find a mature voice with which to clarify and express what I have been trying to say.

I am grateful to Taylor and Francis Ltd. for the permissions to reprint the following chapters and journal article:

Lanyado, M. (2006) 'The playful presence of the therapist: "anti-doting" defences in the therapy of a late adopted adolescent patient'. Chap. 8 in M. Lanyado and A. Horne (eds) (2006) *A Question of Technique*: 13–148. London and New York: Routledge.

Lanyado, M. (2008) 'Playing out not acting out: the development of the capacity to play in the therapy of children who are "in transition" from fostering to adoption'. Chap. 9 in D. Hindle and G. Shulman (eds) (2008) *The Emotional Experience of Adoption. A Psychoanalytic Perspective*: 155–167. London and New York: Routledge.

Lanyado, M. (2009) 'The impact of listening on the listener. Consultation to the helping professions who work with sexually abused young people'. In A. Horne and M. Lanyado (2009) *Through Assessment to Consultation*: 141–156. London and New York: Routledge.

Lanyado, M. (2012) 'Transition and change: An exploration of the resonances between transitional and meditative states of mind and their roles in the therapeutic process'. Chap. 8 in A. Horne and M. Lanyado (eds) (2012) *Winnicott's Children*: 123–140. London and New York: Routledge.

Lanyado, M. (2016) 'Transforming despair to hope in the treatment of extreme trauma: a view from the supervisor's chair'. *Journal of Child Psychotherapy* 42(2): 107–121. Reprinted by permission of Taylor and Francis Ltd, www.tandfonline. com on behalf of Association of Child Psychotherapists.

Introduction

In the best of circumstances, ordinary families struggle at times with all the demands of parenthood and need as much help as they can get if they are to give their best to their children. A baby born to a young mother with mental health problems, a father who is drug and alcohol addicted, both unsupported by the extended family because of problematic relationships, poor housing and barely any money, has nearly all the cards stacked against him or her from the start of life. Without substantial help, parents such as these may neglect and traumatise their babies physically as well as emotionally, despite their often desperate wish not to do so.

Some of these parents are offered, and accept, help from specialised social care and perinatal resources; some are offered these resources but aren't able to make the commitment that this entails. Others aren't offered sufficient help when it is most needed. Some are offered help but cannot change sufficiently emotionally to be able to become good-enough parents. Or they might refuse the help offered because they are suspicious of those who are offering the help. In the meanwhile, the baby or young child is extremely vulnerable and possibly suffering significantly due to lack of care. Time is not on their side. Whilst they are not receiving the ordinary parental care that is essential for babies and young children to grow into emotionally healthy children, teenagers and adults, they are becoming more and more at risk of having serious relationship, mental health and social problems as they grow up and enter adult life.

But there is an area of uncertainty involved with these risk factors that allows room to act, and try to find a way of navigating the best possible path forward for these very unfortunate children and those who try to care for them. This book may be hard to read because of the awful and heart-wrenching life experiences described in it of the children and their parents. However, it is important to remember whilst reading these pages that there have been, and often remain, many people involved in these troubled lives, who are trying to help, and keep on trying to help. Hope requires a determination to try to change for the better, and find a way out from desperate relationships, feelings and circumstances.

As Solnit notes:

> Hope locates itself in the premises that we don't know what will happen and that in the spaciousness of uncertainty is room to act. When you recognise

uncertainty, you recognise that you may be able to influence the outcomes, you alone or you in concert with a few dozen . . . others. Hope is an embrace of the unknown and unknowable, an alternative to the certainty of both optimists and pessimists.

(Solnit 2016: xii)

Although each attempt to help may not be as effective as is hoped for, it can be a small step in the right direction, along the very difficult and demanding life journey that many of these children have to make. These small steps can accumulate into significant life changes, internally and externally. There are many people who choose to give deeply of themselves to nurture these children: foster and adoptive parents, children's home workers and the many professionals who choose to do such demanding work with the children. There are also many alarming mistakes that happen along the way, from which we have to learn as much as possible.

It is too easy to allocate blame to others in this emotionally charged work which very readily challenges our faith in humanity by exposing the worst side of human nature. When realistic hope cannot be maintained or is eroded, it is not possible to carry on doing the work. This is why, as well as being about the children themselves, this book is about sustaining the buoyancy of the professionals who at times despair about whether their efforts can have any effect at all on their very needy clients and patients. The many examples in this book, together with the theories that provide a framework for understanding and thinking about this work, show that it is possible to help some of these children and their families to transform the despair that they feel when they first come to therapy, into a more hopeful future. It is this that makes all the effort worthwhile.

The structure of the book

I have worked with this group of severely neglected and traumatised children, in one capacity or another, for all of my professional life. Since retiring from clinical practice, my role as a clinical supervisor and theoretical seminar leader has increased and I have been in the interesting and privileged position of hearing about many of my colleagues' work with these children. Being a clinical supervisor has enabled me to observe and learn from what has helped or hindered each unique patient–therapist couple in their work together. In many ways, this has been an informal naturalistic research experience. The clinical examples throughout the book come from my own and my supervisees' work and I am very grateful to them for all I have learnt from our work together.

Inevitably when reporting my supervisees' clinical work, some of the immediacy of the emotionality of the transference–countertransference experience is diluted. The examples from their work in Chapters 1, 3 and 4 are therefore more in the form of quite detailed clinical vignettes which, depending on the subject of the chapter, serve as examples of neglect, trauma, complex attachment relationships and loss. They also give insight into the therapeutic process over time.

As a theoretical seminar leader on the topic of severely neglected and traumatised children, and bereavement and endings, I have tried to think about which theories, ideas and research I have found helpful in providing some understanding of the complex therapeutic problems and processes, and the changes of clinical technique that are often required for these children.

This book is a combination of relevant selected papers published since I wrote *The Presence of the Therapist: Treating Childhood Trauma*, and four new chapters which provide an overarching theoretical, social and historical perspective on psychoanalytic psychotherapy with severely neglected and traumatised children (Lanyado 2004a).

The first chapter, 'The far-reaching consequences of neglect and trauma in childhood', describes the nature of childhood neglect and trauma which can lead to the need for local authorities to remove a child from their birth family. The consequences of this removal are manifold. The child now needs adults who can nurture him or her, and a new physical home. This need is responded to in varying ways in different countries. In the UK (for reasons that are expanded on in Chapter 2) children tend to go to foster homes and sometimes they move on to adoptive homes. Some older children might go to children's homes. This whole process has many problems, not the least of them being the fact that these children have highly ambivalent feelings towards family life with all its intimacies. Plus, foster and adoptive families often need much more support than they are offered and are inadequately prepared for the task. In other countries that have different policies and responses to the children's needs for a stable home, I am sure that there are other disadvantages and dilemmas. The underlying problem is the same: the impact that neglect and trauma have already had on the child before he or she is removed from their birth home, what kind of home is subsequently best provided for the child, and what therapeutically can be done to try to help them to recover from their very unfortunate starts in life. Child and adolescent psychoanalytic psychotherapists have been working with these children for many years and have gathered a wealth of clinical experience. A case example is given which illustrates some of the clinical, theoretical and technical issues involved including the central problem of finding the appropriate balance between remembering and forgetting the neglectful and traumatic past.

The second chapter, 'The historical and social context: influences on the treatment of severely neglected and traumatised children today', gives a more comprehensive perspective on the treatment of childhood neglect and trauma in the UK. Psychoanalysts Bowlby, Anna Freud and Winnicott were greatly affected by their wartime experiences of trying to help children who were separated from their families due to evacuation. This was reflected in their ideas and theories, during and post-war, about ordinary and disturbed children. Some years later, first the physical and then the sexual abuse of children was fully recognised. Understanding the enormous impact of major child abuse scandals helps in understanding how we have arrived at our present-day social policies in the UK about child protection. The debate about the advantages and disadvantages of residential care and foster and adoptive homes is expanded, with particular emphasis on the need to adequately support all the adults trying to provide this care. The value and tradition of good residential therapeutic child care is described. Psychoanalytic psychotherapy with severely neglected and traumatised children has developed within this broader context. For example, parent–infant psychotherapy, together with the contribution of developmental psychology research and neuroscience, has enriched understanding and treatment of these children. As always, there is a concern that financial decisions and cuts inevitably affect the quality of care and treatment that is possible. The short-sighted nature of not investing in treatment and prevention, when it is possible in childhood, needs to be set against the long-term consequences, often inter-generationally, of providing too little too late.

Chapter 3, 'The absence of "holding" and containment, and the absence of parental protection', discusses in more detail some of the psychoanalytic theories which are central to the understanding and treatment of these children. Winnicott's ideas about ordinary devoted parenting and all the emotional responsiveness that this requires are contrasted with the lack of caregiving that neglected and traumatised children have experienced (Winnicott 1960). Bowlby's emphasis on the centrality of the parent's caregiving and protective function, understood in a biological and evolutionary context, highlights the significance of the real-life extreme vulnerability that these babies and young children are exposed to (Bowlby 1953, 1979, 1988). As we sadly know too well, when parents have not only failed to protect their children from harm, but have actually perpetrated terrible harm on their own children, babies and young children can die. Some of the children discussed in this book have been rescued from homes when they were taken into care, just in time. They had sustained shocking physical injuries and, as neuroscientific research is now showing us, their brains and whole body systems have been terribly affected in the long term, as a result of living in prolonged situations of fear. The clinical example in this chapter is about a child like this. Bion's concepts of projection, introjection and containment are central to the therapeutic process and are described in detail (Bion 1962). Hurry and colleagues' ideas about the therapist functioning at times as a developmental object for the patient are introduced and form a backcloth for understanding the child's gradual recovery from parental neglect of these developmental emotional needs (Hurry 1998).

In addition to neglect, trauma and abuse, the level of loss that severely neglected and traumatised children have experienced is dreadful. There has been one complex loss after another in their lives, with no chance to begin to recover from one loss before another loss occurs. Their distress, anger or, for some, level of dissociation frequently has a profound impact on anyone who tries to form a new relationship with them. Their complex losses and the necessary and extreme defences that the children have needed to use to protect themselves from overwhelming pain are heart-breaking, but become known in the course of their psychotherapy. This subject is discussed in Chapter 4, 'Complex traumatic childhood losses: mourning and acceptance, endings and beginnings', together with the very difficult issue of how and when to end therapy with such a needy child. Clinical examples which highlight the complexity of these children's losses are given.

These first four chapters are followed by five papers which are relevant to the subject of this book and have been published before. Each paper is published here in its original form, even though this means there are some overlaps of ideas in parts of the chapters as readers may choose to read a chapter at a time rather than read the book as a whole. With this in mind, I have added to each chapter a brief preface which links it more specifically to the themes in the first four chapters.

Chapters 5 and 6 both highlight the importance of 'playing' in the Winnicottian sense, within the therapeutic relationship. Chapter 5, 'Playing out not acting out: the development of the capacity to play in the therapy of children who are "in transition" from fostering to adoption', is one of several papers I have written about the extraordinary and paradoxical emotional tasks of moving a young child from their foster home, to their adoptive home (Lanyado 2002, 2003, 2004). The importance of new transitional phenomena which can emerge in therapy at such times, what I have referred to as 'therapeutic transitional phenomena', is discussed, as are the multiple traumatic losses of the young child whose transition from fostering to adoption is the focus of the clinical example. Chapter 6, 'The playful presence of the therapist: "antidoting" defences in the therapy of a late-adopted adolescent patient', develops these ideas and includes a discussion of the value of the playful availability of the therapist (Lanyado, 2006). The technical challenges of working with such patients are discussed in some detail, as is the therapeutic value of 'moments-of-meeting', as described by Stern and his colleagues (Stern *et al.* 1998).

Chapters 7, 8 and 9 are all concerned with different ways of helping psychotherapists and other professionals who work with these children, to be sustained and supported in this emotionally demanding work. Possibly because of my awareness of the toll that working with such painful emotions can have on the practitioner, including of course myself, for many years I have been concerned with trying to strike the best possible work–private life balance (Lanyado 1988, 1989, 1993). Having seen some of my colleagues succumb to stress, burnout, stress-related illnesses and significant physical illness possibly related to overwork, I take this balance very seriously. One of the ways that I have found to be very helpful to me for many years is meditation. However, it is probably only in the last ten years or so that it has become more widely acceptable to try to integrate ideas about meditation and psychotherapy, within mainstream psychotherapy practice and publications. Chapter 7, 'Transition and change: an exploration of the resonances between transitional and meditative states of mind and their role in the therapeutic process', is a more detailed discussion of my thinking around this interesting subject (Lanyado 2012). The preface to this chapter adds some further ideas that are not in the chapter itself. The chapter brings together my thoughts about the importance of transitional experiences and phenomena, an idea which has run through my writing for many years (prompted by the patient discussed in Chapter 5), in relation to meditative states of mind in the therapist. The clinical example in this chapter is from the end of the therapy of the patient discussed in Chapter 6.

Chapter 8, 'The impact of listening on the listener: consultation to the helping professions who work with sexually abused young people', describes my work as an external consultant to the staff of a small residential unit (Lanyado 2009). Staff in these units have an incredibly difficult task and well-run units have carefully structured daily and weekly staff meetings of many different kinds, in which to try to understand, digest and work with the feelings which the very disturbed and disturbing children evoke in them. This enables the staff to continue to offer the most caring and understanding relationships that they can to the children, often in the face of the aggressive, violent and distressing experiences which are a daily part of life in such units. These meetings also facilitate the communication of conflictual and painful feelings within the staff group itself, enabling them to be thought about and worked on. This process contributes to the resilience and strength of the staff group in helping and understanding the children. Often a consultant who is 'outside' the staff group, and therefore able to have more of a perspective on the staff group dynamics, is central to the functioning of the unit. I had always appreciated the importance of working with these group dynamics, but hadn't been trained in this work. I was very fortunate to be supervised by Isabel Menzies Lyth for a number of years whilst I was consulting to the staff group discussed in this chapter. This experience both helped me, and in turn helped me to help colleagues, working in these settings to make more sense of what was going on. This experience also enabled me to gain a better understanding of the difficult group dynamics which can emerge in the professional network surrounding any child who is fostered or adopted. This has proved very valuable.

The final chapter, 'Transforming despair to hope in the treatment of severe trauma: a view from the supervisor's chair', comes from my more recent experiences of clinical supervision of psychotherapists in training and experienced colleagues (Lanyado 2016). This stimulating experience has prompted me to think a lot about what happens in the supervisory process which is helpful to the supervisee and in turn the patient. Having been on the receiving end of supervision and teaching which has sustained me in my work, it has been intriguing to have the opportunity to explore what has been so helpful to me in the past, and what is helpful to my own supervisees in the present. This chapter implicitly gives a picture of the continuity of learning that is passed from one generation of psychotherapists to another through the supervisory process. The title of the chapter has become part of the title of this book because it seemed to capture the essence of what psychotherapy with severely neglected and traumatised children is trying to achieve.

1 The far-reaching consequences of neglect and trauma in childhood

Some of the greatest literature of the nineteenth century tells vivid stories of children who were orphaned, rejected, abandoned or subjected to cruelty by those who were meant to be protecting them. Charles Dickens' *Oliver Twist* opens with powerful descriptions of the misery and deprivation of nine-year-old Oliver who has no parents and is being raised in the Victorian workhouse (Dickens 1837). Having dared to ask for more food he is literally sold into an 'apprenticeship' with an undertaker because the misery and unhappiness of his facial expressions make him an ideal person to accompany the hearse in funeral processions.

Oliver runs away from his apprenticeship because of the cruelty and physical abuse he suffers there, and is befriended on the streets by the Artful Dodger, a child thief, who lives with a gang of other child thieves under the protection of Fagin. Oliver has no other choices of how to survive and joins the gang, living under the criminal Fagin's protection. None of the children in the gang have families; they only have each other and Fagin, who teaches them how to pick pockets and live a life of crime. Fagin exploits the children but provides a bed and food away from the streets on which they would otherwise have to try to survive. He also provides a parody of parenting and the other boys in the gang provide a perverse sense of family. But this is only for as long as they carry on stealing for Fagin. If, like Oliver, they try to escape from the gang, they are ruthlessly pursued and brought back to the gang, because they 'know too much' and could tell the police about Fagin and his criminal contacts.

Although the book has a fairy tale-like happy ending for Oliver, *Oliver Twist* is a powerful description and statement by Dickens about the sordid lives and plight of poor, exploited, neglected and abused children in his time.

Victor Hugo, in his complex and moving book *Les Misérables*, created the child character Gavroche, who was about the same age as Oliver (Hugo 1862/1994). Unlike Oliver, he was not an orphan but had been thrown out of his rejecting, abusive and criminal home at any early age. He was expected to, and managed to fend for himself on the streets. He is a more resourceful character than Oliver and his name has become somewhat synonymous with the image of a loveable (and sentimentalised) Parisian street urchin. Gavroche managed to make himself useful to other street characters in a less criminal way than the boys in Fagin's gang, but he mostly lived on his own in odd scavenged nest-like places that he found around Paris. He did not trust any adults and chose self-sufficiency.

Hugo, like Dickens, was concerned with social reform and the vulnerability and desperation of the poor, the 'Misérables' of the title. Gavroche's fate is quite different from Oliver's. He is shockingly and deliberately killed by soldiers on the Parisian barricades of the short-lived student uprising of 1832, whilst trying to make himself useful to the students.

Great literature enables the reader to identify with characters such as Oliver and Gavroche, and briefly get a sense of what it would be like to live their lives. Great literature also survives the test of time when the issues in which it immerses the reader remain so pertinent and a part of ongoing life. The complex problems of how to help children who are so unprotected from the worst aspects of adult behaviour remain, even though there is much improvement in the attitude of responsible societies towards how this is best achieved. The children that this book is about are the survivors of similar starts in life to Oliver and Gavroche.

Whilst the impact of the reality of childhood trauma, particularly in the form of physical, sexual and emotional abuse, has received a great deal of attention since the 1950s, the subtle and pervasive effects of neglect have been much more difficult to recognise (Music 2011b). However, it is often as a result of parental neglect (however unintentional this may be) that children become vulnerable to being abused. My previous writings have focussed on the impact of trauma, and the psychotherapeutic processes which aid recovery (Lanyado 2004a, 2009). To redress this imbalance of not having paid specific attention to the impact of severe childhood neglect, the first four chapters of this current volume place the emotional significance of neglect in the foreground, setting the scene in which trauma takes place.

This group of children suffer from many serious difficulties which is the reason why it is so hard to care for and help them, particularly when they have had to be removed from their birth parents' home by the local authorities. In the UK, they are initially likely to be placed in foster homes and in time, if deemed appropriate by the courts, they may be adopted. They are likely to be highly reactive, frightened and frightening, wild, violent, angry, at times withdrawn and depressed, extremely demanding and controlling in all their relationships, full of hatred and neediness, anarchic, encopretic, eneuretic – the list goes on and on. Alongside these problems, they are often diagnosed as being on the autistic spectrum or attention deficit disordered. They are likely to be intellectually impaired or functioning well below their intellectual ability in school. They can become dangerously violent, self-harming and suicidal in adolescence. They can also become sexually promiscuous, delinquent and drug or alcohol dependent, as well as being diagnosed as mentally ill in adult mental health terms – for example, suffering from psychotic states of mind or paranoia.

In addition, the child is likely to have been very frightened, angry, traumatised and distressed by what happened leading up to, and at the time of being taken away from their birth parents. This is true even if there is relief at being removed from violent and neglectful homes. The loss of what is familiar, however awful that may be, is compounded by the unfamiliarity of the foster home despite the kindness and care they try to offer. Many of these children have needed to be removed from their birth parents' care well before the age of five. They are still very little when all these traumatic events have taken place. Also, the child, because of all the adverse relationships and circumstances of the birth family home, is inevitably deeply troubled, difficult to live with and likely to be resistant to forming a relationship with foster carers. Their basic trust in **any** adults' capacity to care for them has been fundamentally compromised by their birth parents' inability to care for them. This lack of trust is transferred into any potential new relationship including the psychotherapeutic relationship, and results in the child needing to use strong emotional defences to protect him or herself from further distress and trauma. These defences often become self-defeating, leading to further difficulties. The implications for the child of separation from, or loss of, attachment figures for future mental health are well documented and will often be referred to in this book (Bowlby 1979, 1988; Simmonds 2013).

When a child like this comes for psychoanalytic psychotherapy, often some considerable time after these major life events, the remnants of these experiences and relationships inevitably and spontaneously re-emerge within the therapeutic process. They are expressed, sometimes in obvious ways and at other times in extremely subtle ways, within the transference–countertransference relationship, which is the aspect of the therapeutic relationship in which the child's past is re-experienced in the present. This is a form of unconsciously repeating in the present what cannot be consciously remembered from the past (Freud 1914). This transference of the past into the present can colour the child's internal world in ways that make the child misunderstand the better external relationships and life experiences that have subsequently become available to him or her. The child cannot help but unconsciously understand the present through the distorting lens of the traumatic past. It is the therapist's efforts to understand what the child is unconsciously repeating within the transference–countertransference relationship and to disentangle this from the contemporary and new developmental relationship with the therapist, which facilitates the process of developmental change which subsequently emerges (Hopkins 2000; Hurry 1998, Lanyado 2004c, 2017).

Paradoxically, it is from within the present, developmental relationship with the therapist that the impact of neglect can be seen in many small ways. This becomes evident as the therapist gradually realises what has **not** happened (that is the deficits) in the child's emotional life. As a supervisor of many therapies of severely neglected and traumatised children, I have been struck by the ways in which, as therapy progresses, the intensity of the therapist's attention to the details of the child's emotional life, replicate the ordinary parent's detailed attention to their child. This detailed knowing of the child, within the therapeutic context, is the result of the therapist's efforts to listen to and contain the child's anxieties and preoccupations as discussed in more detail in Chapter 3 (Bion 1962). This intensity of thinking and knowing about the child's internal life can be utilised to detect very early signs of more ordinary developmental growth, so that they can be noticed and nurtured from their fragile beginnings. It is in this way that the therapist becomes a 'developmental object' for the child in the present relationship. This provides some opportunity to compensate for significant aspects of parenting that did not happen whilst the child was being neglected; this is discussed in Chapter 3.

It is much more difficult to capture the emotionality of the transference–countertransference relationship when reporting other clinicians' work. Whilst these feelings do come alive within the supervisee–supervisor relationship, as discussed in Chapter 9, the case illustrations in this chapter, and Chapters 3 and 4 of this volume, need to be read as therapeutic vignettes which capture the overall treatment issues as well as some of the detail of the therapeutic interactions. The following example is interesting because, rather unusually, this child was not neglected for the first twenty months of life and as a result, in comparison with children who were neglected during this same period of time, he is remarkably able to recover from subsequent terrible trauma, neglect and painful separation. I am grateful to the supervisee and her colleagues for permission to use their work as an example.

Eddie was removed from his birth mother's care at birth because she was unable to care for him properly. This does not happen lightly and careful assessments and legal processes must have been involved in this difficult decision. He was placed with an experienced foster mother and lived with her for twenty months in a loving relationship. She wanted to adopt Eddie but a distant relative of his birth mother came forward in the last stages of the adoption process, and wanted to adopt Eddie. This kinship adoption application was given preference and went ahead and a new adoption process was started. Eddie moved to the relative's home but after a number of months it became very evident that all was not well in the placement. The social worker noted that Eddie looked neglected and waiflike. Having been a chubby sociable little boy when he left the foster home he seemed frightened and watchful when social workers visited the home. Concerns mounted and resulted in Eddie being removed from the prospective adoptive home, and fortunately going back to his original foster mother. He had not gained weight or height over ten months of living with the prospective adopters. As well as having been severely neglected, there was significant evidence that he had been sexually abused which the social services and police investigated.

Eddie was referred for therapy when he was three and a half years old. He was a bright and expressive little boy who, from early on in the therapy, was able to make good use of the relationship with the therapist whom he clearly trusted, and towards whom he could express a healthy range of emotions: playful, cheeky, loving, angry, aggressive. From the beginning of his therapy, he communicated in various ways to his therapist about the traumatic events, separations and losses he had experienced. For example, there was a strong sense in the transference–countertransference relationship that leaving his foster mother to go with the therapist to the therapy room, and then leaving the therapist to return to the foster mother at the end of the session, repeated at an unconscious level the intense anxiety he had felt when going between the foster and prospective adoptive family, and back again. The level of watchful fearfulness which was projected into the therapist at these times was of a very different nature to the ordinary separation anxiety that many young patients feel when they are getting used to going to the therapy room without their parent, and alerted her to the traumatic roots of this emotional experience.

Early in the therapy Eddie could at times be very rejecting of his foster mother, saying he wanted to go back to his 'other' mummy. Fortunately, this mature and understanding foster mother (who was by then again in the process of becoming his adoptive mother) could see the distress, confusion and above all anger, which lay behind these difficult times and could respond lovingly despite the rejecting things that Eddie was saying. It was because Eddie felt secure enough in his relationship with his foster/adoptive mother that he was able to express these feelings at all, and they would then return to their more usual loving and affectionate relationship. In attachment theory terms, the behaviour that Eddie was showing was that of a child re-united with a trusted attachment figure to whom he could express his confusion, anger and love in whatever way these feelings tumbled out of him.

Eddie made very good progress in his therapy and it was evident that he was a bright child and learning well. He made the transition from nursery school to reception class in primary school with delight in all that he was learning, and was clearly able to think and reason. This is in great contrast to many children who have been neglected and traumatised from the start of life and struggle to be able to think and function intellectually at an age-appropriate level. Very significantly, Eddie had had a good start in life with his foster mother and this showed in his curiosity and ability to reflect on his life experiences, to think about them and to ask some very important questions – all before he was five years old.

Eddie's return to his foster mother after the awful neglect and abuse he had suffered at the hands of his relatives, and his subsequent adoption by his foster mother, was almost like a fairy tale in which one would like to say 'and they all lived happily ever after'. Whilst they did live happily together, there were many painful emotions and memories which needed to be processed in Eddie's therapy, as well as his mother's parent work. Eddie was full of questions and distressing memories. In particular, once he was adopted, he often pleaded with his adoptive mummy never to send him away again to what he called the 'faraway' family. When he gradually but still confusingly understood that his foster/adoptive mummy had not been able to do anything about this decision at the time, had also been very upset by the loss, and had missed him a great deal, this raised new questions. Why could social workers take a little boy away from his foster mummy – who of course he had felt then, and felt again now, **was** his mummy? If they could do that when he was little, he was very worried that they could do it again now. This raised the question for the therapist and adoptive mother, was he also aware that there was yet another mummy that he had been born to?

This was all discussed carefully between the adoptive mother, therapist and parent worker. To what extent could/should the gaps in Eddie's life history be shared with him more fully, particularly as he was still so young? Would talking to him more about it, help him to recover and to deepen his sense of security in his adoptive home? It was important to enable him to find his own narrative with the help of the grown-ups, but at the same time, he needed some straightforward information to fill in some of the gaps that he couldn't make any sense of. Whilst these discussions were taking place, Eddie had come to his own conclusions based on what he had talked about with his adoptive mummy. He told his therapist that there was yet another mummy, his birth mummy who as he told his therapist, no doubt based on what his adoptive mummy had told him, 'cannot come back'. However, there was a theme of being abducted as well as rescued that he expressed through play in his therapy, that took a number of months to be worked through. During this time he had many nightmares, found it difficult to sleep on his own and became very clingy to his adoptive mother. At this point in his therapy these issues were foremost in his mind and needed to be talked about with his adoptive mother and his therapist, so that his memories could gradually become more conscious and bearable rather than repeated in nightmares which he was unable to control (Freud 1914). Any conscious memories that he might have had about the sexual abuse that there was physical evidence that he had experienced, remained inaccessible.

This brief example from a lengthy psychotherapeutic treatment raises just some of the questions that this book addresses about how best to help children like Eddie. Strikingly, whilst the experience of forming a therapeutic relationship with each child is unique and individual, the presenting problems are very similar and are the result of neglectful parenting which has made the child highly vulnerable to traumatic experiences. As already indicated, Eddie was unusual because he received good mothering for the first twenty months of his life and as a result, despite the terrible trauma he subsequently experienced, he had developed the secure emotional foundations on which to build his inner world. However, his life story and this clinical vignette also illustrate the enormous emotional challenges children such as him have to negotiate.

Although it is beyond the scope of this book, it is important to note that an increasing number of unaccompanied young asylum seekers are being accommodated by social care in the UK and are needing psychotherapy for the many terrible traumas that they have experienced – such as witnessing the death of loved ones, being tortured, suffering physical and sexual abuse, and homelessness. From within the therapeutic experience, psychotherapists have good reason to believe that many of these young people come from secure family relationships and had good emotional starts in life before they had to flee for their lives. Whilst different practices in child care and family structure in their countries of origin are likely to play their part in this clinical observation by British psychotherapists, there is nevertheless evidence from within the therapeutic relationship itself that, despite the severe levels of post-traumatic stress disorder that these young people experience, they have a firmer bedrock to their personalities and internal worlds than children who are known to have been neglected from birth (Melzak 2017b, personal communication). In this respect, these children have much in common with Eddie and can eventually, with sufficient therapeutic help, go on to study, make valuable contributions to the new communities that they join and form loving relationships, if they are given a chance to do so. (For detailed accounts of this work see Melzak (1992, 2005, 2017a) and Papadopoulos (2002)).

The broader context: finding a new home for the child

A number of the children may go backwards and forwards between birth and foster homes whilst efforts are made to help the birth family to provide better care for the child. Other children may rapidly lose contact with their birth family, siblings and extended family. Legal processes are involved in attempting to work out what is in the best interests of the child. Some birth parents argue their case in court and try to have their child living with them again. Access arrangements between the birth parents, siblings and extended family may need to be specified by the courts, if this is to be allowed at all. Very difficult decisions may need to be made about whether it is in siblings' best interests to be fostered or adopted together or separately. Specialised clinicians and social workers write reports for the court and many professionals need to be involved with informing the courts so that wise decisions can be made. Some parents and infants or children are placed in special residential units to see if the parents can respond to help. Dowling has written thoughtfully about her role in assessing these painful situations where it is not clear if a baby or young child can stay with the birth parent/s or not. Her work, in an in-patient as well as an outpatient setting, gives vivid clinical examples including some from parent–infant psychotherapy, as well as providing helpful theoretical models (Dowling 2006, 2009, 2012). In a thought-provoking paper, Sternberg writes about how a child psychotherapist's way of assessing a child's emotional difficulties can help courts to make wiser decisions about placements for children who present risks to others (Sternberg 2016).

Currently, only a small number of children in the UK are looked after in small children's homes. The history of the debate in the UK about which provision is best for severely neglected and traumatised children – fostering and adoption, or children's homes – is enlarged on in Chapter 2. Regardless of which kind of provision is the social policy for the care of these children, regular support of the adults trying to provide this care is fundamental to whether it succeeds or not. Too often these adults do not receive enough help and the care of the children suffers because of all the stress and distress it inevitably entails for the carers. An example of the consultation process to the staff of a residential therapeutic unit, who were struggling to digest the impact of their work with sexually abused children, is given in Chapter 7.

What is initially meant to be a short-term foster home of a few months, may easily become a more long-term foster home lasting for well over a year in many cases. This might be because other more suitable long-term placements are not available when it becomes clearer that this is what the child needs. Meanwhile, the child and foster parent/s and family may be managing to form deeper relationships which come to an end when a long-term placement becomes available. So there is further loss for the child, and a significant loss for the foster family who might take some time before they feel emotionally ready to foster another child because of the upset of parting with a previous foster child.

The level of uncertainty which underpins foster children's lives constantly runs counter to their need to try to form more secure new attachments. It can be very difficult to balance the parents' rights with those of the child. Whilst all this indecision continues, time is passing and the child's development and emotional well-being are at stake. These massive instabilities and uncertainties in the children's lives arouse not only confusion and distress but anger, particularly in relation to their helplessness and dependency on the adults (professionals and foster carers) who are making such life changing decisions on their behalf. This can become one of the roots of the severely controlling defences that many of these children subsequently develop in their relationships.

Foster families offer the most extraordinary service to society by taking such difficult children into their homes and trying to form secure enough relationships with them. Whilst foster carers are usually carefully selected and offered some training for the work, the quality and quantity of support they are given by professionals in order to do their work varies greatly from one part of the country to another. Whilst the focus of this book is on severely neglected and traumatised children, without a well-supported foster home, adoptive home or children's home, these children cannot benefit from psychotherapy. Their need for a caring home is paramount. Foster carers are paid a salary for their work, but it is much more than 'ordinary' work. It is often extremely stressful and exhausting work and there is rarely any time off from the emotional and physical needs of these children. Planned respite with families known to the child happens too rarely. The foster carer may well have his or her own children, whose lives are greatly affected by the needs of the foster child. Jealousies and rivalries are inevitable.

An additional stress is the risk of children making false allegations of abusive or neglectful behaviour by foster carers. Whilst some false allegations might be made to deliberately cause harm to the foster carer, or to bring a child's foster placement to an end, others arise from the child's emotional confusion of past and present adult behaviour (as described above), in which ordinary parenting can be perceived by the child as being frightening or abusive. Such allegations always have to be wisely investigated as unfortunately, we also know of foster and adoptive homes where children have been abused, mistreated and neglected, as was Eddie's experience. However, wisdom doesn't always prevail and un-thought through procedural responses to allegations can be deeply unjust to good, solid foster and adoptive parents, who can feel that they are treated as if they are presumed 'guilty' and have to prove their innocence.

Foster carers and their children and families not only have to cope with the actual behaviour and emotions of the foster child, they also have to find ways of managing the repercussions of this on their own internal and external lives. It is striking that the foster and adoptive families that seem to be most resilient are those where the family is a part of a large and supportive extended family, or a part of a local community that supports them and is able to be tolerant and understanding of the child. Most foster families become strongly emotionally attached to these children and go to great lengths to try to help and care for them. However, under the long-term pressures they try to survive, 'compassion fatigue' can eventually set in, leading to the breakdown of good foster placements and great distress to the children and foster families who can no longer continue to care for them. The risk of foster placement breakdown may be more intense during adolescence when some teenagers can become violent to their foster or adoptive parents as well as worryingly promiscuous (Selwyn *et al.* 2014).

A far-reaching research study 'Compassion fatigue and foster carers', which involved 546 foster carers online, followed by 4 focus groups of 23 foster carers in all, came to important conclusions regarding the need to improve support to foster carers (Ottoway and Selwyn 2016). Of particular relevance are the following conclusions: foster carers need to be better prepared for the impact of fostering traumatised children and the need for a therapeutic approach to parenting; agencies need to be able to identify and support (without judgement) foster carers who are suffering; there is a need for local inter-agency and independently run support groups; peer support groups for foster parents should be actively encouraged; and there needs to be a greater investment in regular and familiar respite provision for the children. The report also notes the need for those who support foster families to have an understanding of the effects of trauma and attachment difficulties on children and young people.

Child psychotherapists researching in this area have come to similar conclusions. Many therapists emphasise the importance of working with the professional network around the child, including the foster and adoptive parents, sometimes as a precursor to working with the child, or quite often instead of working directly with the child (Robinson *et al.* 2017). Directly addressing the problems of foster placement breakdown, Sloan Donachy describes the 'loss of sense of self' that foster carers experience over time when trying to cope with the demands of fostering, and how this can eventually lead to foster placement breakdown. She argues for the need to understand better the emotional impact of attempting to care for a child who has experienced abuse and neglect (Sloan Donachy 2017).

However, when the foster placement is well supported, foster carers experience 'compassion satisfaction', are deeply committed to the child and delight in small improvements in the child's emotional and physical well-being. Their relationships with the children often continue long after the child has stopped living with them, particularly if it has been a long-term foster placement and the child has turned eighteen. By this time, the foster home is truly the young person's home, and although all financial support from the local authorities will usually have stopped, the relationships, in one way or another, are for life. Young people who have had the good fortune of having a good enough fostering experience speak of the importance to them of the relatively trusting, secure and loving relationships they have established with the foster carers and their families. These relationships, which are of course not without their continued difficulties, provide the comparatively secure base from which they can try to make as much as they can of their lives. It is not unusual to hear of foster families where several children have been fostered over the years, have grown up and started to live independently and remain very much a part of the family's ongoing life.

For those foster children who are less fortunate, their hardship is compounded by the fact that somewhere between the age of sixteen to eighteen, depending on the way policies are implemented in different parts of the country and the young person's educational situation, they will have to leave their foster homes and are effectively on their own. They are expected to be able to live independently or semi-independently with little support or preparation for adult life. Many young people of this age from ordinary families would quickly find themselves in all sorts of financial and emotional difficulties.

Sadly, these young people who have to leave their foster homes and are effectively cast adrift into the world, are likely to be the young people who become drawn to crime and gang cultures as a means of survival. Some of these young people have always expressed the wish to return to their birth families and are now free to do so. Drug and alcohol abuse, prostitution, violence, imprisonment and homelessness are common, as are mental health difficulties. Alarmingly quickly, these young people can become parents themselves, totally unequipped for the demands of parenthood, and the cycle of neglect, deprivation and trauma repeats itself in a new generation. The consequences of not investing enough help in this group of children and young people are extremely far reaching.

The provision of a permanent home

When it is clear that some children, particularly if they are already in mid-childhood, cannot go back to their birth family but, where there are no legal grounds for severing contact with their birth families, long-term fostering is a valuable option. Some kind of supervised contact with the birth parents and family may have been agreed by the court. This can be very complicated for the child and full of potential conflicts for the foster family and the birth family. The emphasis is on 'coping' – and the painful acceptance of many conflicting feelings and losses. It is very hard to know what is in the child's best interests and what he or she can realistically cope with: to keep some kind of regular contact with the family and try to cope with the emotional upheaval that can often be entailed around contact, or to have very occasional contact but have to try to cope with the child's missing of birth parents and anger at the lack of contact. These meetings cannot help but be bitter-sweet and tense and involve a very confusing mix of anticipation, longing, frustration and anxiety for all involved. Quite often, and for a variety of reasons, birth parents and families gradually fail to come to contact meetings. The child then has to cope with the disappointment of hoping to see their birth parent/s as well as the anger at being let down again. This can, in time, lead to access being stopped altogether by the courts, in the child's best interests. These difficult decisions are rarely clear cut and more often amount to having to choose between the 'least bad options'.

In other circumstances, when a child clearly cannot go back to his or her birth family and is judged by the social workers and courts to be suitable for adoption because of their younger age and potential to settle with adoptive parents, the legal ties with the birth family have to be severed. There can be a heart-breaking 'goodbye' meeting of the child with the birth parent/s. Once a year letter box contact might be allowed by the courts, but can be disturbing of the new adoptive relationships. It can also be at this point that many adoptive children lose contact with siblings because adoptive families cannot realistically manage full sibling groups. Some children adopted separately from their siblings might still have occasional contact after the adoption, but this can also be very fraught for everyone involved.

The decision for a child to be adopted also means that there is further loss for the child – the loss of the foster family where the child may have started to make some healthier attachments. The transition from fostering to adoption can be helped through psychotherapy and sensitive social work support as discussed in detail in Chapter 5, but is inevitably a difficult process for the child and foster family to go through. Several of the clinical examples in this book come from children who have either been adopted, or permanently placed in kinship guardianship with relatives such as grandparents. Child psychotherapists Boswell and Cudmore, in their research about the child's actual experience of moving from fostering to adoption (which currently in the UK, after all the careful selection and preparation for the child's move has taken place, happens in a period of seven to fourteen days) note how the professionals and foster and adoptive family can lose sight of the child's distress about the loss of the foster family (Boswell and Cudmore 2017). They conclude that individual and organisational defences against loss function to protect the adults involved with this difficult transition, from becoming overwhelmed by anxiety and distress. This can lead to these adults feeling that the children are 'fine' rather than trying to look deeper into the child's state of mind. In agreement with Ottoway and Selwyn's findings (above), one of their recommendations is fuller training and support for foster carers and adopters on the psychological processes involved.

It is important to remember that adoptive parents and kinship guardians have often been through distressing times themselves. Adoptive parents may well have struggled with fertility problems before being approved as adopters. Kinship guardians, particularly grandparents, can offer a great deal to their grandchildren, but also need help to process the difficult relationships they might have had, and might still have, with the child's parent/s (that is, their own children). There is an example in Chapter 4 of grandparents having kinship guardianship of their grandchildren. All of these parents have been very carefully scrutinised by social services departments and/or adoption agencies, and often desperately want to prove that they are good parents. Against this background history some of these adoptive parents find it very difficult to ask for and accept help. Others find it difficult to find appropriate help.

Specialised post-adoption services offer a variety of forms of therapeutic help to these families, including psychotherapy. The patient discussed in Chapters 6 and 8 was adopted and, although she still presented many problems in adolescence, was in a much better emotional state than other children who had not had the bene-fits of many years in a secure home with loving, patient parents. With the numerous difficulties and painful situations that have to be faced, it is remarkable that fostering and adoption can be as successful as they are at times. But it is also important to accept the limitations of the degree of recovery that is possible for the children and the toll that loving and looking after them can take on their new families. Seeing the happiness of these families, at times when life starts to get easier, makes all the effort worthwhile; but the struggles involved to reach this point should wisely never be under-estimated (Simmonds 2008).

Psychoanalytic psychotherapy with severely neglected and traumatised children

Child psychotherapists have a long history of offering therapy to these children and this is described in more detail in the next chapter. A recent survey into the differing ways in which child psychotherapists were working with looked-after and adopted children in the UK, found that there was a wide range of psycho-therapeutic activities (Robinson *et al.* 2017). Direct work with the child could vary from seeing the child monthly, weekly or sometimes three or four times weekly, over several years. Some therapists worked for periods of time with the child and foster or adoptive parent/s in the room together (see Chapter 5). Others worked across the transition from fostering to adoption. Some therapists were seeing these children in Child and Adolescent Mental Health Service (CAMHS) clinics; others were working in specialised clinics where their therapeutic work was an integrated part of the general social care of the child; some psychotherapists were a part of larger- scale fostering organisations which offered psychotherapy for the child and support for the foster carers as a significant aspect of their overall service.

As mentioned above, recent research found that child psychotherapists place great value on working with the network of professionals surrounding the severely neglected and traumatised child (Robinson *et al.* 2017). This can range from facilitating various kinds of groups for foster carers and adopters, more formal teaching about the needs and difficulties of these children, consulting to social care teams on a regular basis and working closely with social workers in specialised clinical teams (Ironside 2004, 2009). Some child psychotherapists work within specialised residential therapeutic communities, whilst others offer outside consultation to the staff of these communities as discussed more fully in Chapter 7 of this book (Ward *et al.* 2003; Wilson 1999/2009; Sprince 2002).

Following referral, the decision about what is the best way for a child psychotherapist to help the child, will be reached after several initial consultations, which may involve a combination of meeting with the foster or adoptive parents, the social workers involved and the child him or herself. Local resources and pressures on the treatment team are bound to play a significant part in what kind of treatment plan is suggested, and this is likely to be a pragmatic blend of what it is felt that the child needs, and what is possible. Comparisons between, for example, different kinds of intensity of treatment (once, twice or three times weekly work), are difficult to make because the treatment plan will depend greatly on the ways in which the foster or adoptive parents are being supported in the clinic, the level of involvement of the professional network, including the school and the level of the child's disturbance.

More intensive work does not always mean that there will be greater improvement in the child's state of mind. Some children cannot cope with the level of intimacy that therapy involves so that, for example, it may be contra-indicated at the time of referral for the child to be offered more than fortnightly therapy. The foster or adoptive parents may be offered regular 'parent work' meetings with another member of the clinic team or possibly the child psychotherapist if a colleague is not available to do this work. Treatment plans can also be changed according to the child's changing needs over time. The therapist will try to meet regularly with foster and adoptive parents (and social workers if involved) to review the progress of the therapy as well as holding additional meetings when there is a crisis in the child's therapy or ongoing life. Some psychotherapists may see children in their school and develop good working relationships with the teaching staff, as in the example in Chapter 3. When the child has many problems at school, the therapist may have meetings with the school staff to try to support them and aid understanding of the child's behaviour. This can be very beneficial to the child and help the child to remain at school rather than be excluded, as well as aid their gradual ability to settle in class and learn. It is also very helpful for the therapist's understanding of the 'whole' child, to hear about how the child manages in the classroom, with his or her peers and educationally.

The problem of remembering and forgetting

All of the issues that have been raised in this chapter about the disjointed and difficult life journey that children like Eddie have experienced, make the possibility of them developing a coherent and integrated sense of Self extremely challenging. The to- and -fro, complex inter-relatedness of what has happened in the past, and what is happening in the present, means that somehow the problem of the balance between remembering and forgetting the past must be addressed. As well as illustrating the complexity of the different relationships and experiences in Eddie's young life, his example raises important questions about how to try to enable even a very young child, to think about some of the awful losses and events that have happened in his or her life. What happens to the child's traumatic memories and feelings and to what extent, and when and how, does the child need to be told about what happened in his or her life, that is not a part of these memories? The narratives that children like Eddie tell themselves, and others, about their lives, will change according to their stage of development and who is available to help them to try to process all that has happened. Is it helpful for the therapist to try to reconstruct what has happened in a child's life as a part of the therapeutic process and how is the therapist best advised to make use of information that they have about the child, which the child may only dimly remember?

These are all very difficult questions which can only be responded to on an individual, child by child, basis. The risk of re-traumatisation is always close at hand, and there are periods in the child's recovery when it may well be better that they 'forget' all that they have been through, in order to move forward in their lives (Alvarez 1992). This idea in itself is complex, because there is also a need, in whatever small measure is possible, to mourn the losses of the past as discussed in more detail in Chapter 4. In many ways, the cues come from the child, with the sensitive parent or therapist becoming aware of a growing readiness in the child to explore painful memories or questions at different times in their lives. In Eddie's case, he was asking important questions about all the mothers in his life, some of which could be answered. He was also developing well emotionally and was able to express his feelings and thoughts, and to play in an age-appropriate way. Not to answer his questions as wisely as possible and to fill in, a bit at a time, the gaps in his life story that made no sense to him could have been a mistake. His distress, as shown in his play, and fear of abduction, as well as his nightmares, were entirely appropriate and could be processed with his adoptive mother's knowledge and understanding of the life experiences he had. She, in turn, could be supported through this difficult time by her parent worker at the clinic.

All of these issues are interdependent and interwoven. As a child such as Eddie changes and becomes more secure in his relationship with his foster or adoptive parent/s, he feels more able to express his deepest verbal and non-verbal anxieties and memories, knowing that his foster or adopted parents will do their best to listen to and contain these communications. These, in turn, are emotionally processed by the parents who help them to become more digestible. This is a very difficult task as it is so distressing to know in such a visceral way what the child that you love has suffered. However, in trying to meet this need in the child, the adult, over time, helps the child to discover that it is possible to communicate previously overwhelming emotional experiences in such a way that they can be survived, and in turn become survivable for the child. These processes of non-verbal 'projection' of feelings (by the child) into the parent, who 'introjects' them and 'contains' them before communicating them back to the child in a more tolerable and less toxic form, will often be referred to in this book and are discussed in more depth in Chapter 3 (Bion 1962). The containment offered by the adult in turn strengthens the loving attachment relationship and helps to increase the level of security that the child is able to experience.

Often the body 'remembers' traumatic events that the mind cannot and this can be expressed in psychosomatic symptoms which hold distinct meanings for the individual (McDougall 1989). Plus, our knowledge of how the brain is affected by frightening and abusive early experience further helps us to appreciate the real physical and physiological difficulties that some neglected and traumatised children are trying to overcome. Important neurophysiological research developments in this area are discussed in Chapter 3 alongside a clinical example. Being able to remember traumatic events, however small a slither of a memory it might be, is very significant because this may provide the hidden (forgotten) link between odd repetitions of self-destructive behaviour that it has not been possible to learn from. These ideas are embedded in classical psychoanalytic theory and provide some understanding of the 'compulsion' to repeat distressing experiences and not to learn from them – because they have not been remembered (Freud 1914).

These questions are bought into particular focus when 'Life Story' work takes place and can be very helpful when carefully timed. However, whilst there is a need to have a record of a young child's life before adoption, if it is not invested with real meaning or is not carried out by a specially trained professional it can become an empty exercise. Awful life events can become so sanitised during this process that they don't begin to reflect the child's experience. Despite this, sometimes in later years, children spontaneously bring their Life Story Books to psychotherapy and these become a means for further and deeper exploration of the child's life history (Cant 2005, 2008; Lanyado 2012 and Chapter 8 of this volume).

Whilst this chapter has attempted to describe the consequences, scale, complexity and broader context of the emotional damage that severely neglected and traumatised children and young people are trying to overcome, it also draws attention to and pays great respect to all the foster and adoptive carers, as well as the many professionals who persevere in all their efforts to help these children.

Despite often feeling that they cannot make a difference in a child's life, the moments when small positive changes become evident make it clear that their efforts are not in vain. Progress is made up of many small steps, as I hope this book demonstrates.

2 The historical and social context

Influences on the treatment of severely neglected and traumatised children today

Months after the outbreak of World War II, Bowlby and Winnicott, together with another leading child psychiatrist Emmanuel Miller, wrote a letter to the *British Medical Journal* voicing their concerns about the emotional impact of the large-scale evacuation of small children from cities to the countryside, to live with allocated families whom they had not met before. They stressed that, based on their clinical experience, this kind of premature separation of the young child from their mothers and family homes could lead to much more than an ordinary sadness. It could amount to 'an emotional blackout' for the child (Bowlby, Miller, and Winnicott 1939, cited in Phillips 1988: 62). Their emphasis on the immense importance of the early mother–child relationship for sound mental health in childhood and adulthood, further influenced by their wartime experiences, was continued in their theories, clinical practice and research after the war and is directly relevant to helping severely neglected and traumatised children today.

It is important to note that the number of these patients who need the help of child and adolescent mental health clinicians today in the UK, takes up a high proportion of clinical time and effort. This has not always been the case. It is with this in mind that the historical and social context of this chapter is offered. Social policies have changed greatly since the 1970s as a result of necessary changes in child protection measures in the UK after the prevalence of physical and sexual abuse of children became more widely recognised. These social policies have repercussions, as already discussed in Chapter 1, and enlarged on from a historical and social perspective in this chapter.

Psychoanalytic influences

Bowlby was a child psychiatrist at the London Child Guidance Clinic in the 1930s. His early research and clinical interests into juvenile delinquency came to the conclusion that 'prolonged separation of a child from his mother (or mother substitute) during the first five years of life stands foremost among the causes of delinquent character development' (Bowlby 1944, 1951, cited in Holmes 1993: 39). Bowlby's thinking about the significant repercussions of separation of a young child from his or her mother came to powerful fruition in his landmark popular book *Child Care and the Growth of Love* (Bowlby 1953). The book was based on the report Bowlby had written for a study commissioned by the Social Commission of the UN in 1948, carried out by the World Health Organisation in the wake of the war, to look at the needs of homeless children (but not refugees from war or other disasters) post war (Bowlby 1951). Bowlby was a psychoanalyst as well as a child, adolescent and adult psychiatrist and at the start of this book he made the uncompromising, and for the times, bold statement:

> ... what is believed to be essential for mental health is that an infant and young child should experience a warm, intimate and continuous relationship with his mother (or permanent mother substitute – one person who steadily 'mothers' him) in which both find satisfaction and enjoyment. It is this complex, rich and rewarding relationship with the mother in early years, varied in countless ways by relations with the father and with the brothers and sisters, that child psychiatrists and many others now believe to underlie the development of character and mental health.
>
> (Bowlby 1953: 13)

Winnicott, who qualified as a psychoanalyst in 1934, had been a child psychiatrist and paediatrician working at Paddington Green Children's Hospital before the war. During the war, his responsibilities for evacuated children, whose placements with ordinary families broke down because of psychological disturbance necessitating placement in evacuation hostels, led him to realise that these were children who had not had good-enough family relationships before evacuation. His work with the children, their families and the hostel workers helped him to recognise that the children had carried these problems with them into the foster homes and evacuation hostels. Being involved with the setting up of these hostels gave him the experience and opportunity to think about what kind of 'environmental provision' would help these troubled children to recover. This wartime experience became incorporated into his theories about ordinary good-enough parenting and the significance of providing a facilitating environment in which children could develop emotionally.

In the early days of Winnicott's clinical practice, children's medicine did not distinguish between paediatrics and child psychiatry and, as a result, his rich experience of working with many ordinary babies, children and their families, helped him to formulate his important ideas about good-enough mothering and ordinary emotional development. His enthusiasm for sharing his thinking with many different professional groups as well as the general public resulted in his ideas becoming well known by non-psychoanalytic audiences. This is particularly evident in his BBC radio broadcasts in the 1940s and 1950s which were addressed to ordinary parents and resulted in the publication of his books *The Child and The Family*, and *The Child and the Outside World* in 1957, which were combined into *The Child, The Family and the Outside World* in 1964 (Winnicott 1964).

Anna Freud was also deeply concerned about the impact of the separation of young children from their mothers and families. Having set up nurseries in Vienna before the Second World War and been very positive about the influence of psychoanalysis on education, she established the Hampstead War Nurseries in 1941 after her family had sought refuge in London from the Nazis, in 1939. These nurseries provided a home for hundreds of children whose homes were broken by the war. Midgley gives a fascinating account of Anna Freud and Dorothy Burlingham's work in the Hampstead War Nurseries, and the ways that this influenced their thinking along similar lines to Bowlby (Freud and Burlingham 1944; Midgley 2013: Ch 5). In the same volume, Midgley also describes the impact of James and Joyce Robertson's work on the effects of separation on young children in their ground-breaking 1953 documentary film, *A Two Year Old Goes to Hospital*. This film had such a powerful effect that rules for visiting sick children in hospital were changed as a result (Midgley 2013; Robertson 1953; Robertson and Robertson 1989).

Each of these psychoanalysts made distinctive contributions to the ways in which we think about neglected and traumatised children today. Their theories remain relevant and helpful for understanding and offering treatment to the children and their families and will be returned to in many of the chapters that follow. (For further historical and contextual information, the reader is referred to Caldwell and Joyce 2011; Edgecombe 2000; Holmes 1993; Midgley 2013; Phillips 1988). From our modern-day perspective, it is striking that prolonged separation from, and the injury or death of, fathers during wartime was barely considered. Possibly these traumatic wartime losses and experiences needed a greater passage of time to allow for reflection on their significance for child mental health and healing, and it was too soon for them to be integrated into these theories. The role of fathers in the emotional development of their children has changed enormously in the last seventy years and this is inevitably reflected in the theories of the times.

The recognition of the 'battered child syndrome' and its impact on Child Protection policy

The reality of adult cruelty to children was not a new phenomenon but, when it first came into the public eye in the 1950s, the recognition of the deliberate harming of children by their parents and other family members was shocking to the general public and professionals alike. The realisation that 'non-accidental injury' was much more widespread than it had formerly been thought to be was, in large measure, due to the ground-breaking and courageous work of American paediatrician Henry Kempe. He brought to professional awareness the reality of the cruelty and physical abuse shown to children when good-enough parenting was absent. A ground-breaking paper, written in 1962 together with colleagues including Silverman, a radiologist, provided graphic and distressing x-ray and photographic evidence of the children's injuries (Kempe *et al*. 1962). In the abstract of their paper entitled 'The battered child syndrome', they stated:

> The battered child syndrome is a clinical condition in young children who have received serious physical abuse, and is a frequent cause of permanent injury or death. The syndrome should be considered in any child exhibiting

evidence of a fracture of any bone, subdural hematoma, failure to thrive, soft tissue swellings or skin bruising in any child who dies suddenly, or where the degree and type of injury is at variance with the history given regarding the occurrence of the trauma.

(Kempe *et al*. 1962: 17–24)

Kempe was the first to identify child abuse and demand better diagnostic interventions from the medical profession when they observed unexplained and life-threatening injuries in children, in the American equivalent of accident and emergency units. Whilst adults' abusive and cruel behaviour to children was sadly nothing new, Kempe's work drew attention to the many sadistic ways that children were deliberately injured, and how vulnerable and unprotected they were if those who had harmed them were also their parents or other family members. The x-ray and photographic evidence that Kempe and his colleagues provided was convincing. This research led to international recognition of physical child abuse (non-accidental injury) and placed responsibility for reporting it on any professional who came into contact with it. Kempe's researches and papers led to changes in the law around the world, and many of the child protection procedures that we are so familiar with today. He was twice nominated for a Nobel prize for his work.

The problems of how to identify when children are at physical risk from their family members continue today as the evidence can be covered up or explained in other ways if challenged by doctors, teachers, social workers or police. High profile cases in the UK, such as the death of seven-year-old Maria Colwell in 1974, eight-year-old Victoria Climbié in 2000 and seventeen-month-old 'Baby P' in 2007, have resulted in public enquiries and many procedural changes to try to save the lives of children who are at risk. However the inquiry into the death of Maria Colwell at the hands of her step-father 'highlighted the serious lack of co-ordination within protection services' – as did the enquiries into subsequent deaths (Batty 2004). For further helpful information on the historical timeline of child welfare, child protection law and sexual abuse in the UK, the reader is referred to Batty (2004) and Delap (2015).

Efforts to tighten up Child Protection procedures can at times lead to the right 'boxes' being ticked, but straightforward observation and common sense being over-ridden so that appropriate action is not taken. Child protection procedures can also have the reverse effect when over-rigorously applied so that apparently suspicious looking, but in reality perfectly ordinary injuries are not thought about in the context of other information about the child and family. There can be a confusing mix of over-zealousness and lack of communication between those who are responsible for the reporting of any possible child protection issues. Added to these complicated and stressful issues is the under-resourcing and under-financing of professional services in all areas related to child protection. In practice this means that many of these professionals are trying to help so many troubled families that they are overloaded and do not have enough time to think carefully about the wisest course of action.

However, as a result of Kempe's work, many children are removed from abusive families in good time, or sometimes only just in time. Abusive adults are prosecuted. Children are placed in loving foster or adoptive homes. But they continue to bear the emotional and physical scars of their physical abuse and often need psychological treatment in later years (Simmonds 2013). The case illustration in Chapter 3, 'Amber', is an example of what can happen to children who have been physically abused.

The impact of the recognition of child sexual abuse

It was only a matter of time before the widespread incidence of sexual abuse within the family, and sadly also in children's homes, foster homes and adoptive homes, came forcibly to public and professional awareness. In 1977 it was Kempe again, who was one of the first paediatricians to recognise the prevalence of child sexual abuse in his paper 'Sexual abuse: Another hidden paediatric problem'. He states:

> In our training and in our practice, we paediatricians are insufficiently aware of the frequency of sexual abuse; it is, I believe just as common as physical abuse and the failure to thrive syndrome.
>
> (Kempe 1977)

Child mental health professionals were shocked and disturbed by the fact that they had not previously recognised the reality of widespread sexual abuse. It was possible that many of their past patients might have been abused but didn't think they would be believed or could trust these professionals enough to reveal what had happened to them. And indeed, sometimes if they had managed to speak to trusted adults about sexually abusive experiences, they had not been believed. What they had said was often seen as being a product of their general emotional disturbance rather than a possible cause of it. In addition, the shame that they felt as a result of what they had experienced made it very difficult to speak about. As a part of the abuse they had often been told that they were bad, dirty, seductive and had 'asked for it', that they the victims were to blame for the abuse they suffered. The children and teenagers had often been threatened that, if they spoke about what had happened to them, they or someone they loved would be harmed.

The question of whether child sexual trauma was a reality or fantasy was contentious and controversial from the start of psychoanalysis (Freud and Breuer 1895). Even with our recognition of the reality of child sexual abuse, in each clinical case the entanglement of reality and fantasy, as well as the issues of what is remembered and what is forgotten or repeated, are often central to the psychotherapeutic process as discussed in Chapter 1. There are times when this raises particularly complex problems for therapists, such as when child protection issues may need to be raised as a result of what a child has communicated in a therapy session. There are clear guidelines for how to proceed in these circumstances which have to be followed and careful discussion in the clinic team is vital at such times. In these circumstances, the external world issues have to be attended to whilst listening to and working in the transference-countertransference relationship through which these issues become alive and 'known' by the therapist. An ongoing theoretical issue is that some psychoanalytic thinking seems to prioritise the importance of the impact on the child's internal world over the reality of the actual, and externally corroborated experience of child sexual abuse. This has been, and to some extent remains, an important discussion as it affects the ways in which clinical material is responded to in more everyday sessions where fantasy and reality need to be thought about in a balanced way. This possibly indicates a significant difference between psychoanalytic work with children where external reality is always very present in the therapist's mind, and adult psychoanalytic work where, because of confidentiality, the analyst has no contact with the patient's external world.

In today's twenty-four-hour news society, we are bombarded through the media with sexual allegations, to the extent that we almost become somewhat de-sensitised to the suffering that lies behind such news. However, when child sexual abuse first came into the public eye, it had a truly seismic effect leading to intense journalistic activity which resulted in services such as Childline (the UK confidential phoneline) being set up by journalist Esther Rantzen in 1986 and run by the National Society for the Prevention of Cruelty to Children (NSPCC) since 2006. The response to this service which offered frightened children the opportunity to talk confidentially on the phone about abusive experiences was far beyond what had initially been anticipated. In addition, in a thought-provoking and integrative book, Bacciagaluppi notes the impact of the feminist movement on the recognition of child sexual abuse 'because much information was obtained from adult (female) survivors of sexual abuse' (Bacciagaluppi 2012a: 87). He provides a fascinating psychoanalytical historical view on trauma which draws on similar sources to this chapter (Bacciagaluppi 2012b).

We, as individuals and society as a whole, find it very hard to hear about sexual violations because they are so distressing and 'unbelievable' to those who have not had direct or indirect experience of them. Unfortunately this has played into the hands of sexually abusive adults. The breaking of sexual boundaries, which we now realise have been broken by women and well as men, with young boys as well as girls, from babyhood into their teenage years, across all social groups, results in a potent mix of disbelief and anger, horror and shock in the vast majority of the population.

It is important to keep in mind how disturbing the idea of sexual abuse of children is to any of us. It is possible to think about the confusion and many flawed attempts to find some wisdom in how to respond to the problem of sexual abuse, as being an example of Freud's views expressed in one of his early works, *Totem and Taboo*, about the many ways in which different cultures try to enforce boundaries against committing incestuous acts (Freud 1913). Drawing on anthropological studies of the time (early twentieth century), Freud noted the universality of the incest taboo and how deeply seated this was in societies of all kinds, as well as in the individual. Whilst there has been a great deal of debate about Freud's views on sexuality, he also drew on the much older powerful Greek myths, such as Oedipus, to describe and name the fundamental sexual taboos which remain as abhorrent in society today as they were millennia ago. The fact that these myths and tragedies are still as moving and powerful as they are today is because they capture aspects of the human condition that remain timeless.

It is these very deep-seated sexual taboos and boundaries between the generations, which have been broken when child sexual abuse has taken place. These sexual taboos extend beyond incestuous relationships, to sexual relationships between adults and children in general. There are sexual boundaries between the generations which feel universal, and it causes great distress and outrage when they are broken. Chasseguet-Smirgel discusses this in detail, in her disturbing and powerful paper 'Perversion and the universal law' (Chasseguet-Smirgel 1985). As a result of the widespread recognition of the reality of sexual abuse the question of whether patient's accounts of being sexually abused were fantasy or reality had to be re-addressed from within psychoanalysis and, as already indicated, that debate continues.

The first high profile sexual abuse enquiry in the UK was the Butler-Sloss enquiry into sexual abuse in Cleveland in 1988. Over one hundred children had been diagnosed by two paediatricians as having been sexually abused, by using a controversial simple physical examination. These children were immediately removed from their homes by social workers, without enough further corroborating evidence, investigation or forethought. The social workers and paediatricians were subjected to widespread criticism for being 'overzealous' and 'intrusive', and this eventually led to the children being returned to their families, in some cases despite clear additional evidence that the child might be at serious risk. Something similar happened in the Orkney Child Abuse scandal and subsequent enquiry in 1991. Whilst it was obviously very important that the abuse that was being exposed was recognised and stopped, there was utter confusion about who was to blame, how best to protect the children and how to help them to recover. In addition there was significant concern about the thoughtlessness with which action was taken by social workers, which did not take into account the need to consider carefully how best to provide for the needs of the children themselves. There was very public disagreement between experts on the subject about whether abuse had taken place or not. In the midst of all this tremendous uproar, there were parents and professionals who were falsely or wrongly accused.

At the time of writing this book, there are a number of historical abuse enquiries ongoing in the UK under the aegis of the Independent Enquiry into Child Sexual Abuse, where adult survivors of childhood sexual abuse are coming forward. Plus there have been convictions of well-known public figures and personalities, as well as some posthumous investigations, where groups of victims of historical abuse have given convincing evidence to the courts. Disturbingly, those convicted of serious sexual offences include police officers, social workers, mental health workers, teachers and doctors – often people who had been well-regarded in their professions. The record of cover up, disorganisation, lack of accountability or joined up thinking by the public authorities who should have been properly investigating these allegations at the time is deeply troubling.

Changes in social policy and the closure of children's homes

During the 1970s and 1980s, in the UK, there were some children's homes which had to be closed down because of cruelty, physical and sexual abuse of the children by the staff. At that time, children who had to be removed from their parental homes were likely to be placed in children's homes, in preference to being fostered or adopted, unless they were very young. From the accounts of these children when they became adults to public enquiries at a later date, it seems possible that this institutional abuse was often known about but a blind eye was turned to it or it was minimalised or rationalised. It would possibly also be fair to say that many other children's homes which were not abusive, were far from restorative or healing for the children in their care.

The public and professional awareness of these severely deprived and disadvantaged children's further vulnerability at the hands of their professional carers led to children's homes in general being disgraced and policy decisions to close as many of them as was possible. In addition there was probably a financial pressure to close many of these homes in the belief that fostering would be less expensive, as well as some political dogma which insisted that however difficult a child found it to trust adults and family life after the harm they had suffered in their birth family's homes, family life was better than the group life in a children's home. The blanket decision to close so many children's homes ignored the fact that some children really could not cope with family life, nor could any family be expected to cope with them and their extremely disturbed behaviour. Some good children's homes were closed alongside the bad. Building on the findings of Bowlby's attachment theory, the policy of all children in need being placed with families, when first removed from their birth family because of child protection issues, became the main policy of trying to provide for their emotional needs. The situation that we now have in the UK of some children being adopted following fostering, gradually came into being as the result of the Children's Act in 1991 when the importance of the 'permanency' and security of the home for the child was recognised, as discussed in Chapter 1 (Simmonds 2008, 2009).

The needs of childless adults who desperately wanted to have children were put together with the needs of children who needed lifelong families and, as a result, adoption in the UK today is likely to be of much older children than would have been thought possible in the 1950s and 1960s. One of the effects of changes in social attitudes towards 'illegitimacy' was that parents who wanted to adopt children found it increasingly difficult to adopt a baby. For a number of years, these parents were able to adopt babies from other countries but this has also become increasingly difficult. Many of the children who are now adopted in the UK have had neglectful and traumatic starts in life. The difficulties encountered by these families, where both the adopted child and the adopting parents long to have loving and intimate relationships which take many years to achieve, are well documented by child psychotherapists (Hindle and Shulman 2008).

From his child and adolescent psychiatric clinics Winnicott knew that, in extreme circumstances, some very troubled children could not be cared for within families or the children's homes of the time, but needed specialised residential therapeutic care. For many years he consulted to Barbara Dockar-Drysdale, who founded the Mulberry Bush School in 1948. Dockar-Drysdale's ideas about therapeutic child care were very influential. In particular she argued that children who had not experienced good-enough care at the start of life (i.e., had suffered from a failure of emotional environmental provision) needed the opportunity to have this 'primary experience' in a residential setting, provided by extremely dedicated staff.

Dockar-Drysdale described these children as initially being 'frozen' and unable to think or play symbolically, or to experience guilt and felt that they were 'pre-neurotic'. In his foreword to Dockar-Drysdale's book *Therapy in Child Care* Winnicott wrote that he liked this idea as it 'gives us the defence organisation that has value to the child in that it brings invulnerability, an idea which carries with it the idea of potential suffering' (Dockar-Drysdale 1968: p.ix). This was one of the issues in which Winnicott differed from Bowlby, in that although Bowlby's idea of the 'affectionless child' in *Child Care and the Growth of Love* is descriptive of a child who has suffered maternal deprivation, for Winnicott the emphasis was too much on the external behaviour of the child and did not indicate that the child had become 'affectionless' as a defence against the vulnerability that many, such as Dockar-Drysdale, were so aware of. Interestingly, the idea of a 'frozen' defence is exactly what neuroscientific research is helping us to understand further, when children are described as physically expressing 'fight, flight or freeze' responses as a result of the automatic reaction of their autonomic nervous systems to frightening experiences. This response and its clinical and neurophysiological implications are discussed in relation to a number of the case examples in this book, as well as in research terms later in this chapter.

Other impressive specialised residential settings which were a part of the therapeutic communities' movement for children and young people who could not live in families were the Peper Harow Foundation, the Cotswold Community and the Caldecott Community. Schools for children with emotional behavioural disorder (EBD) were also often residential and embraced therapeutic community thinking in their everyday functioning. For a more detailed history of this work, the reader is referred to Kasinski's chapter in *Therapeutic Communities for Children and Young People* (Kasinski 2003; Ward *et al.* (eds.) 2003) and 'Reflections on the evolution of the Mulberry Bush School and Organisation 1948–2015' (Diamond 2015). Melvyn Rose, Director of Peper Harow for many years, wrote in detail about his work and philosophy in his book *Healing Hurt Minds: The Peper Harow Experience* (1990).

Good therapeutic child care resources such as those described above (for example, The Mulberry Bush and Peper Harow) have struggled to survive because the staffing levels need to be high, staff need to be well trained and well supported in their work and they are inevitably expensive to run (see Wilson 2009). This is not work that can effectively be done on a financial shoestring. An example of consultation to the staff of this kind of specialised residential facility is given in Chapter 7 of this volume.

Changing social norms and family structures have bought a new set of challenges for family relationships. For example many mothers choose to have children without a partner and the stigma of illegitimacy has largely disappeared in Western culture; divorce is much more common than in the past; the tremendous changes in sexual behaviour resulting from the advent of the contraceptive pill and the feminist movement have enabled women to have some control over their sexuality and fertility. Many of the children who currently end up in local authority care come from very complex families where there are a number of siblings, often from different fathers who may or may not continue to have contact with their children after they leave the family home.

It is important to remember that these young men are also often the product of the intergenerational cycle of neglect and trauma and get very little help and support to become better fathers to their children. They readily become marginalised and efforts to help them to change are few and far between. (For an interesting research project on this subject see www.familyandchildcaretrust.org/young-dads-collective.) Unfortunately where there is contact, it can be intermittent and unreliable. The lack of stable caring father figures in these families is concerning as is the level of domestic violence and abuse which can force mothers and their children to escape from their homes and seek shelter in special Refuges. However, there is also the problem that perfectly innocent men can be suspected of being physically or sexually abusive, simply because they are men, when in fact the mothers or other women in the child's life have serious mental health problems and the father, with help, might have been able to be a more competent parent. It is extremely difficult and disturbing to have to recognise some women's complicity or active engagement in various forms of abuse and neglect. There is still something more shocking about reports about mothers and other women who are abusive towards children, than men.

It is sadly not uncommon to meet neglected and traumatised children in whose extended birth family there has been hardly any stable lasting relationship between any parental couple. Instability of the core family and loss or separation from **either** parent is a cause of great distress to children. The absence of the father as a positive role model may be particularly significant for adolescent boys, and one of the factors contributing to delinquent behaviour in the teenage years. Fathers who unpredictably come and go from their relationships with teenage sons cause distress which can become well-disguised by angry and generally delinquent behaviour. Underneath this defence are feelings of being rejected by their fathers, low self-esteem, alienation and loss. In an insightful chapter about the roots of delinquency and the psychodynamics of psychotherapy with these patients, Wilson reminds the reader that juvenile delinquency relates to much more than transgressing the law in ways that would be classified a crime if committed by an adult. He relates delinquency to the lack of a state of mind in which 'responsibility and honesty, both in relation to oneself and to others', matter (Wilson 2009). He draws attention to the fact that delinquent behaviour is an important aspect of the consequences of neglect and trauma. This can almost get lost in all the concerns about child protection, drug and alcohol addiction, prostitution and self-harm which can become such common features of these children's adolescence. Delinquency is related to the breakdown in the trust of adults which is a fundamental consequence of family breakdown and separation from birth parents (Wilson 2009). Horne has written about delinquency from a Winnicottian perspective (Horne 2012).

Unfortunately anti-social and violent behaviour in this group of children can become out of the control of foster and adoptive families in adolescence, leading to the breakdown of previously sound placements. Many foster families express this concern when they take a young child into their home. They are not sure that they will be able to cope with the child's adolescence and this can be the reason why a placement cannot become a long-term commitment. Some of these teenagers, possibly particularly the boys, end up in prison with very few prospects in life when they are released. As indicated above, they may also become young fathers with extremely limited internal resources to meet the challenges of fatherhood. More attention needs to be paid to their needs. They are often marginalised and given up on by society – labelled as 'no good' and incapable of change. However this group of young men need similar support to that available to young mothers who have been neglected and abused as children, if they are to try to break the cycle of neglect and abuse of which they are a part. They might get this from within the criminal justice system if they are fortunate enough to get onto a scheme which tries to offer rehabilitation and foster their entry into the workplace. In addition, innovative programmes which draw on community resources can play a vital part in helping them to change. For example a current 'Young Fathers Collective' community project is enabling these young men to talk about their needs so that public services can understand them and help them to become better fathers (www.familyandchildcaretrust.org/young-dads-collective). It is possible that, as realised by Fraiberg and her colleagues, just as young women have a powerful incentive to try to change in order to become a good-enough mother, becoming a father may also potentiate a readiness to try to change in a young and troubled father (Fraiberg *et al.* 1980).

Research influences on child and adolescent psychotherapy with severely neglected and abused children

In my experience, child patients who were known to have been sexually abused were rare until the 1980s, and when they did start to be referred for treatment it required a great deal of emotional work on the part of the therapist, to be able to fully listen to and receive the very disturbing communications that they needed to make. (For a fuller discussion and clinical example of this issue in the context of psychotherapy with a sexually abused child within a residential setting, see Lanyado (1988)).

In the UK in the 1960s, it was extremely rare to be offering psychoanalytic psychotherapy to severely neglected and traumatised children. Specialist colleagues, then known as Child Care Officers, would be working with these children and their families and the child would not be referred to the local Child Guidance Clinic or Child Psychiatry Departments (the precursors to Child and Adolescent Mental Health Service (CAMHS)). As indicated above, if a child needed to be removed from their family home because of neglect or cruelty, it was more likely that they would go to a children's home than a foster home.

The overarching policy of moving a child from his or her birth family to a foster family barely existed at this time, and neither did the idea of moving a child on from a foster family to an adoptive family. Prior to this, children had tended to be adopted as babies and the idea of 'late adoption', such as we know it today, of children in their nursery or primary school years, was unheard of. The adopted children who were referred for therapy before that time had been 'illegitimate' and had usually been adopted as babies with the consent of their mothers through adoption societies. They were not children who had been removed from their birth homes by the courts because of serious child protection issues before being legally freed for adoption.

In the 1950s, the times were so different that Bowlby devotes a whole chapter in *Child Care and the Growth of Love* (1953), to the discussion of the impact of illegitimacy and widowhood on childhood maternal deprivation. If adopted children were referred to Child Guidance Clinics, their difficulties were more likely to relate to a feeling that they did not 'fit' into their adoptive family. Or they might have lost both parents at a very young age (Lanyado 1985 and 2004 Chapter 2). Perhaps significantly, they did not present the complex and destructive behaviour that is described in this book.

Yet we are now at a point in time where a Family Division Appeal Court Judge was quoted as saying that Britain's relatively high forcible adoption rate is 'rare across the world' (Bowcott 2017). In the article the Judge notes that greater efforts should be made to promote family drugs and alcohol courts, as they might offer a way of 'breaking the cycle of vulnerability, addiction, confrontation with authority and failure, which is so often the hallmark of families who come back and back before the family courts because, without intervention, they are placing their children at risk'. The Judge also voices frustration with the current social policies and legal system surrounding these children as well as the lack of research indicating the outcomes of current social policy (Bowcott 2017).

One of Bowlby's more strongly held views (but which he modified over the years) was that such severely deprived children could not respond to psychoanalytic or any other kind of psychotherapy. He took the view that the damage to their mental health was virtually irreversible. However, the referrals for psychotherapeutic help for these children nevertheless were growing, and in 1983 Boston and Szur (Editors) published their study based on the treatment of eighty children offered psychotherapy, and discussed in a workshop at the Tavistock Clinic for psychotherapists working with severely deprived children (Boston and Szur 1983). They demonstrated that these children could respond to psychoanalytic psychotherapy and that despite the level of emotional damage they had experienced they were able to recover in some measure. This was controversial at the time, but proved to be a breakthrough. In addition psychotherapists had been publishing papers about these children for some time (for example see Henry 1974). Hunter drew together her extensive experience in this work in her book *Psychotherapy with Young People in Care* (Hunter 2001).

Daniel Stern's *The Interpersonal World of the Infant: A View from Psychoanalysis and Developmental Psychology* is a book which changed psychoanalytic paradigms for many psychotherapists in the 1980s (Stern 1985). This extraordinary book manages to do what had felt virtually impossible before this time – to explore and develop the relationship between the psychoanalytic thinking about infancy, and the infant developmental research tradition. Stern's innovative and important ideas about the infant's subjective experiences of the 'sense of self' were based on his extensive knowledge and experience of developmental psychology research and his clinical psychoanalytic practice. The use of videoed research material was a comparatively new research tool, which enabled the researcher to see the detail of minute interactions between parents or researchers and babies in ways that conventional psychoanalytic observations could not. This technology, using frame-by-frame analysis of data, together with increasingly sophisticated research methodologies and analysis of research findings, were catalysts in thinking about the infant in entirely new ways. The infant as seen through psychoanalytic theory and observation, and the infant as seen on video in the lab, relating to the researcher or parent were similar in some ways and strikingly different in others.

Stern's findings and theories (based on his own and other researchers' findings) about the ordinary busily relating infant who was highly sociable and curious once his or her needs had been met had significant effects on many clinicians because there was a sense of a new psychological validity to what he was deducing, which had been felt to be lacking from previous research. For example, in her paper 'The perpetuation of an error', in the light of the highly sociable infant that Stern described, the child psychotherapist Tustin, whose writing about autistic states is internationally renowned, changed her views about the earliest stage of normal infant life being an autistic phase (Tustin 1994). Stern used the infant's state of 'alert inactivity' when basic needs for food and sleep had been met, as a 'window' through which 'questions can be put to new-borns and answers can be discerned from their ongoing activity' (Stern 1985: 39). Stern and his contemporaries' ingenious research methodology enabled researchers and clinicians to see that they could share and further develop a mutually beneficial language about parent–infant research in particular.

Significantly for the subject of this book, the advances in what can be understood about 'ordinary' infant and young child development – through developmental psychology research like Stern's, and neuroscientific research as discussed below and in subsequent chapters – enable clinicians to comprehend the enormity of what has **not** happened in the lives of severely neglected and traumatised children. Rather than solely relying on psychoanalytic theories based on direct baby observation, or extrapolating backwards in time from experiences in the consulting room with patients who do not represent the 'norm', we are now able to triangulate our knowledge through these different disciplines and shape our clinical practice accordingly.

The 1980s also saw the beginnings of an important new form of treatment, parent–infant psychotherapy, which was first named and developed by Selma Fraiberg and her colleagues in her book *Clinical Studies in Infant Mental Health: The First Year of Life* (Fraiberg (ed.) 1980). This book had an enormous and very encouraging impact because, as well as indicating that it was possible to break the inter-generational cycle of deprivation and abuse, the positive results of the treatment were achieved in a startlingly brief period of time. For therapists accustomed to the need for lengthy therapeutic interventions with very deprived patients, Fraiberg's work demonstrated that, contrary to previous thinking, the first year of life was an extraordinarily fruitful time to be working with struggling parent–infant couples. This was possible if the therapist worked through the parent–infant couple's relationship, crucially with the infant in the room. Fraiberg's work, and particularly her and her colleagues' chapter 'Ghosts in the nursery: a psychoanalytic approach' (Fraiberg *et al.* 1980), has remained inspirational for a whole generation of psychotherapists who have developed these ideas. There is a rich literature on the subject of parent–infant psychotherapy, for example Baradon (2010), Daws (1999), Dowling (2006, 2009, 2012), Hopkins (1994/2015), Joyce (2010), Jones (2010), and Onions (2009).

Hope can be supported and sustained by greater understanding, and, in this respect, one of the most exciting developments over recent years has been the dramatic technological and research advances of neuroscience. These have been growing dramatically since the mid-1990s. We are now able to understand why children who have been severely traumatised can be so hyperactive, or so closed down. Levels of cortisol in their brain, triggered by the autonomic nervous system – fight–flight or freeze when in danger – get stuck on 'override' as a basic physiological protection against danger. Technological advances which enable us to see what is going on in the brain, such as fMRI scans, show us what we in many ways already know clinically, but add an important new dimension – the physicality of our emotions, particularly our most primitive emotions. The alarming impact on the baby's brain during the first two years of life, of constantly living with fear, illustrates how vital early intervention through parent–infant psychotherapy can be (Gerhardt 2004a). This emphasis on work with babies and children under five as a significant clinical intervention, as well as a preventative measure against later emotional disturbance, is well recognised in child mental health services today, many of which offer specialised clinics for these young patients and their parents.

We live in our bodies and our emotions are expressed within our bodies as well as our minds. Neuroscience has enabled us to think in a much more holistic way which challenges the old body–mind dichotomy and helps us to realise that it is not a dichotomy at all, but that the mind and the body are different sides of the same coin. This understanding of the body's response to trauma, particularly in infants and young children, leads to greater insight and potentially more tolerant responses to some of the more disturbing behaviour of these children who are essentially at the mercy of their primitive bodily responses to fear. Encouragingly, we can now also appreciate that new neural pathways involving the thinking cortex can be laid down which, given enough time, can supersede old destructive more primitive brain reactions. To quote Music

> One hopeful feature of recent neuroscientific findings is that the brain remains plastic throughout life . . . New learning can give rise to new neuronal connections and new brain organisations throughout life. We might never erase old experiences and their related brain circuits, but we can build new experiences, new expectations and new pathways.
>
> (Music 2011a: 95)

This is a valuable and healing part of the everyday experience of these children's lives in foster and adoptive families, and in the psychotherapy consulting room. However, these changes can take many years, and in the meanwhile the children and adults who try to care for them have to try to survive as best as they can and need a great deal of support and therapeutic help.

There is nevertheless alarming evidence from fMRI brain scans that trauma and neglect can result in actual and, to some extent, possibly irreversible brain damage when it happens at a very young age. The impact is clearly serious and enduring and there are limitations to how much change is possible. In the absence of a protective adult, the baby becomes dependent on the most ancient part of the human brain, often referred to as the reptilian brain, to react to perceived danger on a life-preserving basis (such as fight, flight or freeze), without the mediation of the cortical part of the brain that can help inappropriate fear responses to be moderated by thought. It is through the inter-personal relationships of early childhood that the cortex of the brain develops in normal childhood. Severely neglected children have not had enough of this kind of relatedness. They have effectively been left to the mercy of the most basic reptilian response system for survival, which is unable to show any discernment about different kinds of danger but simply reacts as a part of the autonomic nervous system's response to fear. Such children struggle to play, learn or form relationships because they are constantly on high alert for potential danger, even though the danger of their early years has long disappeared. All of the children described in this book will have suffered to some degree in this way and their bodies and brains will have been affected by these experiences to the extent that it is necessary with children like Amber discussed in Chapter 3, to regard them as trying to live with a physical condition akin to being brain damaged in other circumstances.

It is all too easy to lay the blame for this at their parents' door, but in the main it is very unfair to do this. Few of these parents intend to be the neglectful and traumatising parents they nevertheless become. They are often sad, overwhelmed, unsupported, young and very lacking in their own experiences of having been adequately looked after as children. As discussed above, they are often part of an inter-generational cycle of emotional deprivation, neglect and misfortune, which may only begin to be changed when their child is removed from their care, or they are offered some form of treatment and help before this becomes essential for the child's safety.

A very big investment of professional time is needed for a number of years if lasting change is to be possible. There is no quick fix option. And clinically we are now clearly seeing the inter-generational effects of **not** treating the children, who despite their often genuine wish to be better parents than their own parents were to them, may become neglectful and traumatising to the next generation in their family. The sequelae of being a severely neglected and traumatised child, in cultural and social terms, are serious. These are the most vulnerable people in our society who are likely to have significant mental and physical health needs throughout their lives, end up in prison and altogether live unhappy and impoverished lives. We cannot afford to ignore them and hope the problems will go away. Quite the contrary, the problems continue through subsequent generations if appropriate help and intervention is not offered.

3   The absence of 'holding' and containment, and the absence of parental protection

At the core of thoughts about what is meant by neglect is the idea of an *absence* of something that is needed. And at the core of thoughts about trauma is the idea of the overwhelming *presence* of something that is harmful. What is it that is needed but absent when a child is being neglected and how does this almost inevitably open the door to the presence of trauma?

In thinking about what is missing when there is neglect, we need to have in mind theories about ordinary, good-enough emotional development in infancy and childhood. What is it that ordinary babies 'have', which neglected babies do not have? There are several key psychoanalytic concepts that help to build up a picture of the emotional life of the ordinary infant, by which I mean the pre-verbal baby during roughly the first two years of life. Winnicott emphasises the importance of parental physical and emotional 'holding' of the baby; Bion describes the detail of early communication between the baby and the parent which helps the baby to experience the 'containment' of his or her anxieties: Bowlby underlines the life-preserving function of parental protection of the young in his theories about attachment (Bion 1962; Bowlby 1988a; Winnicott 1960). These ideas have different and, to my reading, complementary contributions to make to the understanding and treatment of severely neglected and traumatised children and are expanded on, together with a detailed case illustration, in this chapter. Severely neglected and traumatised children suffer from such a multiplicity of problems that it is highly unlikely that one unifying theory can comprehend them and point the way to try to help them. We are bound to need several key theories, each of which may have its place and time in the understanding of the psychotherapeutic process with a particular child. This kind of pluralistic thinking can provide structure for the understanding of the therapeutic process, which can enable therapists to tolerate better the enormous demands of the work.

Whilst all of these psychological processes and relationships are operational in some form throughout childhood and the life cycle, the focus in this chapter is mainly on infancy. It is during this early and extremely vulnerable phase of life that the children discussed in this book have suffered the most damaging neglect. This is because what does or does not happen in these early months of life, forms the bedrock of the ways in which the individual learns about relationships and is the foundation of the individual's mental health. This view is supported by developmental psychology and neuroscientific research as described in the previous chapter. It is not that later stages in child development are less important, more that the process of emotional development is cumulative. One step leads to another. Neglect appearing in many forms and intensities can happen at different stages of a child's life with differing repercussions as discussed by Music, as well as intermittently over many years (Music 2009b, 2011b).

A sound understanding of ordinary infant and child emotional development becomes a guiding principle in the therapeutic process, as it helps the therapist to recognise the earliest signs of when healthy emotional development is starting to take place. This is one of the reasons why a detailed two-year, hour-long weekly observation in the home of a baby and his or her parents is so central to the training of child and adolescent psychotherapists (Sternberg 2005). As a result of this training, the first important signs of new development can often be more readily noticed by the therapist within the intensity of the therapeutic relationship, than in the everyday lives of previously neglected and traumatised children. When the therapist draws attention to them, these tiny new shoots of growth need to be nurtured by the child's parents, carers and teachers as well as within the present therapeutic relationship. This concerted effort of all the adults involved in the child's life helps the child to put down healthy roots for new emotional development (Hurry 1998; Lanyado 2017).

In a carefully argued and important paper, based on Anna Freud's ideas about developmental help, Hurry comes to the conclusion that 'The distinction between developmental and psychoanalytic work is (thus) a false one: psycho-analysis is in itself a particular type of developmental therapy' (Hurry 1998: 34). She adds 'In psychoanalytic developmental therapy, patients find or create in the therapist an appropriate "developmental" object.' (Hurry 1998: 35).

These ideas are very helpful in understanding the multi-tasking approach that is needed in severely neglected and traumatised children's therapy. Hurry argues that just as the good-enough parent is mindful of when his or her child is becoming able to manage the next developmental step, there are also times when the good-enough analyst in effect gives the patient a subtle 'nudge' towards the next developmental stage. If the nudge is well-judged and well-timed, the patient will be able to respond to it; if the nudge is not well-timed or inappropriate, the subtlety of the nudge may simply mean that it will pass unnoticed by the patient. If the nudge is really mis-attuned to the patient it will be a therapeutic mistake, the consequences of which will need to be addressed as with all other mistakes. When the therapist is being used as a developmental object in the therapy, he or she is inevitably more active and present than when working in the transference relationship. These processes are inextricably interwoven within the total therapeutic process particularly with severely neglected and deprived children (Hurry 1998). When children have suffered serious developmental delay because of neglect at the start of life, it makes sense to encourage development as much as possible when the child recovers enough to show signs of getting back on a more normal developmental track. The clinical material throughout this book draws on this thinking and is expanded in a recent paper where the interplay between the therapist as a developmental object and the therapist as a transference object is discussed from the perspective of technical dilemmas in the therapy of these patients (Lanyado 2017).

'There is no such thing as an infant'

In his work as a paediatrician, Winnicott observed and consulted to thousands of ordinary parents and babies whilst their early relationships were developing: families who were in the midst of the demanding reality of feeding and sleeping difficulties, developmental milestones and delays, childhood illnesses and so on. This contributed to his great respect for the 'ordinary devoted mother' whom he directly addressed in his BBC radio broadcasts, as well as in the opening chapter of the book based on these broadcasts *The Child, The Family and the Outside World* (Winnicott 1964). This enabled him to incorporate what he learnt from his paediatric practice into his child and adolescent psychiatric and psychoanalytic practice and writings.

The importance of the reality of the quality of the baby's physical care at the start of life, which is the literal embodiment of the parent's love of their baby, together with the emotional counterpart of trying to understand the baby's needs, became Winnnicott's paradigm for parental 'holding' of the psyche and the soma (Winnicott 1960). This emphasis on the holding of both the body and the emotions of the baby helps us to understand the many variations and intensities of neglect that can happen. For example in some instances the body may be well looked after by the parent but the emotional needs may be left largely unmet. It is against this template of the ordinary good-enough parent–infant relationship that Winnicott's writings about emotional disturbance can best be understood.

Bowlby and Winnicott challenged psychoanalytic theories that were essentially atomistic – that is, isolating the individual baby and not taking into account the actual experience of how a particular baby was cared for by his or her parents. (However, Winnicott was critical of what he felt was Bowlby's lack of attention in his theory of attachment behaviour, to the internal life of the infant and young child and this remains a significant difference between their theories.) Winnicott's 1960 paper on the parent–infant relationship emphasises the fundamental importance of what he calls emotional and physical 'holding', at the time of the infant's maximum dependence on the parent's care. As a footnote in the paper, he makes what has become one of his best known statements about infancy:

> I once said 'There is no such thing as an infant', meaning, of course, that whenever one finds an infant one finds maternal care, and without maternal care there would be no infant.
>
> (Winnicott 1960: in Caldwell and Joyce 2011: 168)

During this period of time when the individuality of the child begins to form, the baby is totally dependent on maternal (and more generally parental) care as expressed through the physicality of this caring relationship, for the experience of a dawning sense of continuity of selfhood and the earliest integration of mind and body. This is what I understand Winnicott to mean when he writes about the individual's growing experience of 'continuity of being' as facilitated by parental care. The baby needs to be held in the mind, heart and enveloping arms of the parent which includes the presence of parental loving touch of the baby. In the ordinary parent–infant relationship, parents go to extraordinary lengths of devotion and preoccupation to do this (Winnicott 1956).

At first the ordinary physically and emotionally demanding tasks of simply trying to work out when the baby needs feeding, cuddling, nappy changing, burping and putting down to sleep are all-absorbing and exhausting for parents. Amidst the happiness and celebration of the baby's arrival, the parents suffer from sleep deprivation, and the mother may suffer from sore nipples, painful breasts, an aching body from all the carrying of the crying baby and attempts to sooth him or her, lack of seeing friends and so on. Winnicott drew attention to the very special state of mind that was needed in the mother in particular, for her to be able to devotedly give this care. He called it 'primary maternal preoccupation'. He went so far as to say:

> I do not believe that it is possible to understand the functioning of the mother at the very beginning of the infant's life without seeing that she must be able to reach this state of heightened sensitivity, almost an illness, and recover from it.
>
> (Winnicott 1956: 302)

He argued that this heightened sensitivity and state of mind develops during and particularly at the end of pregnancy and lasts with great intensity for a few weeks after the birth of the baby, slowly diminishing as the baby becomes less dependent. Gradually the baby becomes more comprehensible and the mother comes to know what the baby needs, and when he or she needs it. As the baby grows into a child, the child is always in the parent's mind with the potential for the intensity of this early preoccupation to come to the fore again if the child is in any kind of difficulty. In ordinary relationships, there are periods of calm and contentment for the baby and parents, which reassure the parents that they are being 'good-enough' (Winnicott 1949). Developmental psychologists refer to this developmental process as 'attunement' of the parent to the baby (Stern 1985). This process, which is particularly important during the first six weeks of the baby's life, roughly coincides with the period that Winnicott describes as the parents' most intense 'primary preoccupation' with the baby. Observation of babies during these early weeks of life (possibly significantly before the baby starts to smile at around six weeks and reward parents for all their efforts) offers a profound sense of anticipation, of something coming-into-being which Stern has termed the sense of 'Emergent Self' in the baby (Stern 1985). Interestingly, when patients are on the cusp of important emotional change in therapy, this sense of Emergent Self can reappear in the clinical experience as Stern has suggested.

Winnicott argues that if the 'good-enough' parent is able to immerse him or herself in this primary preoccupation, the baby's 'own line of life' is disturbed very little by experiences which are not reasonably congruent with his or her needs. And indeed, again we can observe ordinary parents going to remarkable lengths to make sure they fit as closely as they possibly can to whatever the baby seems to need. For a number of weeks at the start of a baby's life, most households revolve around the baby, until there is a sense in the parents that the baby is more able to wait a bit to have his or her needs met. (For a detailed and delightful account of 'the business of parenting' see Daws and de Rementeria (2015)).

The counterpart of the parents' fierce need to protect the baby's sense of continuity of being by staying as close as possible to whatever the baby seems to need, is that life inevitably throws up all sorts of obstacles to providing this rather idyllic state for the baby. This is why Winnicott's idea of the 'good-enough', not perfect parent is such a relief to so many parents when they come across it. All parents cannot help but fail some of the time in trying to make sense of what the baby needs and trying to provide it. Winnicott calls intrusions into this aspect of the infant's sense of continuity of being, 'impingements'. If these intrusions happen too often or are too overwhelming for the baby they become traumatic. Winnicott argues that when this happens, the baby can suffer a sense of utter 'annihilation' and he goes on to state dramatically that at this early stage in life 'being and annihilation are two alternatives'. He says that

> ... in the extreme case the infant only exists on the basis of the continuity of reactions to impingements and of recoveries from such reactions. This is in contrast to the continuity of being which is my conception of ego-strength.
> (Winnicott 1960 in Caldwell and Joyce 2011: 165)

and

> If maternal care is not good enough then the infant does not come into existence since there is no continuity of being: instead the personality becomes built on the basis of reactions to environmental impingement.
> (Winnicott 1960 in Caldwell and Joyce 2011: 167)

With these quotes in mind it becomes possible to see more clearly, from a Winnicottian perspective, what has been *absent* in the parent–infant relationship at the start of life, when there has been early neglect, and how devastating for the baby's future emotional well-being the consequences of this absence can be. Winnicott is clear that traumatic impingements can much more readily intrude on the baby's emotional life when parents cannot become 'preoccupied' with their baby. Whilst he is not directly writing about physical harm to the baby in this paper, his thoughts about the emotional consequences of 'environmental failure' are enlarged on in his thought-provoking paper 'Hate in the countertransference'. This paper draws on Winnicott's wartime experiences of consulting to hostels for disturbed evacuated children, many of whom had suffered from the kinds of neglect and trauma that are the subject of this book, as well as his and his wife's experience of trying to foster such a child (Winnicott 1947/1949). He discusses frankly the feelings of hatred that children like this (as well as borderline/psychotic adult patients) can arouse in their therapists and how this goes back to the original environmental failure in which love and hate could not be integrated. The therapist's difficult task in the countertransference is to 'maintain an analytic attitude and not retaliate in the face of intense provocation' (Caldwell and Joyce 2011: 72). Amber, discussed below, provides a good example of the countertransference struggles that the therapist has to engage with in order to help the patient. In an insightful paper, Dowling develops Winnicott's ideas about the therapist's efforts to understand the therapeutic implications of hatred in the work of child psychotherapists with children, parents and within the professional network (Dowling 2012).

The importance of parental containment of infantile emotions

Bion's concept of containment and Winnicott's concept of holding, both describe very early forms of communication, with Winnicott emphasising the significance of good-enough physical care of the baby at the start of life. The absence of early emotional containment of intense infantile anxieties can be seen very graphically in the behaviour of a neglected and traumatised child. Alvarez describes Bion's concept of containment as follows (Bion 1962):

> Bion's idea is of a container receptive to and working upon projections of a powerful and active kind. His idea of containment involves something far more than soothing a distressed baby (or patient). It involves being filled up with feelings that may be highly disturbing, and the attempt to transform these and communicate them back to the patient in a bearable form, is done at considerable cost to the mother (or analyst) – that is, after much work on her own feelings.
>
> (Alvarez 2012: 138)

For these reasons, as Alvarez indicates and many parents will testify, it is very demanding and hard emotional work to be an 'ordinary' parent, even when external circumstances and support are readily available. What is it that makes this emotional work so hard? Whilst non-verbal projection of emotions into another person is a lifelong psychological mechanism, it is particularly intense when words and appropriate actions are not available to express even some small part of the feelings which are being communicated. The ordinary pre-verbal baby relies on the parents' strenuous efforts to listen to the baby and try to make sense of what the baby is trying to communicate. This form of listening involves the whole of the parent's body: for example, feelings of dread or panic which are experienced in the pit of the parent's stomach; seemingly irrational fears that the baby will die if the parent doesn't manage to understand why the baby is crying so much and what the baby needs; feelings of terrifying helplessness in the face of the unknown and incomprehensible causes of the baby's distress. The baby evokes these feelings in the parents in the unconscious to unconscious form of communication that is projection.

Through the same inter-psychic mechanism, patients also evoke these feelings in their therapists who need to have developed a good and enhanced capacity to contain anxiety. Training analysis is a central part of all psychoanalytic trainings. One of the many outcomes of this is that the therapist's capacity to contain anxiety is increased in ways that are essential if they are to be able to contain the intense anxieties communicated by their patients. The other major way in which psychoanalytic training and professional development help therapists to increase their capacity to contain anxiety is through clinical supervision, as discussed in Chapter 9. This capacity to contain extreme anxiety, enhanced by training and ongoing professional development, is part of the reason why child and adolescent psychotherapists are particularly able to help severely neglected and traumatised patients (see Note 1). It is the therapist's role to listen extremely carefully to the patient – with body, mind and soul – and then, as Parsons indicates, to listen to himself listening to the patient. It is from this listening, in two directions – externally to the patient and internally to the feelings and thoughts the patient stirs in the therapist – that understanding, insight and change gradually emerge through the work in the transference–counter transference relationship (Parsons 2014).

The demanding nature of what goes on inside the mind and body of the parent, who is able to listen to and try to transform the baby's inchoate experiences into more understandable experiences, is the reason that many new parents are astonished that they can feel so exhausted from 'simply' being with the baby. On a good day, these parents may feel that they have not done much other than gaze at the baby, talk to the baby, and think about the baby for several relatively peaceful hours. But this belies the fact that this process of listening (introjecting) and trying to transform the incomprehensible elements of the baby's communications (what Bion terms the alpha elements of the baby's communications) into more readily understood elements (Bion's beta elements) can be all absorbing. This is true when the parent muses about what is going on in the baby's mind, when the baby is actively alert and seemingly curious about the world outside them, as well as when the baby is incomprehensibly screaming and nothing seems to help them feel better (Bion 1962). Becoming a parent and trying to meet all of these challenges is transforming and potentially maturing for parents. It is an opportunity for personal growth.

The parent's actions in response to the baby – cuddling, rocking, touching, stroking, talking, singing, feeding, nappy changing and so on – reflect the significant emotional efforts of the parent to understand their baby's needs and respond as well as they can to them. If the parent has got close enough to 'knowing' the baby and what the baby is trying to express, particularly when the baby is crying, and as a result the baby calms, the parent also calms and the previous powerful waves of anxiety diminish within both of them. The baby's anxieties have been 'contained' by this process of communication with the parent, in which their cries and needs have been heard and appropriately responded to (Bion 1962). These are the precursors of feeling known and understood, and not isolated and alone in the world. Psychotherapeutically, when a patient has experienced this kind of communication and understanding in the therapeutic process, through a verbal interpretation or through more subtle non-verbal communication, there can be a palpable change in the quality of the relationship, as well as the clinical material that follows. There are many examples of this in this book.

What looks like a very simple and straight-forward everyday process, is in fact very complicated and emotionally demanding. This becomes even more apparent when parents find it difficult to listen to their baby in this way. The ordinary parent's capacity to contain and transform the very powerful emotions that the baby projects into them, is inevitably impaired when they are struggling with their own everyday needs, feelings and worries. In these circumstances, there is less space in their mind to perform this vital emotional task for the baby. As a result, there may be periods of time when they are less able to understand or to transform the baby's intense and overwhelming feelings so that they can become more tolerable, and integrated into the baby's developmental progress.

In more extreme circumstances, parents who are struggling with, for example, their own significant mental health issues, post-natal depression, adverse social conditions, drug addiction, alcoholism, bereavement, difficult relationships with their own parents, serious tensions and domestic violence in their relationships with their partners – cannot have enough space in their minds to devote to their babies in a steadfast and reliable way. Any one of these difficulties adds significantly to the parental difficulty in caring for a young baby and often, as many of the clinical examples in this book illustrate, several, or even all, of these problems are ongoing in their lives. Most fundamentally, if the parent has not had enough of an experience of having their own primitive anxieties contained by their parents during their childhood, they have a very limited internal emotional capacity to help them to help their babies and children. These parents are much more likely to reach breaking points in which they become aggressive, harmful and rejecting towards their babies and children. They are more likely to feel persecuted by their baby's needs than responsive to them. Their ability to tolerate and not feel overwhelmed by the intense anxiety that their baby or child needs to project into them, is inevitably much more limited than parents who have themselves been well parented.

Parent–infant psychotherapy provides the immediate opportunity (with the parent and baby in the room together) for the parent to engage in the transference–countertransference relationship with the therapist. This can change the parent's internal experience of what it feels like and means to be listened to, from within the therapeutic relationship, and this in turn can have a surprisingly rapid impact on the parent–infant relationships. By containing the anxieties of the parent in the immediacy of the transference–countertransference relationship, the parent becomes more able to contain the raw feelings of their baby (Fraiberg *et al.* 1980; Hopkins 1994/2015).

Whatever our sympathies with these very troubled parents might be, the impact on the child's emotional and physical development is devastating and immediate. Some of these children have bodily scars that have resulted from neglect and trauma, and may have been injured to the extent that they were close to death. There can be evidence of burns or untreated fractures. There may have been severe malnutrition requiring hospitalisation; the baby might have been shaken in ways that caused brain damage. Amber's story, below, is about particularly extreme physical abuse and neglect at the start of life and is an example of the significance and implications of the lack of basic child care leading to cruelty, as well as the lack of containment of extreme feelings at the start of life. Foster and adoptive parents and residential care workers offer dedicated and loving child care to them, but can hit a point where 'love is not enough' and psychotherapy is needed to release the child from the constrictions of their past experiences, so that they can really make the most of the care that is being given to them in the present. Whilst therapy takes them some of the way along this journey, there always remains an intense awareness of how much trauma and emotional damage remains, even when a helpful therapy comes to an end.

The following case illustration describes the complex life history of the patient and its repercussions for her mental health. When a child has had a number of parents – birth parents, foster parents and adoptive parents – his or her sense of 'continuity of being' is profoundly affected (Winnicott 1960). Unlike ordinary children whose parents can remember all the significant internal and external events of their lives, which helps them to understand their growing child, these children inevitably suffer from the lack of this kind of parental remembering, which results from the **discontinuity** of parental care. One of the most difficult and distressing tasks for foster or adoptive parents, is to try to take into their minds and hearts the awful experiences of their child's life, before the child came to live with them. What this in effect means is that when he or she was a vulnerable baby, the child they have adopted and love, suffered (for example) from acute hunger and lived in squalor in a drug dealing birth parent's chaotic and un-protective home. This is very painful for loving adoptive parents to realise, yet it is part of what they need to internalise and utilise to help them make sense of the child's emotions and behaviour (Cregeen 2017).

With this in mind, it is clear that psychotherapists also need to be able to absorb the emotional implications of each severely neglected and traumatised child's life history, if they are to be able to understand them and try to contain the extreme emotions that are projected into them at times. 'Amber' was seen by a supervisee of mine and it is this internalisation of the life history aspect of the therapeutic process that I am trying to illustrate in what follows. Because of this, the example is only partially about the therapeutic process itself. I am very grateful to my supervisee and her colleagues for giving me permission to write about their work with Amber. Care has been taken to disguise Amber's identity whilst remaining true to the important features of her treatment.

Amber is an example of a severely neglected and traumatised child whose chronic level of hyper-alertness, resulting in her being in a constant state of fight/flight arousal and suffering from the effects of 'corrosive cortisol', have been described in Chapter 2 (Gerhardt 2004a).

Amber was removed from the care of her birth parents when she was two years old. She had multiple unexplained fractures and had clearly experienced non-accidental injury of the kind described by Kempe and his colleagues in Chapter 1 (Kempe *et al.* 1962). There were several foster placements which soon broke down because of her very destructive and exhausting behaviour in the home. She was hyperactive during the day and had great difficulty in sleeping at night. She smeared her faeces and urinated wherever she fancied. However, as thankfully happens surprisingly often, when she was five years old she was fostered by experienced foster parents who became very attached to her, as she did to them and their family. Despite her awful behaviour she was still a loveable child. However, over the years the foster parents became more and more exhausted, as well as worried that they were neglecting their own children because of Amber's needs.

Amber was referred to Child and Adolescent Mental Health Services (CAMHS) by her school when she was eight years old because she was hyperactive, unable to concentrate, disruptive in class, stealing from other children and impossible to keep in the classroom. She would unpredictably rush out of the classroom many times a day and end up wandering about the school, quite charmingly engaging other classes and teachers in the process, as well as taking up a great deal of the head-teacher's and other senior staff members' time. This was despite having a learning support assistant with her most of the day, who did his best to settle Amber to various activities.

Amber's therapist fortunately was able to see her in a special room in the school. However, it would be more accurate to say that at the start of therapy the therapist tried to see her in the room – because much of the time was spent trying to get her back into the room after she had run off, just as she did when in class. In following this little girl and trying to get her back to the room, the therapist had the opportunity to see how the whole school – pupils as well as staff – were extraordinarily patient and kind to her. Without actually knowing the details of Amber's past, they seemed to understand her need to be compassionately contained whenever she felt so anxious that she just had to run from wherever she was. Why did Amber still behave in these ways so many years after the extreme neglect and physical abuse she had suffered, and despite her foster carers' concerted efforts to look after her?

The therapist gradually understood that part of the problem was that it was extremely difficult for anyone who knew about the terrible events of Amber's first two years of life really to bear to know the emotional impact this had had on her. Amber was a child who might have been murdered by her birth parents if she had not been removed from home. She had been to hospital a number of times because of her injuries, but had been discharged and put on the child protection register with a social worker monitoring her welfare. This might have been the kind of case where, at the time, there was not quite enough evidence for Amber to be taken away from her parents, or it might have been that Amber simply 'fell through the net' of child protection procedures. She must have suffered extreme and relentless fear of her parents who should have been protecting her from harm, but were in fact the cause of her harm. They were imprisoned for the injuries they had caused Amber. It was striking that throughout the time that Amber was in therapy, and despite numerous requests, hardly any more detailed records about what had happened to her were forthcoming. It seemed that this was too awful to know about. This inability to provide crucial information, which must have been available somewhere in the system, is often an unconscious 'acting out' by professionals of the wish 'not to know' about terrible events in a young child's life, as such knowledge would be intolerably distressing and painful.

What was increasingly apparent to the therapist was that Amber remained fixed in the physiological fight or flight mode of trying to protect herself from danger, many years after she was actually living in safety. Understanding this, and imagining what Amber's first two years could have been like was distressing for the therapist, but also very necessary if the therapist was to be able to understand Amber. There was a meaning behind all of Amber's extremely challenging behaviour. Whilst Amber was still too traumatised and frightened for this to be spoken about, the fact that the therapist had managed to become more aware of some of the details of the source of Amber's extreme fear helped the therapist to understand why she (the therapist) was often so full of the disturbing and frightening feelings with which Amber was strug-gling. This kind of 'knowing' is the process of projection, introjection and containment taking place in the therapeutic setting (Bion 1962).

The therapist often dreaded Amber's sessions with their high levels of anxiety and unpredictability and needed to examine and reflect on these feelings in between each tumultuous session, trying to make some sense of them, in order to face the next session. This was an important part of the parallel clinical supervision process that she engaged in with me, as is discussed in more detail in Chapter 9. At times this inevitably involved thinking about the hatred that Amber could engender in the therapist, as well as feelings of fierce protection (Winnicott 1947/1949). As the therapist gradually became able to understand that the intense anxiety she felt about being with Amber was the result of projection, of the intense anxiety Amber felt all the time, because of the life-threatening physical abuse she had suffered, some of the fear started to be contained and processed by the therapist, and the healthy containment of the powerful early emotions, that Bion writes about and Alvarez describes above, started to take place. As a result, Amber was gradually more able to stay in the therapy room and classroom and to play and concentrate a little bit more than in the past.

This is an example of the therapist's efforts to bear to get close to, and tolerate knowing about, Amber's extreme fear and dreadful past, that is, to contain and transform her emotions into something more bearable. Knowing about Amber's past in any deeper or more sustained way had possibly been too overwhelming for other adults in her life, and it was not until her therapist tried to bear knowing about the fear and pain she had experienced, that it became more possible for Amber to become less overwhelmingly anxious to be with. This is also an example of the therapist becoming a developmental object for Amber. The containment of Amber's extreme and automatic flight behaviour, as seen in Amber's increasing ability to stay in the therapy room and classroom, enabled Amber to make some developmental progress, particularly in her new and growing capacity to play in an imaginative way for increasingly long periods of time (Hurry 1998). This was a child who had not given up trying to communicate her primitive anxieties and had not given up hope that someone might be able to receive and contain them. The therapist's response, like the parent to their desperately crying baby, met some of Amber's needs and enabled her to make some small developmental progress.

As well as seeing Amber regularly for her therapy, the therapist worked closely with the school staff to try to help contain Amber's behaviour. Another colleague from the clinic met regularly with the foster parents. However, whilst Amber did become more able to stay in the therapy room and play in communicative ways, and had become much less aggressive – all of which was a big achievement for her – her foster parents were close to collapse. They needed much more practical support and respite than the social services department were able to provide. In addition, the hard-pressed social worker who had a number of similarly worrying children to work with, became increasingly unavailable, possibly feeling that Amber was getting lots of help through CAMHS and the school, and hoping that this would be enough. But it wasn't. Due to the rationing of therapeutic resources, her treatment had to stop after a year and a half. Although it was a planned ending as discussed in Chapter 4, and Amber was touchingly able to express some of her sadness at losing her relationship with her therapist, which was another important developmental achievement, the placement subsequently broke down, amidst great distress for all concerned.

Amber's fear and anxiety could not be contained in her foster family despite all the professional input there had been. Possibly what she needed was more than any family could provide – that is, a group of adults, who by working closely together, could provide the containment and understanding she had not received when she was so little. Intuitively, the staff (and pupils) at the school in their kindly and patient response to Amber's uncontained behaviour were trying to respond to this need, and succeeded in some measure, particularly when they were able to work closely with the psychotherapist and her CAMHS colleague. They tried to be the group of adults that Amber needed to contain her intense anxiety. But sadly, in this case it was not enough. Amber may well have needed to receive therapy whilst living in a specialist residential therapeutic community, such as described in Chapters 1 and 8, where this kind of intensive containment is constantly attended to as an ongoing part of the staff group process. However, the funds were not available.

On reflection, the hope remained that the developmental gains she had made might continue in her new relationships in her next foster home. Hopefully Amber's experience of some of her emotional needs being met and understood in her therapy stayed with her, even though she might not have had a lengthy enough opportunity to fully consolidate this experience. Her loss of her therapist might have prompted some internalisation and helpful memories of their relationship through some identification with the lost good-enough therapist as discussed in the next chapter (Freud 1917). However, the loss of her foster home where she had lived for nearly half of her life, as well as the loss of the school that had tried so hard to help her, inevitably had further emotional repercussions in her life. This is part of the hit and miss nature of what happens to children like this as they move from one foster home to another.

It is hard to believe that all the emotionally demanding work of Amber's therapy was of no avail, and indeed this is not my view as a supervisor of the case. In the lead up to the last few weeks of Amber's therapy, she started to run out of class again and was sometimes found in the vacant therapy room. When the therapist was told about this by the school, she could imagine Amber curled up in the tent she often made in her sessions, with cushions to make herself comfortable. She had managed to form a new relationship with her therapist which clearly mattered to her, and the therapist expressed hope that Amber might still be able to love and be loved, wherever she was moved onto in life. Unfortunately, it is often not practically possible to find out how children like Amber have fared in the long run. Therapists have to hope and trust that the emotional authenticity of what has taken place in the therapy will sustain the child, and enable the child to recognise further opportunities for growth promoting relationships at later stages in life.

Severe deprivation of stimulation also has a lasting effect on babies' brain development. The horrors of the physical and emotional deprivation and trauma experienced by children in the Romanian orphanages in the 1980s led to some of them being adopted in other countries. The long-term twenty-five-year findings of the English and Romanian Adoption Study are pertinent to these children (Kennedy *et al.* 2016). They conclude that there is a powerful statistical link between severe early deprivation and hyperactivity, which suggests a deep-seated alteration in brain structure and function as a result of the early deprivation. This hyperactivity co-occurred with high levels of quasi-autistic features and is confirmed in the neuroscientific research discussed in Chapter 2.

The implications of this research are far reaching. One of the central considerations in the difficult question of how best to look after these children, is how to secure the greatest stability in their lives, and this includes the further and important consideration of the impact of many placement moves such as Amber's, on the child's education. The negative effects of many moves of home often don't take into account the fact that the child may also be moving schools many times. The emotional disturbance that the child will be suffering because of all the neglect, trauma and losses he or she has experienced is compounded by difficulties in learning and behavioural problems in school. These children are, very ironically, often described as being 'looked after' by the local authorities (LAC for short), as in the quote below. A recent report on early education and looked-after children presented some stark statistics:

> Government data show that LAC (looked after children) have significantly poorer educational outcomes than children not in care throughout primary and secondary school, with the gap widening as the children get older. By secondary level, only 18 percent gained 5 GCSEs at grade C or higher in 2015 compared with 64 percent of children not in care . . . LAC are also four times more likely to have special educational needs than children within the general

population, and almost ten times more likely to have a statement of special educational needs or an education, health and care plan.

(Mathers *et al.* 2016)

The report refers to Sylva *et al.'s* research that attending early years provision can help disadvantaged children catch up with their peers, and argues for early intervention and enrichment programmes in the pre-school years (Sylva *et al.* 2010). Some recovery from the damage to the brain as a result of severe early neglect, clearly is possible, otherwise we wouldn't see the changes we do see when a child is settled in a home which enables them to develop, or the changes that we see in the course of therapy. But these changes are very difficult to achieve. For more detail on this fast-developing field of research, the reader is referred to Gerhardt and Music (Gerhardt 2004c; Music 2011a).

The importance of enabling these children to learn to the best of their ability cannot be emphasised enough as it is through their ability to engage creatively with learning, that these children might eventually gain qualifications and working patterns to be employed in the future. Education is one of the most significant 'ways out' from the deprivations they have suffered in their lives. The school needs to be a part of the network of professionals working to support the child and foster or adoptive family, and needs thoughtful support from mental health workers to find ways of containing difficult, distressed and disruptive children.

The biological necessity of parental care and protection of the young

The later developments and applications of Bowlby's research and thinking into the important concepts of the 'secure base', categories of attachment (particularly disorganised attachment) and the centrality of the capacity to trust and hope have become significant themes for many clinicians and researchers when trying to understand severely neglected and traumatised children (Ainsworth *et al.* 1978; Hesse and Main 1999; Main 1995; Main and Solomon 1986). This chapter assumes some knowledge of Bowlby's theories, the different types of attachment pattern described by Ainsworth, and in particular, the disorganised (D) attachment pattern described by Hesse and Main, and Main and Solomon, which is the attachment category that children who have been severely neglected and traumatised are most likely to come under (Ainsworth *et al.* 1978; Hesse and Main 1999 and Main and Solomon 1986). For more detailed information about attachment theory the reader is referred to Bowlby's clinical essays in *The Making and Breaking of Affectional Bonds* and *The Secure Base: Clinical Applications of Attachment Theory*, Holmes' *John Bowlby and Attachment Theory*, Cassidy and Shaver's *Handbook of Attachment* and Hopkins' paper 'The observed infant of attachment theory' for an integration of attachment theory and psychotherapeutic practice (Bowlby 1979 and 1988; Cassidy and Shaver 1999; Holmes 1993; Hopkins 1990/2015).

Bowlby's ideas about the vital protective function of parents for their young are a major aspect of his ethological perspective on human attachment relationships. The central significance of the parents' caregiving role can often get lost, and it can sound as if Bowlby's theory is only referring to something called the child's 'attachment' as if it exists in isolation from an ongoing relationship. This has echoes of what Winnicott was drawing attention to when he said 'There is no such thing as a baby.' For the survival of the species, the human baby or child has to be attached *to someone* who will care for and protect him or her in their vulnerability and dependence when there is danger. Bowlby talks of the need for parents to protect their young from 'predators' and bases his theories on scholarly studies of animal ethology. He was writing before the widespread occurrence of sexual and physical abuse became as well documented as they are now, although he was well aware of the problem, which he discusses in his paper 'On knowing what you are not supposed to know and feeling what you are not supposed to feel' in *The Secure Base* (Bowlby 1988c). In the past, the word 'predators' seemed rather strong to me: it does not now. The reality of sexually abusive adults 'grooming' children whom they can see are 'rootless and intensely lonely' because they lack a secure base, children who will let an adult give them 'special' attention because their parents are not able to do this well enough, is sinister and real (Bowlby 1979: 132).

This kind of behaviour in predatory adults is not that far removed from animals in the wild, where the youngest or most vulnerable animal in a herd will be picked off and separated from the rest of the herd by predators, and then killed. By contrast, the biological basis of the need for the young to be protected from predators is evident in the wonderful wildlife documentaries that are now available to us. These show the incredible parental care given by many kinds of adult mammals to protect their young, which is necessary for their particular species to survive (see, for example, David Attenborough's BBC Planet Earth Documentary Series (2016), and BBC Frozen Planet Series (2011)). However, what we also see in these documentaries is that the watchfulness of the adult animals' eyes does not have to stray for long before their babies become vulnerable to predators who will kill them. The intensity of the realistic fear and anxiety that vulnerable children, who are unprotected from the basic threats to life, of hunger, thirst and physical attack, experience is very hard and disturbing to imagine. The emotional defences that the child uses to try to protect him or herself from this intense anxiety are bound to be correspondingly intense, as well as necessary, during the time that they are unprotected, for the child's survival. But these defences are often perpetuated long after they have served their immediate function, and the frightened and vulnerable child becomes toughened, hidden, controlling and emotionally inaccessible as a result (Bowlby 1988b).

As is evident in this book, there are many types of misfortune and circumstances which lead to a child's removal from their parental home. The complex issues of determining what is preventative in the earlier removal of the child, when weighed up against the damaging effects of separating a child from their main attachment figures, are a matter for the courts as well as the social workers to decide. As soon as a child is removed from their biological parents, there is a break in an attachment relationship which has its own repercussions.

The point at which a child has to be taken away from his or her biological home, accounts in some measure, for the differing types and levels of emotional damage which these children suffer. The removal is almost inevitably traumatic for the child. There are times, such as for Amber, when a child has been so badly treated that removal of the child only brings relief and is life-saving. At the time of her therapy Amber did not seem to have any sense of her birth parents – other than possibly namelessly, in the form of an intense fear which she kept trying to escape from. However, many children who have to be taken away from their birth parent's care, are very attached to their parents, despite the inadequacy of this care. This plays a significant part in the breakdown of some foster placements and makes it very difficult for the child to form a new attachment. These children remain hopeful that the parents who neglected and traumatised them will change and that they will then be able to return to their birth families. Many, like Dahlia in the next chapter, become a 'caretaker' child, becoming highly attuned to, looking after and feeling responsible for the well-being of their parents, as they have learnt that this is more likely to lead to the parents in turn being able to look after them.

It is important to remember that a child can have different types of attachment relationships to different adults and siblings. So, a child might have experienced a disorganised attachment to his or her primary attachment figure, whilst having more benign attachment relationships to other, possibly more secondary attachment figures. Or a child might become particularly attached to a sibling as a way of coping with the lack of protection and care from a parent. These more benign attachment relationships can play a vital role in the child's subsequent mental health because they provide some good-enough internalised relationships which can be built on later in life, to counterbalance the destructive internalised relationships that have such a powerful negative effect. Qualities of attachment relationships can also change in their intensity so that as a child becomes less troubled, as a result of good and persistent fostering and adoption, specialised residential care or helpful psychotherapy, he or she can become, for example, less severely disorganised in his or her attachment pattern, whilst still having significant difficulty in forming any kind of more secure attachment relationship. However, attachment patterns are very resistant to change and this is part of the difficulty in helping these children to form new, healthier attachments, particularly when they are placed in foster or adoptive families (Hopkins 2000).

Main, Kaplan and Cassidy, in their work on the adult attachment interview (AAI), conclude that the coherency of an adult's account of their life story is a good indicator of how well they have been able to process all the difficulties and traumas they have experienced in their lives, how secure they feel within themselves and their mental well-being (Main, Kaplan and Cassidy 1985). It is not the exact nature of the traumatic events which determines how secure or insecure an adult feels themselves to be, it is how well, or not, the traumatic events have been processed within the individual. This coherent life narrative is greatly enhanced if it has been shared with a secure attachment figure over the years –

such as in ordinary childhood experience, with parents. Severely neglected and traumatised children have not had this opportunity until they are able to allow new attachment figures into their lives. The therapist is one of these figures and because of their training and experience, is particularly able to contain and think about many of the distressing emotions that need to be shared and processed (Hopkins 2000). Becoming able to remember and share good experiences as well as traumatic experiences is a sign of growing strengths in the child's inner world. It is also a sign of an increasingly secure relationship with the person with whom the memory is shared. Being able to remember also prompts mourning and feelings of sadness and loss, the importance of which is discussed in Chapter 4 and will be evident from several of the clinical examples in this book.

Clinical observations with refugee and asylum-seeking children suggest that the attachment patterns described by attachment theory are helpful concepts across cultures and not only relevant to middle class Western cultures. This is in keeping with research overviews in which

> ... cross-cultural studies have not (yet) refuted the bold conjectures of attachment theory about the universality and normativity of attachment ... taken as a whole the studies are remarkably consistent with the theory. Attachment theory may therefore claim cross-cultural validity.
>
> (Van Ijzendoorn and Sagi, 1999)

The theories of Winnicott, Bion and Bowlby, together with the knowledge gained from developmental psychology and neuroscientific research, are sources of insight about the difficulties faced in the therapeutic process with neglected and traumatised children. This chapter has tried to integrate these ideas so that they throw some light on the significance of childhood neglect as a fundamental factor in the subsequent or contemporaneous experience of childhood trauma.

Note

1. Child psychotherapists in the UK undergo a four-year full-time post-graduate training program which involves: a variety of direct supervised clinical experience, usually in a Child and Adolescent Mental Health Service (CAMHS); work discussion seminars; their own intensive training psychoanalysis; specialist clinical supervision of three times weekly work with a pre-school child, a primary school age child and an adolescent; theoretical seminars; two years of once weekly observation of a baby in the baby's home; submitting papers about their clinical work and a research project or Clinical Doctorate. On qualification, they become members of the Association of Child Psychotherapists. For more details see www.childpsychotherapy.org.uk

4 Complex traumatic childhood losses

Mourning and acceptance, endings and beginnings

It is interesting that Bowlby's theories have universally become known as 'Attachment Theory', rather than 'Separation and Loss Theory'. The fundamentally distressing human experience of separation from, and loss of any loved one, is possibly too close to the bone for all of us for it to be conceptualised in professional terminology. So it is important to keep in mind that this often repeated, painful separation and loss from birth parents, foster parents, siblings and extended families, has been the experience of all the children described in this book.

Mourning is an extremely complex process, and the mourning of a good-enough loving relationship is entirely different to the mourning of a highly ambivalent or neglectful relationship. Severely neglected and traumatised children have suffered many losses, compounded often by the absence of anyone to whom they feel reasonably close who can begin to help them with their mourning. Foster or adoption placement breakdown, if it is abrupt and there is no opportunity to manage some kind of planned transition to the next placement, is a sad example of the child being completely alone when trying to cope with multiple losses. The awful image of a child being taken away from his or her birth parents, or moving foster placements, with all of their belongings being put into a black rubbish bag whilst losing everything else associated with the birth or foster home in the process, painfully captures this experience of being a child who is alone in the world.

It is not at all unusual for severely neglected and traumatised children to have had several foster homes before they stay for a few years in a more stable placement. Some children may have lived in well over ten foster homes before they find some stability. All of these moves are also deeply disorienting because the child is expected to adapt to so many different relationships and ways of family life, often as well as many changes of school and locality.

As well as the loss of the relationships with the foster or adoptive family and the wider extended family and friends, decisions might have to be made about the wisdom of keeping siblings together or separating them. These children's losses are more complex than the loss due to the death of a parent. They may no longer have any contact with a parent or sibling who they know is alive. In some instances, they may have witnessed the death of a parent which was the event which precipitated their going into a foster home. In others, they might hear of their parent's death after many years of having no contact with them. In these circumstances, it is very hard to mourn the death or loss of a parent or other important attachment figures in an 'ordinary' way.

It is commonly accepted that most adults are likely to need at least a year before they can begin to recover from the death of a loved one. Severely neglected and traumatised children's mourning process is much more likely to become impeded because they have suffered multiple complex losses, often simultaneously or very close together in time. It is not surprising that they cannot be in touch with sadness and grief, nor move on in life and make new intimate relationships, particularly with adults. The angry and aggressive feelings and behaviour of children who have suffered the loss of being taken away from the care of their birth parents, even though they have been neglected and traumatised by them, needs to be understood in the context of their protest and anger about this loss. This is one of the possible features of impeded mourning. The birth parents often are not the ones blamed by the child for their lack of care, but the world is angrily blamed for separating the child from his parents, whilst the parents are idealised. The real parents can't be mourned because of these idealisations and children remain doggedly loyal to birth parents who may continue to reject them, let them down, hurt them again and again, or totally abandon them.

Before providing case examples of the impact of these losses and how they are addressed in therapy, the concept of multiple complex traumatic childhood losses needs to be put in the context of bereavement and the mourning process in a more 'ordinary' sense. This chapter argues that the impeded mourning processes of these children can be eased somewhat in the course of therapy, and become particularly amenable to therapeutic help when there is a planned ending to therapy. The ending of therapy offers the opportunity to work with loss and mourning from within the transference relationship, with the child well supported by the new adults in their lives.

Ordinary adult bereavement and the mourning process

In everyday experience, the pain and shock following the death of a loved one, particularly a sudden death, can initially induce the feeling that it is impossible to survive the loss. Colin Murray Parkes, in his seminal study of grieving widows, is often quoted for his observation that the pain of loss and mourning is 'the price we pay for love' (Parkes 1972). He also argues that the process of mourning can, in time, bring new strength and increased maturity. In this respect, following the period of mourning, life and love can feel even more precious than they did before. Whilst Parkes' classic study is about the impact of death and bereavement, his findings are very helpful when trying to understand how people respond to other major losses in life.

Bowlby, referring to Parkes, describes a basic overall pattern in adult bereavement in which there are, broadly speaking, four observable phases which vary in intensity and length from one individual to another, and which are interwoven and not necessarily in any fixed sequence (Bowlby 1979, ch.5). These phases, or maybe it would be more descriptive to think of them as states of mind, are helpful in understanding the intense emotions that people who are mourning the death of a loved one, or another painful loss, go through. They are: an initial state of shock and numbness which can be interspersed with extreme distress or anger; yearning, missing, pining, sadness, searching for the lost person; disorganisation and despair; re-organisation and gradual acceptance of the death.

These states of mind have all been written about movingly and painfully in autobiographical accounts of bereavement. C.S. Lewis opens his classic book about the grief he felt following his wife's death, *A Grief Observed*, remarking on how similar grief feels to fear – something he had never realised before. Darwin described the typical facial expressions of grief as being the resultant 'on the one hand, of a tendency to scream like a child when he feels abandoned and, on the other, of an inhibition of such screaming' (Bowlby 1979: 85). C.S. Lewis goes on to describe his ongoing experience of feeling muffled up in an invisible blanket which separates him from the world around him (Lewis 1961).

Joan Didion entitles her autobiography about how she tried to cope with the death of her husband, *The Year of Magical Thinking*, because towards the end of that year, during which she wrote the diary observing her states of mind which then became the book, she realised that she had been trying to reverse time, back to when he had still been alive. She describes the common experience of the bereaved, that they fear they are 'going mad with grief', and painfully notes after she has accepted the passing of time, that she is going over and over the events leading up to her husband's death as she approaches the first anniversary of his passing (Didion 2005). Julian Barnes in *Levels of Life*, his account of his devastation following the death of his wife, describes his irrational anger at friends and life in general, as well as his struggle with suicidal ideas (Barnes 2013).

This is all very powerful and distressing to read about. And these accounts are of talented adults' attempts to cope with their feelings which they are able to express in spoken and written language. We need to transpose, or extrapolate, these intense emotions backwards in time, in trying to comprehend children's experiences of loss. It used to be claimed that young children don't understand what death means and therefore cannot mourn in the same way as adults do. Psychiatrist Beverley Raphael's classic book *The Anatomy of Bereavement*, discusses loss across the life cycle and goes into great detail about the impact of death on a child at different developmental stages (Raphael 1984). Psychoanalyst Judith Viorst discusses loss in a helpful and accessible way in her insightful book *Necessary Losses* (Viorst 1986/1998).

Complex traumatic childhood losses and impeded mourning

A moving account of an ordinary two-year-old boy's brief therapy to help him accept the reality of his mother and baby brother's death in a car crash, has been written by the Swedish child psychotherapist Elizabeth Cleve (Cleve 2002). This little boy was completely unable to acknowledge that his mother and brother were no longer with him, despite having been in the car which his father was driving at the time. Weeks after his mother and brother's deaths, he behaved as if nothing significant had changed in his life and was frozen in the shock of the initial phase of mourning. His father was offered parallel help as a part of the treatment offered by the clinic. Eventually, in his fifth psychotherapy session, the little boy was able to say to his therapist 'A big one and a little one is gone', which became the title of her book, and the little boy's mourning process was able to start. Father and son were then able to share their grief through the help they had received.

In the introduction to her book, Cleve notes how adults who had a loved one who died during their childhood, recount how abandoned they felt in their sorrow, by the then prevailing attitude, that it was wrong to talk to children about a loved one's death, as this was felt to intensify their distress. These adults felt they thus had had to manage their distress alone and that the lack of help after the death gave them greater scars than the death itself (Cleve 2002: xxi).

The difficulty of knowing how to acknowledge a child's bereavement, or even at times the fact that he or she has witnessed the death of a parent, is totally understandable. There is a fear that talking about 'it' will cause the child even more pain, and many well-meaning people are often at a complete loss for appropriate words in the circumstances. It is very hard to know what a child has made of the death of a loved person and maybe the kind of protective numbing, which has been referred to above, provides a very welcome 'invisible blanket between the world' and the child, as described by C.S. Lewis.

There is a similar process when a child has had to be removed from the parental home. Do you talk about it or not? In the initial phases of separation, the child's fear and distress may be so intense that it might feel better not to talk about their mummy and daddy, particularly when it is not at all clear what is going to happen to the child. Is the young child's eventual acceptance of the absence of the parent/s akin to feeling that they are 'gone' or are 'dead' in the child's terms? Is the protest, despair and generally difficult behaviour of the child, part of the mourning process, which needs time before some sadness and loss starts to surface? In addition, there is the child's intense fear and difficulty in understanding what has happened even when initially they might have been very relieved to be taken away from their birth family home. The child is suddenly in totally unfamiliar surroundings living with strangers whom they are expected to trust. It is important to remember that fear is often at the root of violent and angry behaviour.

Green describes the therapy of a child whose mother died in a drink driving accident (Green 2013). Drawing on Freud's classic paper 'Mourning and Melancholia', she addresses the complexity of childhood bereavement as seen in the therapy room, and addresses the significance of the child's identification with the parent who has died, or been lost, as well as the ensuing conflict between accepting his loss through mourning, whilst still searching for a parental figure in the transference who could accept his anger and aggression (Freud 1917). Green also discusses the pain for the child of remembering the parent who died, as well as the irrational shame that often accompanies the loss of a parent in childhood, with the child feeling, magically, that they were not loveable enough to keep their parent alive. The feeling of not being loved enough by parents, together with feelings of shame and worthlessness, particularly when parents have, in reality, been hateful and rejecting towards children, is another painful experience for children who no longer live with their birth parents.

Unfortunately, the death of a parent may be 'just one' of a number of major losses and traumas in the young lives of severely neglected and traumatised children. Onions and Browner, writing about psychotherapy in the residential setting of the Mulberry Bush School, describe the therapy of an eight-year-old boy who, in the year after his father's suicide, was taken into care. Following a number of foster placement breakdowns and finally a more stable foster placement, he started to be a term-time boarder at the Mulberry Bush (Onions and Browner 2012). Whilst all the adults caring for him knew that he had seen his father's body hanging from a doorway in his home, there had not been a therapeutic opportunity to help him with this experience and memory, until it was finally enacted in a therapy session in a manner that deeply shocked the therapist but enabled her to help the boy to start processing the awful experience with her, and with the rest of the staff at the school.

For this little boy, it sounds as if there were no other family members who could care for him, and he then went from one foster placement which failed, to another. As discussed in Chapter 1, this may well be an example of the background reasons why many foster placements break down, because the foster carers are not offered enough support to be able to cope with the distressing facts of the child's past life and their repercussions in the child's ensuing behaviour in their present life. It was not until the little boy was in the stable and containing environment of the Mulberry Bush with a group of carefully trained and supported adults caring for him, that his relationship with his therapist enabled him to communicate his memory of his father's suicide.

In the troubled birth families that so many of these children come from, there has often been alcohol and drug abuse, mental illness, domestic violence and neglect. Sadly, the likelihood of a parent dying is probably higher in these families due to the repercussions of alcoholism, drug overdoses, suicide and murder. There are often complicated family dynamics because parental relationships have broken down and a single parent (usually the mother) is bringing up her children with the father no longer having any contact with them. The mother may then have further relationships from which there are children, whose fathers may also disappear from the family. It is not unusual to find, when an attempt is made at drawing a family tree, that hardly any of the adult couples in the extended family have remained together. The children may have witnessed domestic violence of varying degrees, as well as experienced predatory adults who become abusive, physically and/or sexually, to the children whilst appearing to offer care or protection for the mother and her children. This is sadly the worst end of human behaviour.

Another complex loss is suffered by children when their parents' divorce or separate. The child has to find a way of feeling attached to both parents whilst spending a lot of the time missing the parent the child is not with, but possibly unable to speak about this to the parent the child is with. There is an inherent internal conflict for the child as this is a complicated loss within an existing attachment, which is very hard to cope with or fully resolve (Leach 2016; Wallerstein and Resnikoff 1997; Wallerstein and Lewis 2004). Similarly, when a child is taken away from his or her birth family, however necessary this will have been, the child often remains attached in some way to that parent and will miss them at times. The age of the child, and the way in which separating parents, or birth family and foster family and social workers communicate across this rupture in the child's life at the time of separation, as well as over the years that follow, will greatly affect the way the child tries to integrate this paradoxical and conflicted situation. In therapy, this emotional task which can seem impossible to disentangle at times, can gradually be resolved to some degree so that some acceptance of the sad situation is possible.

When the emotions of sadness and missing start to soak through the layers of defence that have protected the child from the intense pain of loss, this is an important sign of healthy and appropriate mourning processes starting to function within the child, possibly for the first time. Initially these feelings may not seem to be directly connected to the child's major losses. Interestingly, they may be experienced more directly within the new relationship with the therapist who is missed when there are weekend or holiday breaks in therapy, or angrily rejected before or after these breaks.

As the transference relationship grows, the child gets 'under the therapist's skin' in a variety of ways that are helpful to the therapeutic process. This can feel at times like a bodily experience for the therapist who might suddenly feel very distressed and tearful during or after the child's session, without having a clear idea of what has caused so much distress. Often this is a sign that the child is starting to project intensely painful feelings into the therapist whom they have started to trust to be able to receive them fully. This is a good example of the child projecting unbearable feelings of loss into the therapist who then has to experience, wisely think about, and often carry those feelings for considerable periods of time, before they might be put into words or play that can be taken in (i.e., introjected) by the child in a helpful way (Bion 1962). This important non-verbal process has been discussed and enlarged on in Chapter 3 and recurs throughout the clinical material in this book.

Here is an example of the early signs of the mourning process from the therapy of 'Connie' who was the patient of one of my supervisees. I am very grateful to her and her colleagues for giving permission for me to use this as an example. Inevitably, when reporting clinical work which is not my own, something is lost in the quality of describing the transference–countertransference relationship. However, as discussed in Chapter 9, some of these feelings come vividly alive within the supervisory relationship which is part of the supportive structure around the therapist in her work.

Sadly, as with all the examples in this book, there are many children who experience the kinds of multiple and complex losses that Connie had to cope with. Connie is not at all unusual.

'Connie', aged three, was with her mother when she died suddenly of a heart attack. Mother had been addicted to drugs and her relationship with Connie's father was a violent one. He came and went frequently from their home. Fortunately another adult was in the home when mother died. It was assumed by the adults who were there at the time that Connie hadn't seen the panic, confusion, arrival of the ambulance, and above all, her mother's body, and that if she had, she was too little to understand what was going on. Father tried to look after Connie for a few weeks but wasn't able to cope. Then one of mother's sisters tried to give her a home, but this broke down after a few months because Connie was very upset, confused and disturbed in her behaviour. Eventually Connie's maternal grandmother was granted kinship guardianship and this became her new home.

Connie's grandmother was divorced from her grandfather and had a new partner who totally supported Connie coming to live with them. She was referred for therapy when she was five. Although she was well settled with her grandparents (she quickly came to feel that grandmother's partner was her grandfather), and there was a loving and trusting relationship between them, they were worried about all that she had witnessed whilst living with her mother and, in particular, the impact on her of her mother's death. Whilst Connie was aware of anniversaries of her mother's death and went to the graveside, they had not been able to talk much as a family about the circumstances of mother's death and, unfortunately, grandmother had had a difficult relationship with her daughter with which she was slowly trying to come to terms. It remained hard for the family to digest what had happened to Connie's mother. As with a number of grandparents, becoming Connie's kinship guardian was a part of grandmother's wish to repair what had gone wrong in her relationship with her daughter. There can be a strong, conscious, reparative process in these circumstances with grandparents struggling to become better parents to their grandchildren than they had been able to be to their children.

Not surprisingly, Connie needed a great deal of attention and was very demanding and tantrum-y at times, as well as very controlling. This was exhausting to live with. Connie was offered therapy, and both her grandparents, who were in their fifties, came very regularly to see another therapist in the clinic. Social services were supportive of the grandparents and the school understood why Connie was explosive at times in class, and tried to meet her emotional and educational needs as well as they could. Importantly, as noted in Chapter 1, the whole network of adults around Connie communicated pretty well with each other, making it much more possible for her therapy to be effective.

Connie made good progress in her therapy and became less tantrum-y and demanding as well as increasingly attached to her therapist. Having often been noisily and angrily resistant to going to the therapy room when her therapy started, she was now rather passionate about wanting to come to see her therapist every day, and protested when it was time to end the session. Whilst the development of this new trusting relationship was a good indicator of Connie's growing emotional health, there were also important considerations within the clinic team about how much therapy was 'good-enough'. Was Connie sufficiently recovered to start to think about planning an ending of her therapy, in roughly six months' time? By then she would have had two years of therapy, and her grandparents and all the professionals working with her, felt that despite occasional set-backs, she was consistently moving forward in her development and much happier than she had been when referred.

It was during this period, when ending therapy was apparently the last thing on Connie's mind, that the first direct play about a missing mummy started to take place. It was hard to know what had prompted this play, but it was embedded in her trusting relationship with her therapist. Possibly the play was triggered by another patient's very alarming and noisy behaviour outside the therapy room, which Connie quite astonishingly and selectively didn't seem to hear. The therapist felt this denial (or dissociation?) was very possibly the way Connie had coped with the violent behaviour that had apparently often taken place between her birth parents. Connie had effectively become deaf and blind to it. Once the noise had stopped, Connie became much more anxious and there was a sad feeling in the room. For the first time she started to play with a toy phone which said different phrases when different buttons were pressed, to make it more real. One of these buttons said 'Let's call daddy' and she pressed it repeatedly. The toy phone could not actually reply, but children usually started a pretend dialogue with 'daddy' on the other end of the phone. However Connie kept on pressing the button and then protested that she did have a daddy – as if to say, why wasn't he answering? (Her father had disappeared from her life.) Then she pressed the 'Let's call mummy' button repeatedly, but sadly said 'There's no one there.'

These feelings of sadness now came into the sessions increasingly often, but so did some important signs of healthier emotional development. At the same time that this increase of sadness was very apparent in the therapy – and acknowledged by Connie and the therapist – Connie seemed suddenly able to concentrate for much longer on painting and other creative activities. She stopped feeling so readily frustrated when what she tried to make didn't work out, and managed to persevere for a much longer period at what she was doing. It could be argued that she was generally less anxious than she had been and as a result was more able to concentrate and play.

In one session she suddenly announced that she wanted to 'paint the world' (meaning a globe of the planet earth) together with her therapist. Whilst her therapist was taking her turn at painting, Connie played lovingly with a baby doll, pretending to bottle feed it. The therapist found herself close to tears when she observed this. Connie had not played with the baby doll before this, and she fed the baby in an absorbed and very gentle way which the therapist found very moving. It helped the therapist to appreciate that Connie probably had some experience of being lovingly fed by her mother and that this was what had been lost and missed, when her mother died. Connie continued the painting, but then began to paint a big zig-zag in the middle of the earth explaining that she was making a crack down the middle. When the therapist gently said to her that the world, that had looked rather beautiful before, had a big crack in it and looked broken, Connie nodded seriously.

At the end of this moving session, Connie showed more developmental progress when she was suddenly able to read the clock correctly and to know when she was next coming for her session, rather than trying to change the clock time and insist that she was coming for therapy on days that she was not. The fact that all of these changes in Connie were happening at the same time is interesting and, I would argue, not coincidental. Possibly the lessening of the defences against mourning freed some energy that could be used in ordinary developmental processes. Development takes place across the board at times such as these. This process is the 'putting down of roots' that is so important for these children's recovery and needs to be carefully looked out for, and nurtured in therapy as well as in the child's everyday life. This idea is discussed in more detail elsewhere (Lanyado 2017).

It was important to communicate about this change in Connie to the parent worker so that he could alert Connie's grandparents to the fact that she might be more able to share memories and sadness about her mother than she had in the past. Communication with the school was also important so that Connie's teacher could nurture her new ability to concentrate for longer and to enjoy learning.

Significantly, whilst Connie was unaware of the therapist's dilemma about when to start thinking about bringing the therapy to an end, in the therapist's mind, the importance of thinking about how to 'wean' Connie from her therapy was growing because of Connie's growing attachment. To paraphrase Parkes, loss in this therapeutic setting is the 'price' that is paid for deep relatedness and attachment, but can be prepared for, thought about and talked about in new ways, when it happens within the therapeutic relationship (Parkes 1972). It is in this way that the ending of therapy can helpfully prompt the mourning process that has previously been impeded. It is this freeing up of the impeded mourning process that in turn facilitates growth across a spectrum of developmental processes. As in this example from Connie's therapy, the therapist (and foster or adoptive parent) needs to be able, and willing, to take inside him or herself the painful communications of loss from the child, to bear them and then think about them. This enables the child to introject the experience of another human being with a mind that can bear this pain without completely falling apart, and this in turn helps the child to feel and think about the loss without it becoming utterly overwhelming.

Planned endings and beginnings

One of the most paradoxical aspects of psychotherapeutic work is that often after having struggled to establish a therapeutic relationship where some measure of trust and intimacy can be experienced and held by the therapist, it is nevertheless a relationship which has a beginning, a middle . . . and an end. Especially when the patient is a very needy child, it can feel cruel to subject the child to yet another loss of an important relationship when therapy comes to an end. It is also extremely difficult to try to judge when enough developmental and therapeutic progress has been made to justify planning an ending, when it is obvious that these patients require so much help because of all that has happened to them. And yet, clinical experience of planning the end of therapy, with as much time as possible in which to work with all the feelings and memories that ending therapy inevitably stimulates, demonstrates that this is also an opportunity to grow through coping with loss in a new way (Coltart 1996a; Holmes 2001a; Lanyado 2004b; Ryz and Wilson 1999)

The planned ending of therapy, ideally with a period of many months in which it can be thought about and the feelings generated can be explored with past and present experiences becoming somewhat more integrated, provides the possibility for some preparatory mourning to take place whilst therapy is still ongoing. Whilst ambivalence within the therapeutic relationship is inevitable, the loss of the relationship with the therapist is of a different kind to many of the child's previous losses. If therapy has gone reasonably well, the child has experienced a relationship in which great effort has been made to listen to, understand, accept and hold all aspects of the child. This will have been an authentic relationship which is bound to have been very difficult at times and emotionally demanding for the therapist as well as the patient, but also very rewarding when important changes have become apparent in the child's inner world. A planned therapeutic ending is very different to a traumatic loss where there has been little or no opportunity to prepare for a parting, or to express feelings of protest, anger, betrayal and abandonment, to the person who is lost.

It is one of the therapist's responsibilities to help the patient in the often complex circumstances which surround the decision to end a child's therapy, to bring it to a close in as therapeutic a way as possible. One of the central considerations has to be that this ending will be different to the complex traumatic losses of the child's past. The therapist has to be alert to the unconscious pressures to repeat these past traumatic endings as a part of the unconscious repetition compulsion of traumatic loss that Freud has described, and is discussed in Chapter 1 (Freud 1914). This kind of traumatic repetition can be an unconscious pressure within the therapeutic relationship as well as in the network of professionals working with the child and family (Lanyado 2004b).

The compulsion to repeat past traumatic losses can also be expressed through the parents' response to the ending of therapy. For example, despite the therapist emphasising how important the last few therapy sessions are for a child, parents may casually say in the final days of the therapy that they are thinking of booking a holiday at short notice, which means these final sessions cannot take place – thus creating a much more abrupt and immediate end to therapy than had been anticipated. If this were to happen, it would replicate traumatic and more unplanned endings and losses from the child's past. It may well be that when this is pointed out to the parents they are rather shocked that they hadn't thought about this before, and they change their plans and are able to stay with the painful tensions and sadness of therapy coming to an end. Parents also experience a sad loss when the child's therapy comes to an end. Their work with the parent worker is likely to stop around the same time, and they have felt supported by the child's therapist as well as the whole clinic setting. The pull towards this kind of rather obvious repetition, often only becomes clearer with hindsight and is much easier to recognise in others than in oneself.

A planned therapy ending involves the parents or carers of the child, as well as the social workers, school and any other agencies involved with the child, in the preparation for the ending. There will have been meetings with the professionals as well as the parents to think about what the end of therapy means for the child, and how and when this ending needs to take place. All of these adults (including the therapist) are then able to support the child through the complicated feelings of sadness and loss about the ending of therapy, as well as to receive support for themselves in thinking about the implications of the ending and how best to continue with the child's day-to-day care.

When this kind of careful thought and planning is given to the ending of a child's therapy, as had started in the therapist's work with Connie, it can become a 'moving on' in life, as in the latter stages of the mourning process. The experience of feeling appropriate and bearable sadness is often an important and new feeling for the child during this ending phase of therapy. The idea of missing the therapist, and the therapist missing the child and feeling sad to say goodbye, is also often a new experience at this time. In this respect, the ending of therapy offers possibilities for the beginning of a new phase in the child's life. The child learns that it is possible to survive the ending of a relationship and that loss is not automatically a catastrophe. These ideas are also discussed with regard to 'transitions' in life, in Chapter 5 in relation to how a young child was helped in therapy to leave his loved foster home and move to his adoptive home.

When there has been sufficient time to work on this ending in therapy, a positive internalisation of what has been gained in therapy is carried forward into everyday life for the child. In this way, the therapist remains within the child as someone they were able to trust and become close to. Dahlia's therapy, which I was fortunate to supervise, is a good example of this process.

Dahlia's mother was severely alcoholic and could become violent when drunk. Mother's unpredictable and unreliable behaviour meant that Dahlia's basic needs were often unmet. She was neglected over many years, but remained below the radar of social services as she somehow managed to 'get by' using her intelligence to fend for herself, her siblings and her mother. She was a classic 'caretaker child'. Dahlia felt it was her responsibility to look after her mother and told her therapist about how hard she had tried to stop her mother drinking when she was still living at home. The fact that she wasn't able to do this made her feel very guilty and responsible for her mother's alcoholism. It was not until she was nine years old that Dahlia was taken away from her mother after a drunken street brawl, which Dahlia witnessed, where mother was arrested. This had happened many times before but this last fight was particularly brutal and action was finally taken.

Dahlia worried a great deal about her mother and lived in the same neighbourhood as her mother after she went to live in her foster home. She told her therapist that she was sure her mother would drink herself to death – which was sadly very possible. She was fortunate to have been placed with experienced foster parents, who were very patient with her. She did not go from one foster home to another before she settled and was a bright girl with potential to do well in school. Fortunately, she had not needed to move schools when she went to her foster home. Part of her knew that she needed to be fostered and could not live with her mother and she did not present any major behaviour problems. But despite all of this, her wish was always to return to her mother so that she could look after her again and try to keep her alive. This preoccupation dominated the early stages of her therapy. The intensity with which Dahlia was identified with her mother was often painfully apparent when Dahlia would behave like a down and out drunken woman in her therapy. This was excruciating for the therapist to witness, particularly as the therapist was very aware of Dahlia's potential to live a very different life to her mother's, and felt this identification was harmful for Dahlia.

Unusually, the therapist hardly ever heard about Dahlia's life with her foster carers in the therapy and, although they brought her very reliably for her therapy sessions, there was little sense from Dahlia of any relationship between them. It was as if they barely registered in Dahlia's emotional life. Fortunately, these foster carers were part of a large extended family, very compassionate and mature and just continued to give Dahlia good consistent care. They received regular help from another member of the clinic team which enabled them to accept that Dahlia simply could not cope with another intimate relationship. Dahlia did not actively reject their efforts, but it was as if her heart was closed to them. There was only room for her mother.

Slowly, Dahlia and her therapist formed a very touching relationship, which as described by Hopkins enabled her to start to thaw in her relationship with her foster parents (Hopkins 2000/2015). It was very hard for Dahlia to allow her therapist to be the adult who tried to help her, the child, with confused, angry and distressing feelings about her life. Like all caretaker children she wanted to be self-sufficient and in charge, but gradually she became able to share some of her distress with her therapist, when her mother failed to attend one access meeting after another and was then finally stopped from having any contact with her daughter. When the therapist, in a review meeting with her foster parents around this time, shared her awareness of a softening of Dahlia's heart towards them, the foster mother burst into tears as it was the first time in the three years she had been fostering Dahlia, that she had had any sense that she mattered to her.

The feelings of painful separation and eventual loss that Dahlia was consumed with were central to the work of the therapy. When therapy came to a planned ending, after three years of work, the loss of her therapist was of a very different nature to the loss of her mother. The ending of therapy had been planned six months before the last session and there were many opportunities to communicate and think about what this ending meant to Dahlia. The therapist described their last session as follows:

> She came with a big bunch of lovely flowers and we had our last session after the three years. She talked about how she was not sure if she was happy or sad. Both, she concluded. She talked about

> her unremitting disappointment in her parents and her sad sense
> that she has grown beyond them and that her foster carers (who
> had become her permanent carers) are her family now. She fears
> that her mother will die from alcohol and that is a thought she still
> finds unbearable.

> The therapist concluded this account saying 'I was very moved to
> see how proud she was of herself when she left the clinic.'

In this account of the ending of a long and intense therapy, it is possible to see how the patient, who by now was in her early teens, was also at the beginning of a new phase in her life (Ryz and Wilson 1999). The sense of achievement that such patients can justifiably feel when therapy comes to a satisfactory conclusion, moves increasingly to the fore as therapy draws to a close. Alongside the anger, sadness and regrets that are inevitable, it is also a time when it becomes possible to look back at the way the child was when he or she started therapy, and all the growing up and change that has taken place since then. Holmes discusses the ending of therapy from the perspective of attachment theory, and Coltart from the perspective of adult psychoanalysis in ways which are very relevant to child and adolescent psychotherapy (Coltart 1996a; Holmes 2001a). Memories can be shared, and possibly made more sense of, from the greater maturity that the child has achieved since being in therapy.

There is often a lot of discussion between the child and therapist about how to mark the very last therapy session. This varies greatly from one child and therapist couple, to another. Quite often, the sense of loss and preparatory mourning is very painful for the therapist as well as the child, and can reach a climax in the session before the last one. The actual goodbye session however, can have a very different feel about it.

Some children are allowed to choose several special toys from their personal therapy toy box to take home and keep after the last session. Having been encouraged to keep drawings, paintings and all sorts of paper or playdough models made in the sessions in the therapy room whilst therapy is ongoing, the end of therapy is the time when the child can sort through and choose those that he or she wants to take home and what should stay with the therapist. Some children want to bring and share a celebratory snack to have in the very last session and, within appropriate boundaries, therapists agree to this. Some therapists give a specially prepared card to the child in which they write about how they will remember the child and how they have changed during therapy. Some clinics have established rituals where the child is given a certificate of some sort. Religious and secular ritual helps a great deal with ordinary bereavement and losses (such as moving from primary to secondary school), and this is something to be thought about carefully for children who are ending their therapy and who have suffered so many losses.

Therapists would often love to know how a child is getting on over the months and years after therapy has ended, but have to restrain their curiosity and their own missing of the child to whom they have in many respects been an emotional 'caregiver'. This is the aspect of the attachment–caregiver relationship which has grown within the therapist during the therapy. The ending of therapy has many similarities to the parental experience of having to let their child separate as a developmentally appropriate task, and the question of whether, when and how to offer a follow-up appointment to see how the child is faring is complicated, and will vary from one child–therapist couple to another. Sometimes the parents continue to have help at the clinic, or simply keep the therapist informed. Sometimes the child asks to see the therapist to confirm that he or she is well and has survived the end of therapy. Some children want to know that they will be able to come back and see the therapist after a few months and are pleased to have a follow-up appointment confirmed when they have their final therapy session; others prefer to know that they can get in touch with the therapist in their own time. In a helpful paper, Schachter *et al.* discuss the ways in which post-therapy or post-psychoanalysis meetings can fruitfully augment the gains of the therapeutic work (Schachter *et al.* 1997).

The hope that emerges at the end of therapy is that the child will have internalised their experience of the therapist as an adult, who has not only tried very hard to survive and understand all their difficulties, but has become a trusted internal voice which provides strength and sustenance, and importantly, remains with them in memory or in feeling, in a positive way. It is likely that the child, who has been severely neglected and traumatised in the past, still has a long way to go in their recovery. Forming long-term intimate relationships may well be very anxiety provoking. Traumatic memories may continue to surface, but in the process of being in therapy, the child will have started to trust adults somewhat more. The relationships with foster and adoptive parents, as well as residential workers, will have opened up, some of the defences against intimacy will have softened, and the child will have become more able to love and receive love.

This internalisation of the therapeutic experience and relationship can then form a kind of blueprint within the child, for judging whether other relationships and people that they meet throughout life are, as one adopted boy told me, 'for' him or 'against' him. He felt that his therapy had helped him to develop a kind of emotional antenna, which he trusted and which helped him to navigate his way through the choppy waters of life, making the most of those he recognised could help him, and, importantly, trying to keep clear of those who would lead him astray. With all these thoughts and ideas in mind, when therapy comes to a helpful end, loss can become a gain.

5   Playing out, not acting out

The development of the capacity
to play in the therapy of children
who are 'in transition' from
fostering to adoption (2008)

This chapter was originally published in 2008 and is a case study of 'Sammy' a four-year-old patient I saw in the 1990s from whom I learnt a great deal about the importance of playing and transitional phenomena (Lanyado 2008b). As indicated in the text, I have written about Sammy from other perspectives elsewhere. He was referred for therapy to help him in his move from his long-term foster home to his adoptive home, and in the process of going through these enormous life changes surprised me again and again in the diverse ways he made use of his therapeutic experience. This chapter provides more detailed insight into the therapeutic processes that can help children find a path through these potentially traumatic changes as creatively as possible.

Many severely neglected and traumatised children have great difficulty playing in a free and imaginative way, and are more likely to act out aggressively than play out their fantasies. Winnicott's extensive writing about playing and transitional phenomena continues to enlighten me about these processes and I have written further about this patient, and the patient in Chapter 6 from the perspective of technical issues when working with this group of patients (Lanyado 2017; Winnicott 1971). In the context of the earlier chapters in this book, I would now add that the impact of early neglect led to me becoming a new developmental object for Sammy, and that the multiple complex losses that he suffered form a backcloth to what follows.

Anxieties about change and managing transitions are bound to be intense during the weeks in which a young – and inevitably emotionally damaged – child has to find a way of parting with the comparative security of a foster home and joining the (hopefully) lifetime adoptive family that will continue this caring. The responsibilities of all the adults involved, to try to make what feels like a bodily transplant of a young and vulnerable child from one family to another, 'take' rather than be rejected, are enormous. The child's anxieties are naturally greater, given all the failings of adults in their past.

What can be done, therapeutically, to help this change to fulfil its potential? This is the question that I wish to address by thinking about the nature of 'transitional anxiety' and how a growing ability to play can lead to the creation of transitional objects and experiences which can 'hold' this anxiety, so that it does not get acted out in destructive ways (Winnicott 1971b/1953).

The ideas about transitions in life that I wish to discuss in this context inevitably move freely between internal and external reality, often attempting to stay in the paradoxical 'no man's land' which lies at their interface. This is a rather large grey area in which, during the actual process of change, two apparently conflicting internal and external realities have to co-exist as best as is possible. This is about the 'both-ness' of this extraordinary situation of a child being adopted, not the 'either-or-ness'. It is about trying to stay in touch with the painfulness of the loss of the foster and birth family – which inevitably re-evokes earlier losses – whilst trying to be as open as possible to the positive potential of making and experiencing new loving relationships in the adoptive family.

Generally speaking, it has been thought unwise to offer psychoanalytic psychotherapy to a child whose external living situation is considered to be too changeable to withstand, and adequately contain, all the ups and downs of the child's therapy. However, this has at times led to children who are in stable foster homes and considered suitable for adoption being denied treatment which might help them to make the extraordinary emotional changes that are expected of them – in being able to form new loving relationships with their adoptive families. Referrers, usually foster parents or social workers, have found this frustrating and difficult to understand.

Psychotherapists have responded by voicing their concerns about the potential for additional loss and discontinuity that will be experienced by the child becoming engaged in therapy, and then having to end therapy, if they are placed with a family who – for a variety of reasons – may be unable to continue to bring the child for therapy. One way of offering psychotherapeutic help in these circumstances has been for the psychotherapist to consult with the professionals, foster and adoptive parents over the process of transition. This has been helpful in many ways. However, this chapter argues that – provided that the therapist and all other professionals, as well as the foster and adoptive parents, work closely together throughout this process – it can be very helpful to offer therapy to a child who is 'in transition' from fostering to adoption. By working together in this linked-up way, the adults who are important for the child can create enough of a sense of continuity of emotional containment for the child, for the therapy to feel grounded in the stable environment that is needed for it to 'work'. The surprising rewards of therapy offered under these conditions are illustrated in this chapter.

In order for this kind of treatment model to work, the therapist and the other adults who are concerned about the child need to make a commitment *before therapy starts*, to consult regularly and thoughtfully with each other, and to keep each other properly informed about the child's emotional state of health. It may be important to have a clear written agreement on this way of working from the most senior member of the social work team – so that, if there are changes in the child's social worker, key decisions about the child's future are not made without consulting with the therapist. Efforts to communicate as effectively as possible about the child – knowing that there will inevitably be many 'blips' in this communication – have to be maintained throughout the process. If there are significant doubts that this is achievable, then it might indeed be better not to embark on therapy but rather to offer consultation to the professionals already working with the child.

By stating these conditions for effective treatment to take place, it becomes clear that therapy with these children will require the therapist's readiness to be much more involved in the external world of the child than might ordinarily be the case. This is one of those clinical situations where the therapist, possibly as well as a colleague in the inter-disciplinary team, may need to attend review meetings and meet with foster parents and adoptive parents on a regular basis. In addition, wherever possible, the therapy for the child needs to be supported by parallel therapeutic work with foster and adoptive parents, by a colleague.

In my clinical experience, it is important for the child's therapist to have direct contact with these important adults in the child's external life, as well as working with the child's internal world. In this way, the therapist can act as a kind of 'interpreter' of what is going on in the child's internal world to the important adults in their life. This is *in addition* to the therapeutic work and the case management that colleagues are offering to the adult network around the child. This is necessary because of the extraordinary external situation that these children and families find themselves in, which calls for a similarly 'extra' ordinary response from the child's psychotherapist. Indeed, these very deprived children seem to claim 'extra' in a multitude of ways from their therapists, as many accounts of therapy with 'looked after' children illustrate (Edwards 2000; Gibbs 2006; Hindle 2000; Hunter 2001; Ironside 2002; Lanyado 2006).

The active presence of the therapist within the professional network is very helpful in monitoring the risk of acting out in the network (Lanyado 2004a). Their intimate knowledge of the child's inner world enables them to spot the potential for destructive repetition within the network and thus reduce its possible impact. The difficulties of preserving a child's privacy whilst being in contact with so many people in their external world are, I feel, outweighed by the advantages of the improved level of containment of anxiety that results from the contact between all adults working with the child.

My interest in working with children who are 'in transition' arose out of a thoughtful referral from a social worker, who was concerned about a boy, Sammy, whom she was preparing for adoption. She was worried that he was going to find it distressing and possibly re-traumatising, to face the loss of his loved foster mother and family. The social worker was also very concerned that the loss would make the foster mother and family unable to face fostering any more children, even though they had clearly given so much to Sammy. I learnt a tremendous amount from my work with Sammy, which encouraged me to offer therapy to other children in similar circumstances.

Sammy was only four years old when he started to see me, and had spent half of his life with his foster family. He had been deprived and neglected as a young child, but had clear memories of his young birth mother, whom he had clearly loved, and who – despite her inadequacies as a mother – had very much wanted to keep him. Like many other young children in these circumstances, his behaviour in his foster home was often impulsive and aggressive. He could be very destructive of toys and furnishings, and when angry would deliberately wet and soil in the home. He had great difficulty concentrating on anything, and was unable to play in any age-appropriate way for more than a few minutes before he became distracted and moved onto something else. He was a 'handful', but he was also capable of being loving and remorseful, particularly when he had annoyed or upset his foster mother. When he first came for therapy, he was in a state of emotional turmoil, knowing that he was going to be adopted. His head was full of confusion and anger about three sets of parents – his birth parents, his foster parents and his fantasised adoptive parents – all of whom at various times he both idealised and felt rejected by. All of this was going on in the heart and mind of an emotionally derailed four-year-old child.

The disruption of ordinary emotional development

Children like Sammy are usually accompanied through their troubles by fat files of information about their short and highly traumatised lives. There are many reports, describing the abuse, neglect and trauma which led to them being 'looked after' by the social services. Within these reports there is the child's history of attachments, separations and losses – sadly repetitive accounts of parent–child relationships that have failed; adult relationships that have failed; mothers and fathers, and step-fathers or partners, foster families and adoptive families who come and go from the child's life; and siblings, grandparents and extended family with whom there is now little or no further contact. The complex impact of all this on the incredibly sensitive emotional life of the baby and young child is enormous.

Winnicott's (1965) model of ordinary emotional development is very helpful in trying to understand what has crucially *not* happened for these children at the start of their lives. Winnicott emphasises the importance of the facilitating environment (emotional and physical) in providing the fertile soil that the embryonic 'self' of the infant needs if it is to achieve its unique potential. One only has to think about how hard it can be for ordinary devoted parents to be 'good enough' parents in their own eyes – providing protection, understanding and continuity, as well as unconditional love – to realise what a nightmare world the children who end up coming into care have been born into.

Drawing further on Winnicottian thinking about emotional development, these children have not been held in the centre of a caring adult's mind in a totally preoccupied way, because the adults in their lives had so many issues of their own, which made it mostly impossible for them to do this, however much they may have wanted to. Their children have not experienced the quiet holding of their anxieties, or the fact that their parents are able to withstand their periods of primitive fury or terror and help them to survive these times. They have not felt safely protected from danger by their parents. Their utter helplessness and vulnerability in life often remains unthinkable, and only thinly masked by their infuriating defences of omnipotence and control in their relationships with those who subsequently try to help them. Their early, most basic, physical needs – which contribute vitally to their early emotional well-being, in terms of food, basic hygiene, or comforting when crying in pain or fear – have often not been adequately met. Most of the fundamental building blocks that are needed to 'create' a human being have been, in some way, compromised. It is in the details of how these experiences have been processed, or not, by the growing child, that we find the full developmental repercussions of the innocent-looking word 'neglect'.

Winnicott (1971b/1953) linked the development of the ability to play with what he called transitional phenomena and objects. He described these as, for some children, emerging in response to the need to bridge the space between one emotional state of mind and another. Classically, this is seen in ordinary development – in the baby or young child's need to have a particular toy or blanket, or particular rituals to help him or her to move from waking to sleeping. Much to many parents' embarrassment, this transitional object acquires a life of its own – together with a particular smell and feel that must not be interfered with. At the height of its emotional significance to the child, parents will go to enormous lengths to make sure that it is available when the child faces any anxiety-provoking situation, or needs it to go to sleep.

Children who have had very poor starts in life – such as those under discussion – often have not reached the developmental stage where they have been able to create such an important transitional object in their lives. And sadly, often if they have had these special toys and possessions, they have been lost in the moves from one placement to another. Their re-emergence, or emergence for the first time, is therefore an emotional event of tremendous consequence because of their ability to help the child to hold anxieties that would otherwise feel unbearable.

Not surprisingly, many of these children are unable to play in a free, communicative sort of way. They might play briefly with one toy, but then become distracted or dissatisfied with this and move on to another. There is likely to be little evolving fantasy or narrative in the play, and more probably a rather static or defensive quality to the play, which remains focused on the toy itself, rather than the fantasy world that the toy might potentially evoke for the child. Toys are thus 'things' rather than a means whereby the child is able to communicate non-verbally about internal preoccupations. Many of these children may be described as having difficulties with attention, concentration, impulsivity and hyperactivity. Importantly, for the theme of this chapter, it is more than likely that the playing is barely able to hold aggressive fantasies within the play itself, before the child actually becomes aggressive or physical in some way. Thus the child 'acts out', rather than being able to 'play out' his or her deeper anxieties, pains and angers. And these children do have a great deal to be angry about. This primitive rage is evident in their violent responses to many apparently ordinary situations. Through these responses they are frequently expressing their *outrage* at what has happened in their short and traumatised lives.

The ability to play in a satisfying way is such a hallmark of a healthy child-hood that it is easily taken for granted – until one is faced with a child who cannot play, and one realises what a sophisticated achievement this truly is. Here I am emphasising the *process* of playing itself and how this develops in early childhood, over and above the content of the play. This ability to play usually grows in the course of any child's therapy which has become well established. However, my focus on paying attention to this ability in its own right, has been intensified by my work with children like Sammy, whose developmental progression in the ability to play moved on significantly when their transitional anxieties were 'held' in therapy during the move from fostering to adoption (Lanyado 2004a). Becoming able to play out their internal conflicts and pains, rather than act them out, is an emotional and a cognitive achievement for children, which once reached paves the way for creative problem-solving as they grow up, and into their adult lives.

I now see one of the primary tasks of the therapy of children like this, as being able to redress this emotional environmental failure, through providing a therapeutic environment in which the child can be offered the opportunity to take some vital emotional steps – with the relationship that develops with the therapist acting as a catalyst. When the therapeutic package described above is working well, what the therapist is providing (in a very pure and concentrated culture during the therapy session), the external world environment also provides through good fostering and adoption and good social work practice – which is supported in its understanding of the child in the ways already discussed above.

The emergence of transitional experiences and phenomena and play, during the crisis of 'transition'

Sammy reached this developmental milestone at a time when the anxiety within him, and in the system of adults around him, was at its height. The adoptive family had been accepted by the adoption panel, and planning was under way about how to introduce them to Sammy. Although he had not yet been told about this, he was finding the waiting for his 'new' family to arrive quite unbearable. It was striking that when Sammy was literally needing to tolerate the paradoxical experience of having to let go of one set of loving relationships before he could be open to new, potentially loving and lifelong relationships, he became pre-occupied with 'in-between' spaces – both physical and emotional – in his therapy. To my initial astonishment, transitional phenomena started to emerge in his therapy and helped him to contain this transitional anxiety.

I would now like to describe the way in which Sammy became able to make these developmental steps. From the start of therapy, a treatment plan was set up in which each session started with Sammy and his foster mother seeing me together, so that I could help them with their turbulent and rather passionate relationship. At some point, depending on what felt right in the session, I would then see Sammy alone. This very fluid arrangement (which was unusual for me) was well suited to the purpose of trying to help them to face their impending separation with as little defensiveness as possible.

For many months, when he was on his own with me, Sammy was a typically distractible child who found it hard to play. He was extremely physical – jumping around the furniture, running out of the room, and throwing toys around when frustrated in the bits of play he managed. However, very gradually there were little oases of calm in this mayhem, when he was able to express his feelings. He liked to play 'Peter Pan', in which he was Peter and I was the wicked Captain Hook, with whom he had energetic sword fights. Somewhere mixed up in this play, I was able to understand and then talk to him about his identification with Peter Pan and the 'Lost Boys' who didn't have a mother and who didn't want to grow up. I was able to relate this to his fears about his future and his defensive fantasy that he didn't need a mother as she would only let him down.

There were times when Sammy started to enjoy playing with the sand in a quiet and absorbed way, during which I would also be very quiet as his absorption in the play felt very positive and healing for him. However, these periods of calm, where some kind of therapeutic reverie could emerge, really were very occasional oases (Ogden 1999; Lanyado 2004a). When they happened, they were also times when Sammy could briefly have the experience of playing because he was 'alone in the presence of another' – where he was able to feel free to play because of my quiet presence (Lanyado 2004a). However, the norm was much more a situation in which I needed to be on constant alert because of his emotional and physical impulsiveness – uncertain of what he might do next.

This was the context of the build-up towards his introduction to his adoptive family. By this point in his therapy, he frequently complained that his 'new' family were taking a very long time to come and claim him from his foster home. He was angry as well as relieved about this. He knew that they were on their way, but the wait felt interminable to him and further proof of how unwanted he was. He started to express his sense of being at an in-between place in his life by insisting on spending a fair amount of time on the stairs between his foster mother in the waiting area and the therapy room itself. This helped us to talk about how he felt in limbo and torn in two directions in his life, not knowing where to 'put' himself emotionally and physically.

During this period, at the end of a particularly painful session, Sammy was suddenly desperate to take a green ball from his box of toys home with him. As we had often battled about his – usually quite arbitrary – wish to take therapy toys home, this was very much against my better judgement. However, on this occasion there was such an imperative in his wish to take the ball that I let him do this, as long as he brought it back to the next session – which he agreed to do. I then said to him that although he knew I did not normally allow therapy toys to go home, on this occasion I would, because I could see it was so important to him, and we would see together what came of this. In other words, I was giving his acquisition of the ball my blessing, rather than letting it feel to him like a theft or a triumph over me.

I agreed to Sammy taking the green ball home because I was intrigued by the way in which this ball – which he had barely noticed before – had suddenly and genuinely become special to him. He seemed to be claiming rights over it, in the same way that a baby will naturally discover and claim his or her own special blanket, or soft toy, that becomes the classical transitional object as described by Winnicott (1971/1953). This felt potentially healthy to me and was quite unexpected in the midst of his generally disturbed behaviour at this time. I wanted to see what happened to this fragile beginning of what might have been his first transitional object.

Throughout the weeks that followed, during which time he was introduced to his adoptive family and left his foster family, the ball came and went from the sessions with Sammy. It was played with and carefully looked after (as well as, at times, aggressively knocked about), both in the therapy session and at his foster home. His foster mother intuitively understood that the ball was important to him. Even when he forgot to bring it to the session, he always referred to it. It was very clearly neither his nor mine, but it was also both his and mine. This paradoxical state of affairs was very much in keeping with his feeling that he belonged to both his foster and his adoptive family, as well as at times that he belonged to neither of them. Winnicott describes how transitional phenomena serve the function of holding this type of anxiety. It was therefore fascinating to recognise that Sammy had created a new transitional object just when it was most appropriate and most needed – at the height of his anxiety about the transition between his foster parents and his adoptive parents. I think that Sammy's use of the green ball may have been important in helping him to cope with the anxiety of the paradoxes of moving from foster to adoptive home, in what became a manageable transition, as opposed to a traumatic discontinuity and loss in his life.

During this period, he also astonished me by his ability to express his growing tolerance of transitional anxiety in highly communicative and moving play. All the adults in Sammy's life knew when he was going to be told that his 'new' family had been found, and there was an inevitable build-up of tension in all of us leading up to this time, each of us wondering how Sammy would cope with the move to his new home. I often found myself deeply preoccupied during his sessions (if I had the chance for this to happen) and in between his sessions, with trying to make sense in my mind of all that was about to happen to him. This intense preoccupation felt similar to primary maternal preoccupation during late pregnancy and was a state of mind in which I was very aware of having Sammy 'in my pocket', as a way of trying to hold and contain his transitional anxiety (Lanyado 2004a: 106).

In his session two days before I knew he would be told about his new family, he became quietly absorbed in 'making cakes' from wet sand. At first this felt defensive to me and I found myself musing aloud to him about how hard it might be for him, knowing that his new family would arrive soon, but not knowing quite when this would be. I wasn't even sure that he had heard me as he just carried on with his concentrated play. He came and sat next to me, again surprisingly quietly. I waited a few minutes and then asked him what was happening in his play, as he still seemed immersed in it. He told me, in a rather patient, teacherly way, that we had to wait a bit now. I wasn't sure what he meant, and then in one of those amazing flashes of connection that Stern *et al.* (1998) call a 'moment-of-meeting' between patient and therapist, I realised that he meant that we had to wait for the cakes to bake. We had to be patient and wait till they were ready.

This was a deeply moving moment on many levels. I was astonished at the appropriateness of the metaphor he had found in his play for expressing his understanding and trust that he just had to wait for his new life to unfold. He seemed to accept this and trust that the adults in his life knew what they were doing. This was a great achievement. His image of the oven with the cakes baking inside them, also implied that he felt contained in a creative way by these adults and felt that something good might come of all their efforts 'to bake' him a new family. Through his growing ability to play, he had found a means of expressing what was deepest in his heart, and then expressing it to me through his play. I don't think it was just me who felt I could smell those cakes baking. The tangible sense of something longed for, but which had to still be waited for, was alive in the room. I was then able to say – probably unnecessarily, as he already understood this – that he knew that it was important to wait till the time was right to take the 'new mummy and daddy cake' out of the oven. If it was too soon, it would not be ready – and if it was too late, it would be 'burnt'. Sammy's ability to communicate in this way, just when it might have been expected that he would be finding it most difficult to contain his anxieties, was a tremendous *developmental achievement*. This seemed to be a part of a combination of inter-related developmental steps, in which he was becoming able to use transitional phenomena to help him contain his transitional anxiety, and he was becoming able to internalise the containing presence of the important grown-ups in his life. It was an example of how a life crisis can have within it the opportunities for dramatic growth and change, as well as the potential for disaster.

The three weeks that followed his introduction to his adoptive parents were like an emotional roller coaster. Sammy brought out his full repertoire of awful confrontational and aggressive behaviour towards his adoptive parents, as well as being very volatile with his foster parents. The green ball was with him a great deal of the time, and it came and went from the therapy sessions as before. Slowly, Sammy was able to see that his adoptive parents really wanted him and that they tried very hard to understand his distress. He gradually became more able to accept them and the inevitability of saying goodbye to his foster parents. As the day approached that he would leave them, he often asked them whether they would cry when he went. They told him truthfully that they probably would – and in fact did. It was very significant for Sammy to know that he mattered enough to them for them also to be very upset at their parting. This was very different from the separations and losses of the past in which he'd felt that the grown-ups were glad to get rid of him.

In this case, Sammy was able to continue with once-weekly treatment for a further six months, with his adoptive parents bringing him some distance to see me. I had met his adoptive parents before he had, and we had talked about his life story and about the emotional difficulties that he had, and how therapy was trying to help him. However I don't think that I had re-negotiated his need for therapy as much as I would do now, and so his attendance for therapy became rather erratic and we eventually agreed on just a few sessions to bring his therapy to an end, although in many ways I felt that it might have been better for him to continue.

The need to be sensitive to adoptive parents' wish to 'claim' their child, and provide for all his or her emotional needs, must be respected by therapists.

Adoptive parents have often been through so many personally intrusive hoops – before being accepted as adopters – that they understandably cannot wait to be left alone to get on with their lives. There can be a fear that if they admit to the inevitable difficulties that they face with their newly adopted child, they will be judged as being inadequate parents. It is important for the therapist to try to overcome this difficulty through the relationship he or she forms with the adoptive parents during the transition, and after the child goes to live with them. This can enable adoptive parents to see the therapist as an ally and not a threat during the difficult early stages of adoption.

The creation of transitional phenomena in therapy – the green ball

I would now like to turn to a more theoretical discussion of playing and transitional phenomena. The idea of transitions, and the manner in which they are not 'either/or', but are paradoxically 'both', is extremely pertinent when thinking about children in Sammy's position. Sammy's use of the green ball as a transitional object helped him to cope with the paradoxes of his life during the transition to his adoptive home. By managing to hold so many paradoxical feelings within him, rather than becoming torn apart by the internal conflicts they represented, he managed to stay remarkably together during a period in his life where he might have literally felt that his mind was 'blown'. Transitional phenomena (objects and experiences) help to contain and transform transitional anxiety within what might be experienced as a terrifying void or chaotic gap, into experiencing that same psychic or external space as being potentially bearable and creative (Fransman 2002). Harnessing the creative potential that is present within a transition can be seen as a significant aim of the psychotherapy of looked-after children.

Therapy, alongside restorative experiences in foster placements, can provide the kind of environment in which new transitional phenomena can emerge. One of the qualities of this facilitating environment is providing the quiet and often repeated experience of what Winnicott (1958) evocatively describes as being 'alone in the presence of someone'. This experience is very relevant to the child's developing capacity to play, which in turn relates to the ordinary developmental creation of transitional phenomena. Through this concept of being 'alone in the presence of someone', Winnicott describes the states of mind that are likely to be present in the 'secure base' image of a child being able to playfully explore the environment in a state of absorption, as long as an attachment figure is present (Ainsworth 1982; Bowlby 1988a).

In essence, I see what I conceptualise as transitional space as emerging slowly from the many small and cumulative experiences that the patient has of being alone in the presence of the therapist. It is an experience that can be thought of as a space in between them, which does not belong to one or the other person. This in-between nature of the space is uniquely created and generated between patient and therapist as the therapy progresses, and is what makes it transitional. It has to do with 'two-ness' creating 'one-ness'. It is similar to the idea that you cannot clap with one hand. Building on Winnicottian thinking, the in-between-ness of the clap itself is what makes these experiences 'transitional'. Initially in therapy, these experiences may be momentary. But if the therapist notices them, and is able to let them breathe a bit and 'be' a bit in the session, they gradually appear more often. Over time the therapist is able to observe more fully formed ideas, and then ideas which are played with – again, briefly at first – begin to emerge within the session. This is the way in which young children developmentally start to play. The ability grows quietly, initially dependent on the presence of the 'other' to keep it going and growing.

So, it is possible to postulate that a child who cannot play nevertheless may have the potential to play, if the relational conditions allow for this. The therapist may be able to provide this kind of relational environment, through his or her concentrated attunement to the patient during the session, together with his or her capacity to notice the tiny beginnings of ideas and play, and then nurture and pay further attention to them. The concentrated attunement on the part of the therapist is what creates the ground for the patient to gradually become aware of being alone in the presence of the therapist, and indeed the therapist to recognise that this is starting to happen.

Lest this description should sound too much like Nirvana, I would like to emphasise that what emerges in the shape of children's play during these times, is often painfully and frighteningly appropriate to their internal dilemmas. The transitional space is a place in which these painful issues can be addressed because the *vehicle* through which they can be expressed – be it play in a child, or free association, dreams and creative thought or expressions in the teenager or adult – have become more available for use. Sammy's 'baking of cakes' is a good example of the painful expression of emotional truths that can become possible in these circumstances.

The transitional space that the child becomes able to enter has certain characteristics that can help the therapist to recognise that the therapeutic journey has reached this place. But it is rather easier to say what this transitional space is *not*, than to say what it *is*. Transitional space is the opposite of a space in which the individual feels trapped, and unable to breathe, think and play. The sense of being stuck in endlessly repeating negative emotional experiences is a frequent complaint of those seeking psychotherapeutic help. By contrast, a sense of freedom and spontaneity characterises experiences that take place within the transitional space. It is in the transitional space that new ideas and possibilities emerge and can be played with in a safe way. It can be like emerging into an open space after being lost in the woods. But it can be very difficult to reach this place.

It is the acceptance of the essence of this space – that it is neither inner nor outer, past or future, the patient's or the therapist's, but paradoxically both – that contributes significantly to the feeling that this is a space in which anything could happen. It is a space full of potential and surprises where paradox – defined in the *Concise Oxford Dictionary* as 'a seemingly absurd or contradictory statement, even if actually well-founded' – can be tolerated. The freedom of playing with ideas relies heavily on the suspension of the ordinary rules of reality, and the suspension of 'either/or' thinking. This is not about the conflict of two opposing forces or feelings, but about the acceptance of their co-existence. This leads to the contemplation of what may seem absurd – such as two opposing feelings being true simultaneously.

It is important to acknowledge that for many very deprived and traumatised children, the creation of a transitional space can prove enormously elusive. The specific difficulties within each treatment of enabling this space to become alive, is one of the processes that therapists have to work with as creatively as possible. A long period of time in therapy may be spent in trying to enable a child to dare to let him or herself to be free enough, just to 'taste' the transitional space for long enough, to become attracted and intrigued by it.

Part of the therapist's task is to keep the possibility of entering this space as alive as possible within the therapy, despite the endless setbacks that inevitably take place in this process. It is often a question of 'trying and trying again'. Winnicott (1971d/1967: 44) writes intriguingly that one of the major tasks of the therapist is 'bringing the patient from a state of not being able to play into a state of being able to play'. This chapter has attempted to describe how this process can evolve in the therapy of children for whom adoption is planned, who are desperately in need of this experience because of the severe environmental failure they experienced at the start of their lives. I have argued that one of the most important functions of therapy is to enable children such as these to play, and through this find their way towards the ordinary developmental processes which will continue in their lives. This is the process of recovery that therapy and well-supported adoptions are able to offer to children who have had such damaging and traumatic starts to their lives.

Note

This chapter is an extension of the thinking in Chapters 5 and 6 in *The Presence of the Therapist: Treating Childhood Trauma* (Lanyado 2004) and includes some sections from these chapters.

6 The playful presence of the therapist

'Antidoting' defences in the therapy of a late-adopted adolescent patient (2006)

The importance of enabling a child to play as a central aspect of the therapeutic process is developed further in this chapter which was originally published in A Question of Technique, *the first of the Independent Psychoanalytic Approaches with Children and Adolescents (IPACA) series, co-edited with Ann Horne (Lanyado 2006; Lanyado and Horne 2006). The difficulty for the therapist of deciding when it is helpful to be playful with a patient, and when it becomes too directive or revealing of the therapist's personality, is raised often in supervisions and seminars. In the same way that 'Sammy' in the previous chapter stimulated my thinking, I also learnt a great deal from 'Gail', different aspects of whose therapy I have written about in several other published papers and chapters. I saw her for therapy for many years and Chapter 7 provides an interesting picture of how she had changed by the end of her therapy. Severely neglected and traumatised patients constantly challenge established boundaries and technical wisdom within the therapeutic setting. As a result, they raise many questions of technique which result in adaptations within the therapeutic process to meet the needs of the patient.*

Consider the following clinical situation. A severely deprived 8-year-old girl, whose plight had been repeatedly unseen and unheard by the authorities, was eventually fostered, but with poor case management leaving her vulnerable to further abuse. Several foster homes later she was placed with a foster family who were able to make a commitment to her and who fought for her to have therapy. In one of her sessions she spent a great deal of time and effort repeatedly trying to build a tent using a blanket and parts of the furniture in the room, in ways that would obviously fail. She couldn't accomplish this task on her own for straightforward mechanical reasons and yet she kept trying to achieve the impossible. She kept on and on trying to build a space that she could physically get inside, in a heartbreakingly futile way, and several times asked the therapist to help, but in a controlling and rather bullying manner which the therapist felt he could not agree to. Finally, in desperation the child shouted at the therapist who had quietly observed these efforts, 'Why won't you help me?'

The therapist, as well as the patient, found the session distressing but the therapist felt that the girl's expression of helplessness and despair was important and needed to be contained and heard, but not actively responded to, and so decided not to help the child to make the tent. Nevertheless, the therapist also felt uncertain about where the therapy was going and what he was trying to achieve and was concerned that he might at times be getting caught in a re-enactment of the past (by not helping when help was so clearly needed) that was not therapeutic for the child.

From an independent perspective, it can be argued that this was a situation where, despite the patient's controlling behaviour, the therapist could have responded to her cry for help, and thoughtfully joined the girl in her play. In this way, it might have been possible to acknowledge the child's desperate need to maintain the controlling defence, whilst also recognising the intensity of the pain that necessitated such a severe and unrelenting defensive structure. However, at the time, the therapist was more highly aware of the child's sadistic efforts to control everyone around her and the problems that this defence was creating in all her relationships. His view was that there was a pressing need to experience and contain the underlying anxieties in the transference relationship and resist what could be seen as a collusion with the defensive structure the patient had erected.

This is a common dilemma and indeed at the root of a significant technical and theoretical divergence about how to analyse anxieties and the defences around them. Traditionally, Kleinian therapists would directly try to analyse the underlying anxiety, whereas Anna Freudians would be analysing the need for such controlling defences. The therapy of severely deprived patients, whom I find it helpful to think of as suffering from 'multiple traumatic loss', seems constantly to present these kinds of technical choices and challenges (Lanyado 2002, 2003, 2004).

Another argument for the therapist agreeing to help the child could have been the opportunity to help the child in her highly significant wish to build rather than to destroy, which was her more usual way of being. Having witnessed the child's struggle, the therapist might even have offered help before being asked, and waited to see whether the child could accept that this kind of building, practically as well as symbolically, was the kind which could not be done alone. It needed two people. The recognition of the need for adult help is another painful experience for children like these, who will behave omnipotently and controllingly in situations in which they actually feel terrifyingly helpless. Indeed, this is a classic defence used by children who are described in attachment terms as being 'detached' or 'disorganised' (see Solomon and George 1999). Thinking in terms of the girl's attachment disorder, it was a significant achievement that she dared to ask for help. It could therefore also be argued that it was possibly a technical mistake *not* to respond to this with a therapeutic gesture that recognised her need for someone who would try to protect her, and help her to build rather than destroy.

Underlying these differences of perspective about what are the child's primary therapeutic needs is the important further question of 'therapeutic priorities' and how to respond to them. In this instance, it can be argued that by appearing not to see, hear or respond to the child's desperate cries for help, the therapist could indeed have been perceived by the child as repeating what had happened in the past, when the adults around her, and the authorities, had not responded to her cries for help. The child believed that the authorities had turned a blind eye to her suffering by not taking her out of care situations which they had placed her in, in which she was being neglected and abused by adults. For children such as these, for a long time in therapy, the therapist's actions can speak louder than words and are needed as an evident accompaniment to the constant therapeutic efforts to contain, internally and externally, the child's pain, trauma and anger.

Additionally, there are times when a reluctance to follow the flow of counter-transference intuition, as a means of exploring what is happening in the trans-ference relationship, can result in the therapist being unnecessarily withholding or even unwittingly sadistic or cruel towards the patient – often in the name of a perceived technical 'correctness'. By contrast, responding more intuitively to difficult clinical and technical situations, can be likened to taking a 'participant-observer' stance within the transference relationship, from which further informa-tion is directly experienced and then thought about through the medium of, at times, highly unusual experiences in the consulting room.

This example helps me to approach one of the central technical questions of this chapter: to play or not to play? Much of my thinking is based on Winnicott's seminal work, *Playing and Reality*, which is an extremely valuable source of thought about the importance of 'playing' in the psychotherapeutic process (Winnicott 1971a). In this book, he develops his ideas about how playing is at the root of all everyday creative and cultural activity and places this process at the heart of the psychotherapeutic process. His key statement about playing, which is explained and explored in great detail throughout his book, comes in a chapter titled 'Playing: A theoretical statement' and is a typically dense Winnicottian statement which has many layers of significance. He says

> Psychotherapy takes place in the overlap of two areas of playing, that of the patient and that of the therapist. Psychotherapy has to do with two people playing together. The corollary of this is that where playing is not possible, then the work done by the therapist is directed towards bringing the patient from a state of not being able to play to a state of being able to play.
>
> (Winnicott 1971d: 44)

It is important to note that, in this statement about psychotherapy, Winnicott is referring to therapy with adults for whom playing with ideas is very central to the therapeutic process, as well as children. He has a very particular view of playing as taking place in an intermediate area of experience, which he also calls a transitional space, between the internal and external world. Winnicott argues for the value of the *paradox* of play being simultaneously both an internal activity in which fantasy is not constrained by reality, and an external activity as it is being enacted through the use of toys, activity and creativity in the broadest sense, in the outside world. The idea of tolerating this paradox is central to his thinking about the creativity of play.

Winnicott sees the ability to play as being facilitated at the start of life, by the presence of an adult who can hold the child's anxieties sufficiently for the child to be able to play in a *creative and free way*. I stress this quality of creativity and freedom in healthy play, because playing can often be very lacking in these qualities. Here I am thinking of the repetitive and ritualistic quality of the play of children who use autistic defences, or the self-destructive acting-out type of play of severely deprived children, some of which is described later in this chapter. Again, it is important for the therapist always to remain discerning about the function of playing at any point in the therapy, and to be alert to the need to distinguish defensive play from creative play – when the actual content may be identical at times.

Of course, people are playful throughout life as seen in the many games and sports played by adults, the ordinary spontaneous play between adults and children, as well as in adults' ability to play with ideas and be creative in the arts and sciences.

The value of having a sense of humour

As well as having this Winnicottian view in mind, there are other considerations that arise when thinking about playing. Playing, as thought about in a more everyday sense, is often accompanied by a sense of fun. The spontaneous use of humour in therapy, and whether or not it is 'right' to laugh at something that is clearly funny during a session, can cause some consternation, particularly to trainees or more newly qualified therapists. There can be a fear that laughter during a session may play into more manic defences in the patient and this may be true sometimes. However, Carlberg's research into turning points in child psychotherapy has suggested that spontaneous laughter in a session can 'open the door' to important therapeutic change (Carlberg 1997). Counter-transference sensitivity to the patient can usually help the therapist to distinguish between the discomfort that is felt when a manic defence against anxiety is operating, and a genuinely funny moment.

Nevertheless, some may lift their hands in horror at the possibility of anything as light-hearted as playfulness or humour in the context of the very serious problems that patients bring to their therapy. Others argue that being able to keep in touch with the relief and insight that humour and playfulness offer, by there being at times a lightness of touch in the therapist's way of responding to what the patient brings, is what may enable the therapeutic couple to keep on working together (Bollas 1995; Coltart 1992; Horne 2001, 2006). This does not mean that the therapist is not taking the patiently seriously or spends his or her time cracking jokes with the patient.

Additionally, I have often observed that a sense of humour, even at times a rather 'black' sense of humour, can help people working with very disturbed, perverse or violent patients to maintain a humane perspective towards those in their care. Organisationally, this might be thought of as an adaptive social defence against the anxiety and pain that the organisational structure is trying to contain (Menzies Lyth 1988). Certainly, a sense of staff in such organisations and units being 'good-humoured', is likely to help staff to continue to work with the most disturbing of patients, as well as be experienced in a positive way by the patients themselves.

Bollas thoughtfully discusses these issues in detail in *Cracking Up* (Bollas 1995). In his final chapter he draws attention to the ways in which 'a sense of humour grasps the absurdities in life'. He links this to the absurdities of unconscious life, particularly as seen in dreams – but of course also as played out by children when playing alone or with others. This is evident in the clinical example later in this chapter. Freud, of course, drew attention to the importance of jokes and humour and their links to the unconscious (Freud 1905). Bollas reminds us of the ways in which in ordinary everyday parent–baby relationships we can see the mother (and of course the father too) exaggeratedly 'clowning' with their baby to stimulate smiles and laughter. Whilst recognising that this comic approach can become 'too close for comfort' and rather manic in some relationships, in others he sees it as 'eliciting our true self's spontaneity' (Bollas 1995: 237). He goes on to say:

> Perhaps a sense of humour is essential to human survival. Amusement in the self and in the other may be a vital constituent part of a comprehensive perspective on life. The mother who develops her baby's sense of humour is assisting him to detach from dire mere existence, from simply being in the rather shitty world of infancy, for example. Such a child can, as an adult, ultimately find humour in the most awful of circumstances, benefiting from the origins of the comic sense.
>
> (Bollas 1995: 243–4)

In offering these persuasive arguments for the place of humour and playfulness within the therapeutic relationship, Bollas is in good company. Coltart, in her memorable essay *Slouching towards Bethlehem . . . And Further Psychoanalytic Explanations*, speaks of her impression that laughter 'can be felt to be dangerous in psychoanalysis' (Coltart 1992: 10). She quotes Bion in one of his São Paulo lectures as saying:

> I wonder if it is in the rules of psychoanalysis to be able to laugh at ourselves? Is it according to the rules of psychoanalysis that we should be amused and find things funny? Is it permissible to enjoy a psychoanalytic meeting? I suggest that, having broken through in this revolutionary matter of being amused in the sacred process of psychoanalysis, we might as well continue to see where that more joyous state of mind might take us.
>
> (Bion 1980: 94–5)

Coltart draws the conclusion 'to put it very simply, that laughter and enjoyment can be therapeutic factors in psychoanalysis. Certainly, I believe that one not only can but should enjoy psychoanalytic sessions' (Coltart 1992: 11). She goes on to describe the therapy of a man who could make people laugh and who, although quite ill, was really amusing in his sessions. She describes how she spent a lot of energy trying not to laugh and analysed the aggression in his jokes and so on. Many years on, she says that she would still analyse the material in this way, but thinks that she would now laugh first if she felt like it. She says that

I am now of the opinion that I deprived both him and me unnecessarily by being so prim. I think I might have got nearer to some true shape or pattern in him *faster*, by responding with a natural reaction and *then* talking about it. If we are too protective of our self-representation and of what we consider grimly to be the sacred rules of True Psychoanalysis, then we may suffocate something in the patient, in ourselves, and in the process.

(Coltart 1992: 12)

In thinking about the potential value of playfulness and humour, particularly in the therapist's way of being with the patient, what I think of as his or her 'presence', there are implications for the ways in which the therapist feels free to use his or her 'Self' during the sessions. The authentic interplay between therapist and patient in the present relationship, as well as the transference and counter-transference relationship, needs to be understood in every treatment. It is this unique constellation of each therapeutic couple, with its extraordinary complexity and essential humanity, that requires that when we talk about psychoanalytic technique, we are inevitably thinking about the therapist's use of a general technical framework as applied in a particular instance (Lanyado 2004a; Tronick 2003). We are not talking about a manual.

Finding and experiencing the uniqueness of each therapeutic encounter

A patient whom I have written about elsewhere, whose letters I literally carried with me during a period of time when she was dangerously suicidal, I believe needed an unusual response like this from me (Lanyado 2001, 2004). She was in such a concrete state of mind at the time that she was unable to believe that she was in my mind between sessions, at this time of crisis. So, I had to meet this concreteness by actually carrying something of hers with me. It was not a problem for me to do this, and by this small therapeutic gesture I felt that I was, in her understanding, authentically meeting her primary and urgent need to feel emotionally held. She needed something 'special' – by which I mean something unique, specific and not general – and she needed it for a particular purpose. I had not done this for any patient before her and, so far, I have not done this for any patient since. Checking the *Concise Oxford Dictionary* on the precise meaning of 'special' highlights that there are several different meanings of 'special'. I would argue that another therapist might have done something else 'special' in the above sense, for a patient in similar need which might have held the same *emotional significance* between them, but it would probably have taken a different form altogether, a point also made by Horne (Horne 2006).

The question of a patient in some instances *needing* to feel 'special' to the therapist is a tricky one. Possibly this is because, in contrast to the type of specialness just described, there is another form of 'specialness' that *wishes and longs* for an exclusivity and a possessiveness of the therapist, which attempts to deny or get rid of the painful presence of other patients and people in the therapist's life. This kind of specialness implies a comparison with other people in which the would-be 'special' person is exceptional and more important than anyone else. There are controlling and tyrannical aspects in this kind of demand for specialness, which relate to its oedipal, three-person-type character (Bartram 2003). However, it should be remembered that these indications of growing particles of oedipal development are, for patients like these, a therapeutic achievement. But at the same time, these oedipal wishes cannot be met and therapy needs to address the pain of recognising this reality.

Where there has been neglect and poor emotional attunement to the baby from the start of life, there is likely to be a need, indeed a necessity in terms of emotional well-being, to feel special to someone. Developmentally, this need can only be met within a two-person relationship. If it is not, there is a deficit in the individual's emotional life at a basic fault level, to use Balint's terminology (Balint 1968). If this need emerges in therapy, the patient may be unconsciously trying to experience feeling special to someone, possibly for the first time ever in a consistent way, within the therapeutic relationship as discussed by Hopkins (Hopkins 1999). This is the form of regression that Balint would think of as therapeutic and could be described as a basic developmental need. It is an example of the therapist at these times being a developmental object for the patient, as described by Hurry and her colleagues (Hurry 1998). This kind of specialness relates to the earliest parent–infant experiences in which the parent recognises the unique individuality of their baby and all of his or her potential. To bring out this potential, some patients have a particularly intense need for their therapists to recognise this uniqueness.

Alvarez also draws attention to this important distinction between needs and wishes and describes how the therapist uses language to express 'the grammar of wishes and the grammar of needs' in all his or her verbal communication (Alvarez 2000). I think of this as an aspect of the present relationship experience between the patient and therapist, which I have written about elsewhere (Lanyado 2004a). Alvarez emphasises that it is not the words themselves but the underlying emotional understanding within the patient–therapist couple, of the difference between the patient's wishes and needs, that is crucial. Whilst it is better for the patient if the therapist expresses the awareness of the difference between needs and wishes within the language that he or she uses, Alvarez argues that the patient 'knows' in a mostly unconscious way what is in the therapist's heart, and is able to 'forgive us the grammar' if we get it wrong with the words themselves (Alvarez 2000: 18). Regarding this sense of specialness that could be thought of as a primary need, if I understand rightly what Alvarez is saying, she argues that trying to find a way to meet this rightful need can be a moral imperative, which is fundamentally life-enhancing. In effect, I think she is saying, as indeed I would agree, that it may be a therapeutic mistake not to acknowledge or meet this need in some small, but emotionally significant way.

In this context of differentiating wish from need, I have been interested to note the ways in which other child and adolescent therapists describe their actions and words with some of the very damaged patients that make up the bulk of caseloads today. There is a growing literature on therapy with these children and young people (for example, Bartram 2003; Canham 2003, 2004; Edwards 2000; Hopkins 2000; Horne 2003; Kenrick 2000). Gibbs discusses and describes the adaptations of technique that she has found helpful with looked-after children (Gibbs 2006). Each of these accounts contains descriptions of unusual technical challenges and responses with which all who treat these children are likely to empathise. For example, Edwards' 6-year-old adopted patient developed an increasing tendency to 'throw himself headfirst onto the floor' and leapt dangerously around the furniture in the room (Edwards 2000: 361). This followed a period of time when the therapist was sellotaped to her chair and forced to witness the disturbing torture of one of the play therapy toys. Edwards says

> There was no question of my remaining in my chair holding Gary with interpretation alone: it was imperative that I follow him physically and link my interpretations to active physical contact at times of danger. In this context, I thought of the earliest interactions between mother and baby.
>
> (Edwards 2000: 362)

Her patient elicited a physical response within the present relationship, in which he additionally and significantly had the *opportunity* to experience this response being thought about in a therapeutic way. This is what Coltart is referring to in terms of the therapist first reacting naturally to the patient and then thinking and talking about it.

Bartram describes playing with her patient. 'She and I had to (pretend to) dress up in sparkling dresses and twirl around in front of Prince Charming' (Bartram 2003: 28). This game seems to have been important for the therapy and gives us a picture of the therapist playing with the patient in a natural and hopeful way, as Zara was admired and increasingly chosen by the prince over Bartram. Bartram did not feel inhibited about engaging in this play and was able to see its therapeutic potential. Hindle describes the therapy of a very challenging patient who spent much of his session up a tree outside the therapy room, or rushing around the clinic (Hindle 2000).

Severely deprived and abused patients often put us in embarrassing, ridiculous and undignified situations, indeed as Bollas says, absurd situations, and seem to crow at us 'now what are you going to do about that?' This is a wonderfully effective way for the patient to explore the more intuitive and spontaneous side of the therapist, which they may need to know about much more than the cerebral aspect during the early stages of therapy. For children who have been severely abused by adults in positions of trust, this need to know who the therapist really 'is' is part of the child's life-preserving defences which sadly have had to be utilised in the past as a way of trying to avoid and/or survive abuse. They have had to use these antennae to try to judge, as one little adopted boy put it, 'who is for me and who is against me'. I have written about this in more detail elsewhere (Lanyado 2004a).

The therapist may well try to digest what on earth has been going on in challenging sessions such as these after the session has ended, and possibly manage to make a bit more sense of it. Psychoanalytic understanding and regular supervision are extremely helpful in sustaining the therapist through these demanding therapeutic experiences with the patient. However, often despite these therapeutic tools, the therapist is left with an increasingly incomprehensible therapeutic experience which can lead to the therapist – let alone the child – dreading the session.

These complex communications in action are rarely easily decoded. Embedded deeply within the extraordinary situations that these patients create in their therapy, there is an experience which the patient–therapist couple have to tolerate and survive before reaching any more thoughtful understanding or resolution. In the process, these patients inevitably get to know much more about the essence of the way in which the therapist's internal world works than patients who bring neurotic problems.

The clinical example which follows emphasises this idea of the opportunity that is contained within a crisis of this type in the course of therapy. It is through the creative challenges of situations such as these that windows of therapeutic opportunity can open and moments-of-meeting take place which are deeply healing (Stern *et al.* 1998; Lanyado 2001, 2004; Ward 2003).

The playful presence of the therapist and 'playful' interpretation

Gail, the patient who made me think a great deal about the question of playfulness in the therapeutic relationship, needed us to develop a special, unconventional form of communication in therapy for a number of reasons which it took me a long while to understand. I probably played with her much more than any other patient before her. Of course, she did not know this consciously, but I think she did know unconsciously that what she received from me in therapy was something that grew inside me for her and her alone. It was specially for her therapeutic needs.

Much of what I wish to say about our work together only gradually made sense to me over time – a sort of crystallising out process from within the therapeutic process as a whole. I would not wish to give the impression that this was readily understood in this way as therapy progressed. However, as Gail made good developmental progress and became much happier and more able to discover who she was as she became a teenager, I was encouraged that what had happened between us had been helpful. I say this as a precursor to describing some unusual clinical events, because I think that whenever something technically unusual takes place in therapy, it is vital to look carefully at the consequences of these actions to see if they have been helpful or not. Whatever the outcome, the therapist will have to work with these consequences. If it has been unwise, there will be the need to repair the possible 'damage' done. If it has helped, it is important to try to understand why it has helped – and to share this with colleagues, as I hope to do in this chapter.

In Gail's therapy, because of her quixotic unpredictability, there were many times when I awaited her sessions with considerable tension and trepidation. What would she do today that would take me by surprise, make me feel silly or touch me deeply? I am grateful to her parents for giving me permission to discuss the issues her therapy raised.

Gail was adopted when she was eight years old. She had been severely neglected and traumatised by her biological parents and had an unusual 'syndrome' that may have impacted on her intellectual ability. Her biological mother had learning difficulties of her own. Both of her biological parents had been emotionally deprived in their childhood and her father was considered to be personality disordered. In addition to these disadvantages in life, both birth parents were congenitally deaf. Gail was able to hear normally and her birth parents had 'signed' to her, but the severe communication difficulties that existed between them were mainly the result of the emotional neglect that took place during the first four years of her life. As a consequence Gail had no ordinary spoken language when she started nursery at the age of three, but was able to 'sign' and 'speak' in a very rudimentary way. There were many complicated, and very subtle, repercussions from this situation as it is likely that Gail and her birth parents developed their own personalised and idiosyncratic communication system – a combination of signing and very simple speech. Facial expressions and gestures were probably an important part of this system.

Gail's adoptive parents had always made it clear to social services that they would want post-adoption funds to be made available for her to have therapy and this had been agreed. Because of this Gail came to see me privately in my home and the treatment was funded by social services. Gail started twice-weekly therapy when she was twelve and going into her first year at secondary school.

Although Gail was chronologically and physically well into adolescence, for the first two years of therapy play was our primary means of communication. I was concentrated in my wish to facilitate the process of play itself, as a means of communication between us. By this I mean that I realised that I needed to be as playfully 'present' as possible to aid the development of communication between us. My demeanour, state of mind, attempts at openness and willingness to play out her scripts, however silly this felt at times, helped us in this process. There were times, when she had been in therapy for over two years, when there were moments of humour in this that we both saw the funny side of, but that didn't stop us in our playful interaction. By then Gail could say, 'we're only playing' and just carry on, in a very unembarrassed way for a 14-year-old girl who was starting to appreciate ordinary 14-year-old girls' interests.

Early on in Gail's therapy, I was allowed to comment and interpret within and outside the transference relationship, but I often felt that what I had said had not really got to the heart of the matter. Indeed, I suspect that, as I got better at understanding Gail, my words became much more threatening and indeed frightening at times. Just as I often wondered before, and during the session, what she would spring on me next, I am sure that she also felt this about my words. She told me to shut up, talked over what I said or, if that didn't work, simply left the room.

I learnt to keep quiet, but at times this was very hard, particularly when something in her play suddenly conveyed a powerful emotional message and I felt that I might 'miss the moment' if I didn't say something fairly soon. On these occasions, I started to literally ask her permission to speak. So I would say, 'Gail, there's something I really want to say about what's happening at the moment. Can I say it?' When I first started to do this, I actually added that it was something 'very small' as I felt that the number of words I would be able to utter before being told to shut up was extremely limited. When Gail asked in a very slightly playful way 'how small?', I spontaneously literally put my hands apart in front of me indicating a small length of words. I can't say that she actually smiled at this, but there was a softening and a faint twinkle in her eyes when she said, 'Oh, alright then, but no more than that.' This dawning playfulness *between* us seemed to make whatever I had to say more palatable. This approach started after she had been in therapy for about four months. As time went on I came to see the expression of liveliness and creativity, that this type of interaction between us allowed, as a powerful *antidote* to her defensiveness. It seemed that by offering something that she could enjoy – playfulness alongside something she found really hard to swallow, she was able to work with me to find a way of 'melting' or 'dissolving' the defences against emotional pain that she had needed so much in the past. I will come back to this idea of play as an antidote to defensiveness later, as well as thoughts about how defences can 'melt' or be 'dissolved'.

I want to give some more detailed material from a session that came a few months after we first started to communicate in this way. It illustrates therapeutic mistakes and what I learnt from them (Casement 2002), as well as windows of opportunity and a 'moment-of-meeting' (Stern, *et al.* 1998). It was a session in which I think that Gail had a real experience of me, as a person, but in a way that I think helped her to feel that I could respond to her primary need to be special, and seen and heard for who she really was.

When Gail had been in treatment for over a year and after a long holiday break she became increasingly desperate to go into all the rooms in my home that she was not allowed into. She felt that my home, and I, were full of doors that were closed to her. I had tried to talk to her about how excluded and rejected she felt by me and how underprivileged and unimportant she felt in comparison with other people in my life. These oedipal longings and rejections were really painful for her so I was particularly aware at this time of trying to keep the boundaries between my home and my practice well protected. Unfortunately, at the start of the session I want to describe, a number of unusual circumstances led to her catching sight of other people in the house. I felt awful about this. She rushed into the therapy room, and, as on a number of other occasions, shut me out of the room ostensibly to rearrange the furniture in the way she wanted it on that day, something that she did at the start of many sessions. This felt like a particularly poignant attempt, in the circumstances, to try to feel she could create a space which was uniquely hers and mine. It was also of course an attempt to make me feel as shut out as she did. Rather than trying to push the door open, I started to wait as I had done during other sessions, until she allowed me into the room.

However, in the confusion that had preceded her session, I had inadvertently left a walk-in cupboard door in the consulting room unlocked. In my experience it is almost only children who have been fostered or adopted who have a need to keep on trying to get into cupboards and rooms which are not 'allowed'. I have come to see this as another way of expressing their constant sense of being excluded from the world of families – be they birth or foster families in which they have such a paradoxical sense of being both a part of, and yet not belonging, to the family. This was also her feeling towards therapy and me – she knew that she had her own unique place within me, but was nevertheless painfully excluded from my family life.

I realised that Gail was in the walk-in cupboard by the noises that I heard from outside the room and went into the room to find her inside the cupboard but not, as yet, doing anything more than look at what was there. In the cupboard were boxes of therapy toys belonging to other children, a large filing cabinet and some clothes. I was angry with her and felt intruded upon – but also frustrated in my attempts to protect her from such obvious and painful evidence of the other relationships and aspects of my life. I said that she knew I didn't want her to go into this cupboard and she must have seen in my face and heard in my voice my anger at this moment. She came out of the cupboard, walked straight past me, ignoring me in the process, and went to the bathroom, locking herself in. I think that this was the first time that she had succeeded in making me angry in such an obvious way – although she had tried hard to do so in the past.

I was now in the consulting room with the furniture all over the place and the cupboard door wide open. Gail was locked in the bathroom and was, I felt, hiding from my anger. These are the kinds of situations where the question of technique becomes increasingly difficult to frame. What to do now? In my view, I had made several mistakes that were hurtful to her. She had glimpsed other people in the house, I had inflamed the already difficult dynamic over 'closed doors and open doors' and she had experienced me feeling angry with her. After a few minutes,

I was again talking to her through a closed door – this time the bathroom door – asking her if she was upset that I had been angry. She said 'No', but I had a sense of her listening, so I said that I had been angry but that I wasn't now and hoped that she would come back into the room so that we could talk about what had happened. To my amazement, a few minutes later, she came back into the consulting room. I was able to talk briefly about her distress, having first got her permission to do this in the way that I have already described. I think that she was probably also aware that I was upset at what had happened so far in the session and that this may have helped her to be curious about what I would do next.

After a few minutes of aimless rearranging of the furniture in the room, she suddenly said, 'I've got an idea for a game'. It was essentially about two girls sharing a room in a boarding school. She was a 'horrible' girl who kept tormenting the girl that I played, by waking her up at night, hitting her over the head, pushing her out of bed. Gail's character also raided the headmistress' office and vandalised it. No one liked Gail's character and the headmistress who had previously been sympathetic to her wasn't any more because of what the schoolgirl had done to her office. Gail wanted me to 'be' the headmistress and told me to tell the other girls at the boarding school that if Gail's character made any more trouble they were allowed to hit her over the head with a log. This play felt so wafer thin in its disguise of Gail's feeling that she was so awful, and that I was so angry with her that I would viciously attack her, that I really felt that I couldn't say this. (This is an example of one of the occasions when I decided I couldn't play purely on her terms.) I said to her that I couldn't say this as it felt wrong. She modified what the girls were allowed to hit her with and eventually changed it to the other girls refusing to be her friend, which I was prepared to say. However, Gail's character then raided the headmistress' office again and was caught red-handed.

I was told that as the headmistress I was to say that she was bad and that she had a 'bad heart'. This play was so powerful that before I knew it, I had blurted out 'But I couldn't say that. You've got a *good* heart!' which is something I truly believe about her. I was really surprised by the spontaneous intensity of what I felt at this moment and the way that the words came out. Without being too fanciful, it really felt as if 'my heart went out to her', tears inadvertently sprang to my eyes, and I was touched by how deeply she was convinced that I would reject and discard her because I was so angry with her. I tried to explain that, although we were playing, we were also saying something very serious to each other and I didn't agree that she was 'bad', I knew that she had a good heart. Amazingly, the session, which had started in such a messy way, ended positively and I felt I knew her better – and I'm sure she felt that she had come to know me better. Most importantly, I think she also knew herself better.

Over time, we were able to build on this 'knowing' of each other through the medium of play. For example, I was very struck by the way in which I gradually realised that, figuratively speaking, I tip-toed up towards her when I wanted to make an interpretation or comment about what was happening in the play. I continued to ask permission, but I could often build on the first permission and say, 'Can I just say a little bit more?' if I could see that she was open to this. This reminded me of a convoluted version of the children's game 'What's the time Mr Wolf'. In this game, one child is the wolf and turns his or her face to the wall and the other children try to creep up on the wolf without being seen to move by the wolf, who can turn around at any moment. If they are seen moving, they are 'out'. The children ask the wolf the time as they creep up on him and he replies – one o'clock' then two o'clock' and so on until it is twelve o'clock. The aim for the children is to tap the wolf on the shoulder before twelve o'clock because at that time the wolf can turn around, chase them and eat them. If someone catches the wolf, he or she in turn becomes Mr Wolf. The fun is in the creeping up (for the children) or being the chasing devouring wolf (for Mr Wolf).

I wasn't sure whether this game meant anything to Gail, but felt it was a useful metaphor for our communication which it was worth trying out. She immediately recognised the ways in which the game paralleled the way we communicated and at her request we subsequently spent a lot of time playing this game as she gradually acknowledged how scary my words were to her. I was like a wolf who could suddenly rush at her and eat her up. I was similarly aware of how unpredictable I felt she was and how she could suddenly turn a session into a situation in which I felt attacked and intimidated. This is an example, like that of Edwards cited above, in which my natural response was followed by words in a manner that, I think as a result, was more communicative than the words alone, because it was couched in the medium of play that had become our special way of communicating.

We reached other extraordinary moments of understanding in this fashion. For a long time, it was very hard for me to get a deep sense of what it might have been like for Gail to try to communicate, as a hearing infant or small child, with a profoundly deaf mother and father. My imagination, as well as the experience within therapy itself, didn't seem able to reach to this. It took me a long while to realise how deeply embedded this experience was in the unusual ways that we played together. I think I finally got the message through some play in the bathroom, where we would quite often play, in which I was asked to play in some particularly silly (but also funny) ways. By this time Gail often said, 'We're only playing' when she felt the play was a bit silly, but nevertheless important to her. She could also see the funny side, but the play had a serious purpose and she really needed me to go along with it.

Gail was the queen who wanted to make me her prisoner. She tied my hands with string (loosely, at my insistence) and told me to stand in the shower cubicle which was the prison', which I did. I felt very silly and unprofessional, and greatly reminded of the kind of silly play that goes on between parents and children at times and can be great fun just because of its silliness. She closed the transparent shower cubicle door and then started silently to gesticulate to me from the other side. Suddenly, I had a vivid image of two people trying to communicate through a sound barrier, but where it was still possible for them to see each other. I was stunned by this. All the months of talking to her at times through closed doors – to the therapy room or the bathroom – suddenly made sense in a new way that connected emotional and intellectual understanding, and this had happened through being prepared to go along with a pretty unusual piece of playing. When I realised this, I was 'allowed' briefly to say how I thought that this could be what it felt like when she tried to talk with her birth mother and father, when they couldn't hear her and she couldn't get her message across. She agreed to this rather disdainfully as if it had taken me a very long time to finally understand this – and she was right.

My difficulty in understanding Gail continued and I felt sure connected with her learning difficulties. It was often painfully evident that Gail's understanding of the way the world works was limited. But she got much better at communicating verbally with me, and when, some time later, I tried to talk to her about how hard it could be for her to understand what was going on around her at times, she retorted, in a very deliberate and loaded way, 'No Monica, it is *you* who don't understand.' With this statement and the way in which she said it, I suddenly felt myself to be like a deaf mother who truly doesn't understand her child. It was an extraordinary experience and I shared it with her by saying, 'You're right. I really don't understand this properly yet. But what you just said has made me realise what it felt like for you not to feel understood by your birth Mum – made much more difficult by her deafness.'

This was a watershed session which led to a surprisingly 'ordinary' conversation in which, for the first time, she was able to talk with me about her early life with her birth parents, followed by going into care and then being adopted. We had become able to talk about her traumatic early life from a more resilient position of emotional strength. This capacity to talk more about her painful past, and her growing ability to bear to think about and bear memories from the past, continued as her therapy progressed. I believe that the unusual playfulness of our earlier relationship, together with the spontaneity that this at times led to in the therapeutic relationship, paved the way for this development to take place.

Playfulness as an antidote to defensiveness

My willingness to play with Gail enabled us to engage with a powerful creative process which emerged from the unique interactions and ways of communicating that became typical of our particular relationship. This creative process can be thought of as helping to melt, dissolve, neutralise and effectively *antidote* the painfulness of the raw and undigested memories and feelings that she carried in her internal world.

Drawing on this clinical example, I would like to hypothesise that the 'playful presence of the therapist' can hold a key position in what can be thought of as a psychic detoxification process. We know that the extremely damaging past experiences and relationships that children like Gail are trying to recover from metaphorically poison the child's internal world. We now also have evidence from neuroscientific advances that the brain is actually changed and incapacitated because of early neglect and trauma (Schore 2003). We cannot remove the poison, but we can antidote it as best we can. Over time, a gradual change in the internal balance between creative development and psychic crumbling away, as a result of this poisoning, can then take place. When this starts to happen, it is as if these new experiences grow around the gradually decaying memories, and the damaged internal world from the painful past.

The session in which I spontaneously told Gail that I thought she had a good heart illustrates Stern *et al.'s* description of the therapeutic impact of a moment-of-meeting on the shared implicit relationship between patient and therapist (Stern *et al.* 1998). Their description of the impact of these special moments in therapy supports my view that it is possible to redefine the therapeutic process itself, as one in which the losses and deprivations of the past are not (indeed cannot be) undone but, instead, something new in the present starts to tip the internal balance of the patient towards greater emotional health and well-being. This reframing of the therapeutic task is very helpful in providing a realistic therapeutic aim when working with children like Gail who have been so severely deprived, neglected and traumatised. Stern *et al.* describe this process as follows:

> In this model there is a reciprocal process in which change takes place in the implicit relationship at 'moments-of-meeting' through alterations in 'ways of being with'. It does not correct past empathic failures through the analytic empathic activity. It does not replace a past deficit. *Rather something new is created in the relationship which alters the intersubjective environment.* Past experience is recontextualised in the present such that a person operates from within a different mental landscape, resulting in new behaviours in the present and future.
>
> (Stern *et al.* 1998: 918; my italics)

I want to finish with some thoughts about why playfulness can be such an important feature of the present therapeutic relationship. From one perspective, I have in effect tried to demonstrate that by 'not playing' the therapist can be closing down therapeutic opportunities, possibly particularly for moments-of-meeting to happen. From another perspective, I have linked the creative potential of playing as emphasised by Winnicott with the whole process of psychoanalytic work. Winnicott sees the therapist's ability to be playful as central to the process of therapy and Stern *et al.* emphasise the importance of the 'personal signature' of the therapist during the moment-of-change, which has to meet spontaneously the uniqueness of that moment. The moment of change notably is a two-way process. Without the openness of heart that playfulness requires on both sides, I think it is much less likely to happen.

7 Transition and change

An exploration of the resonances between transitional and meditative states of mind and their role in the therapeutic process (2012)

The emotional demands on the therapist of working with severely neglected and abused children are very evident and there are significant safeguards built into the training process and professional development to help therapists with these strains. However, the wise work–personal life balance that each therapist needs to find does not get enough attention and this chapter, originally published in Winnicott's Children, *the third book I co-edited with Ann Horne in the IPACA (Independent Psychoanalytic Approaches with Children and Adolescents) series, addressed this issue in relation to meditative states of mind (Lanyado, 2012; Horne and Lanyado 2012).*

For many years, I had found that the calming effects of my reasonably regular meditative practice seemed to help me to cope with the high levels of anxiety I needed to be able to contain for very troubled patients. Attitudes towards meditation practice have changed rapidly over the past ten years in particular. It has been interesting to discover how many of my colleagues have also quietly valued their meditation practice but, like myself, until more recently had not been able to integrate their meditative and psychotherapeutic practice (Lanyado 2008a and 2014; Pozzi Monzo 2014). The ideas in this chapter are different to a direct Mindfulness approach to helping patients. The focus is on the resonances between the therapist's state of mind in facilitating transitional experiences, and meditative states of mind (Bazzano 2014; Lanyado 2014; Winnicott 1971b/1953). Meditation can help to extend the therapist's capacity to contain anxiety in life in general, and more specifically in the consulting room. There is further exploration of Winnicott's writings about transitional experiences, and how meditative states can be thought about from this perspective. The clinical example comes from my work with 'Gail' who is the patient discussed in Chapter 6.

In *Playing and Reality* Winnicott explores a group of interconnected concepts which have great significance for anyone working psychotherapeutically with children (Winnicott 1971a). The book contains his clearest statements about the importance of 'playing', which he sees as taking place in an intermediate area between internal and external reality, later enlarged on as 'the place where we live' and experience life (Winnicott 1971c: 122–129). As I understand it, being fully alive in Winnicott's sense is not an idealised, pain- and conflict-free experience, it is more a connectedness to a life force with as few impingements on this flow of vital energy as possible. He writes that

> . . . no human being is free from the strain of relating inner and outer reality, and (that) relief from this strain is provided by an intermediate area of experience which is not challenged (arts, religion, etc.). This intermediate area is in direct continuity with the play area of the ordinary small child who is 'lost' in play.
>
> (Winnicott 1971b/1953: 15)

Viewing the problems that child and adult patients bring to their therapists as being the result of emotional environmental (inner and outer) impingements which distort natural developmental pathways, Winnicott sees disturbances in the child's ability to play, or the adult's ability to fully experience life, as indicative of early emotional environments which did not adequately facilitate the development of the capacity to play. This could be because of unavoidable external trauma (for example, illness, accidents, loss or political unrest) and/or relational trauma, where the parents have been unable to provide a good-enough emotional environment within which the child's natural potential could take root and grow. In this way of thinking, if the capacity to play is impaired then the ability to live a life, however difficult it may be, in as potentially creative a way as possible, is also impaired. Creativity, in this sense, is not seen as a reparative consequence of the individual's destructive impulses and loss, but as a natural life force towards growth seen throughout the natural world, which is present in all living things from the beginning of life, be it human, animal or biological. It is the key expression of being alive, and not dead and inanimate.

For Winnicott, 'playing' is vitally important as a 'thing in itself', a process which takes time to develop as well as being important for its symbolic content. Indeed, he comments that '. . . in the total theory of the personality the psychoanalyst has been too busy using play content to look at the playing child, and to write about playing as a thing in itself' (Winnicott 1971d: 46).

The development of the creative ability to play spontaneously and freely cannot be taken for granted and this is particularly apparent when working with children who have been severely deprived and traumatised from birth, as well as with children who are on the autistic spectrum. Winnicott embeds in these ideas about playing (or the lack of playing) the concepts of transitional space, transitional experiences and transitional objects, true and false self, and the 'place where we live' and experience life as it happens in the present moment.

Furthermore, Winnicott extends these ideas to the psychotherapeutic process and experience. In the chapter 'Playing: a theoretical statement', we find one of his most iconic statements about play, emphasised with the use of italics in the original:

> Psychotherapy takes place in the overlap of two areas of playing, that of the patient and that of the therapist. Psychotherapy has to do with two people

playing together. The corollary of this is that where playing is not possible then the work done by the therapist is directed towards bringing the patient from a state of not being able to play into a state of being able to play.

(Winnicott 1971d: 44)

Abram summarises Winnicott's therapeutic perspective as follows:

> For Winnicott, the capacity to use the transitional space represented the ultimate in human development and signified the ability to 'live creatively' and 'feel real'. This concept, linked with the capacity for concern and the capacity to be alone, embellished and transformed the concept of transference. Winnicott's *sine qua non* of the analytic encounter became the analyst's ability to play rather than interpret. In this setting, the analyst would limit inter-pretative comments and wait for the patient to discover the ability to play and to search for the answers within.
>
> (Abram 1996: 4)

Patients come for psychotherapy because they have reached a point where they feel unable to change without psychotherapeutic help. They may feel that they are stuck or 'getting worse' and can't do anything about it. Our work as therapists is to help them to change in ways that will enable them to enjoy life more fully despite all the internal and external difficulties they may face. This chapter explores this process of change in Winnicottian terms by exploring the role of the psychotherapist's states of mind when facilitating transitional experiences and playing in therapy. From this perspective, the idea of 'transitions', of 'in between' places, is crucial: the transitional space between inner and outer reality; the transitional overlapping space between two separate people in playful com-munication; the transitional space between one therapy session and another; the tension within the transitional space between past and future, which is about 'now', the 'present moment' and the 'now-ness' of something new emerging.

The treatment of severely neglected, traumatised and abused children, highlights phases of psychological transition, change and recovery which benefit from different states of mind in the therapist. The initial stages of treatment, which are often characterised by the child being verbally and physically aggressive, controlling and reactive, need the therapist to muster as much calm in the midst of the storm as possible, firmly holding boundaries, and trying to understand what is being expressed in, or evacuated into the transference–countertransference relationship. If this phase is survived, a transitional phase towards healthier development starts to emerge, and can be recognised by the emergence of *therapeutic transition experiences* and islands of freer play in the 'presence of the therapist' which gradually grow and coalesce into a fuller capacity to play. This is where the tension between past and present takes place, which is a new experience, a 'now' experience, freer of the past and full of the potential for change. However, it can feel frightening for the patient to cross this threshold into this unknown and much less controllable world, and the therapist's state of mind may be central in helping the patient to take the risk of entering this space which is so frighteningly full of potential.

I have suggested elsewhere that the therapist's state of mind is experienced by the patient as the 'presence of the therapist' (Lanyado 2004a). This chapter is a development of this idea, extended into links with meditative experience and the part this can play in the therapist's ability to facilitate change. Starting with an exploration of ordinary transitional phenomena and playing, links will be made with meditative states of mind and a brief review of psychoanalytic responses to them. A clinical illustration describes these phenomena through the treatment of a late-adopted adolescent girl.

Therapeutic transitional experiences and playing

Closely observing the difficulties a child has in playing at the start of therapy, and the ways in which the capacity to play changes in the course of helpful therapeutic work, is a very useful way of thinking about the therapeutic process. Particularly when working with children who have suffered total environmental breakdown (and have had to be removed from their birth parents by the authorities), or multiple trauma (such as asylum seekers and refugees), the path towards recovery can seem obscure and tortuous. These people have had so many terrible experiences in their lives that the very idea of 'recovery' is complex and full of limitations. And yet these children and adults, with a great deal of courage, better life circumstances and therapeutic help where available, can go on to greater enjoyment of life.

Working therapeutically with people who have experienced these extremes of suffering and trauma provides the opportunity to learn about how human beings can recover, to some extent. Through their therapy, we are privileged in being able to observe how the natural maturational processes that Winnicott draws attention to are able to flow again (Winnicott 1965). This in turn draws attention to the minutiae of ordinary maturational processes within a good-enough facilitating environment, which it is easy to overlook, and the significance of which can readily go unrecognised.

But as in ordinary development, playing within the context of therapy does not develop out of nowhere. Detailed clinical observation provides evidence that the first glimmers of playing are often accompanied by newly emergent transitional experiences in the therapeutic space, which it can be postulated are facilitated by the work that is going on in the transference–countertransference relationship, as well as the accompanying real, new relationship between the patient and the therapist. These two aspects of the total therapeutic relationship are always present, but in differing ratios according to the stage of therapy. The transference–countertransference relationship comes from the past, and is relived in the present, whereas the real new relationship is about the present and the possibility of change (and thus the future). The tension between these two strands of the total therapeutic relationship is all about change and the difficulties of letting go of the past – which, without psychoanalytic understanding, often can seem odd considering how awful that past may have been for some of our patients. Their difficulty at this stage of therapy is to let go of painful experiences. A sort of 'better the devil you know' internal experience. For patients who are recovering, the ending of a *good* experience is often an entirely new thing, which is why the end phase of therapy can be so therapeutically promotive of helpful mourning and growth.

As therapy progresses, greater awareness of the 'otherness' of the real therapist prompts anxious feelings in the child – of vulnerability and dependence on the therapist. These feelings bring a great deal of anxiety, because these are children whose trust that adults can be dependable and protective, has been broken. It is frightening to feel the longing for these experiences again in the context of new relationships such as with foster or adoptive parents or therapists, and many patients struggle with what Glasser has termed the 'core complex' of longing for and being terrified of intimacy (Glasser 1998). However, if the anxiety aroused is carefully understood, held and worked with in the transference, the patient gradually becomes able to tolerate this otherness or separateness. This is often aided by the spontaneous creation of new specifically *therapeutic transitional experiences* which help to bridge the gap between patient and therapist, and between one session and the next. It can be valuable, when these experiences emerge in therapy, to work closely with the child's parents and school so that they are also on the lookout for and can facilitate these kinds of developing experiences, and the newness and potential for growth that they herald.

The clinical illustration shows how this healthy development needs to be distinguished from the situation where the child still needs to ruthlessly control the therapist, thus remaining unable to tolerate that they are two separate people, a clinical scenario which usually precedes the creation of therapeutic transitional experiences. In the former circumstances, for a long while the issue is more to do with firmly and compassionately setting boundaries for a child who may have many reasons for anarchically challenging adult authority. This is part of the transference–countertransference relationship which needs to be survived and understood by the therapist first of all, and is based on the child's often horrific past experience, where this was the only way he managed to survive. This controlling defence is not readily let go of and can be very destructive of new relationships with foster and adoptive parents. It is more helpfully thought about as a defence that slowly dissolves with time, tolerance and great understanding by the long-suffering new adults in the child's current life.

An important stage in this process is when some children who are moving towards therapeutic transitional experiences and a more healthy acceptance of separateness, together with more ordinary emotional dependence on the new adults in their lives, start to want to take home toys or drawings from the sessions (Lanyado 2004a: 88–90). They may also start to bring into the sessions special toys and possessions from home – quite often important soft toys which they want the therapist to 'meet'. Therapy toys and home toys may spontaneously go back-wards and forwards between home and the therapy room, with little or no prompting by the therapist, creating a bridge between the two experiences which is helpful to the child.

It is not that toys start disappearing from the therapy room and not returning. If this were so, the issue would probably be more to do with the need to continue to set boundaries. The defence of control would still be more to the fore, rather than there being an indication of the dawning of a new developmental stage. Other children may create special transitional experiences at the start or end of sessions that help to bridge the gap between sessions, as in the clinical example later in this chapter where the patient at this stage in her therapy *requested* (but didn't demand) a glass of milk at the start of each session. Whatever this toy or experience is, it is spontaneously alighted on by the child and recognised as being emotionally significant and helpful by the therapist. It is wisely not questioned and is understood to 'belong' to both patient and therapist, as a part of their growing relatedness but separateness.

Initially, there is an element of 'risk' here on the part of the therapist. Should the child be allowed to take the toy, or create the unusual therapeutic experience, or not? This usually involves a technical departure from the norm which is very specific to each child's 'choice' of transitional experience. It may be that the sense that the therapist has, of entering a new technical territory if they 'risk' this technical departure, contains projections of the patient's anxiety about taking the 'risk' of entering the transitional space which is full of potential and unknown, but also decidedly 'risky'. And of course, the therapist may get it wrong and then spend some time trying to reassert important boundaries around the therapy. However, there is also the risk of missing the vital moment of change, of missing a therapeutic opportunity. Not all children wanting to take therapy toys home are on the verge of creating therapeutic transitional objects. But some are, and a great deal of pointless and even therapeutically destructive battling can take place on this boundary between therapy and home.

In ordinary development, the baby or young child makes a similar choice of something special, for example a teddy, soft toy, song or way of stroking a blanket, which the parents know is important and not to be questioned. For a significant period of time in the child's life, it is this classical transitional object that helps the child to go to sleep, to be apart from his or her parents, and to generally cope with anxiety-provoking situations. When the child in therapy is getting back on emotional track, it is therefore not surprising to witness the emergence of these therapeutic transitional experiences and objects.

When transitional experiences are starting to emerge in the session, the therapist's state of mind when with the child needs to subtly change. Rather than spending a good deal of time on high alert because of the unpredictability of these children's behaviour (due to the heightened fight/flight responses to past trauma), the therapist's quiet and real 'presence' comes more to the fore as a means of facilitating the growth of small periods of play by the child. It is these small periods of play that eventually coalesce into concentrated 'playing'. It is possible that the 'real-ness' of the therapist in the sense of *being and embodying* her 'true' self is what helps the patient, in response, to move more towards *being and embodying* his 'true' self, and to dare to part from and gradually outgrow his defensive, familiar but nevertheless 'false' self. It is through this process that change at an internal deep level starts to take place.

In ordinary development, Winnicott describes this phase as the capacity to be 'alone in the presence of another' (Winnicott 1958). This wonderfully evocative phrase has several layers of meaning for me. The idea of someone's 'presence' implies authenticity and 'real-ness'. It also implies 'now-ness', and 'being', and as it extends becomes a way of 'dwelling in the present moment' beautifully expressed by the Buddhist teacher Thich Nhat Hanh (Hanh 2005). The idea of 'dwelling' resonates with thoughts about holding, staying a while, residing, and is highly relevant to the ways in which the therapist tries to hold the patient in the present moment, an idea which in turn is closely linked to the still and attentive mindfulness of many meditation states. By managing to stay for increasing amounts of time in 'the present', the ghosts of the past can gradually be de-toxified.

It is here that the links between transitional experiences and meditative practice start to resonate. In addition, it should be noted that meditative experience takes place within the individual's 'intermediate area of experience which is not challenged (arts, religion, etc.)' (Winnicott 1971b/1953: 14), as quoted earlier in the chapter; that is, within the individual's personal transitional space between inner and outer reality. (As I understand it, Winnicott uses the terms 'intermediate area' and 'transitional areas' interchangeably.) Meditative experience belongs to the present moment, as does 'being alive' in Winnicott's terminology.

Calmness, meditative experience and states of mind

An increasing number of psychoanalytic clinicians are now sharing their experiences about their often longstanding meditational practice and the significant ways in which this contributes to their clinical practice, and their way of being in the consulting room with their patients (Black 2006, 2011; Coltart 1992, 1993, 1996a; Eigen 2008; Epstein 1995, 2006; Parsons 2000, 2006; Rubin 2006). The ideas that follow draw on the writings and experiences of these psychoanalytic practitioners who practise meditation as a regular part of their lives, so much so that it is an integral part of who they are – of their 'true self'. (I am using the terms 'real' and 'true' interchangeably here.) They are eminent clinicians, presumably well analysed during and possibly after their training, and clearly not naively drawn to meditation as a practice which negates the use of psychoanalytic insight.

In the context of this chapter, the philosophical, spiritual or religious thinking around the practice of meditation is not so much the issue as the meditative state of mind itself.[1] The publication of a collection of papers by highly respected psychoanalysts, *Psychoanalysis and Religion in the 21st Century: Competitors or Collaborators?* (Black 2006), from within the Library of Psychoanalysis Series, suggests that discussions about religion, meditation and spiritual matters are becoming more mainstream within psychoanalysis.

Prior to this, there were a number of other thought-provoking publications which contributed to this field and which could possibly be thought of as contributing to the critical mass of writing that was reached with Black's publication (Coltart

1992, 1993, 1996a; Epstein 1995; Molino 1999; Symington 1994; Parsons 2000). Black's more recent book, *Why Things Matter: The Place of Values in Science, Psychoanalysis and Religion* (Black 2011), develops his ideas, which he describes as having had a gestation period of 15 years.

From my own experience, it has intrigued me that whenever I have given psychoanalytic papers and talks which have included ideas about meditation, colleagues whom I might have known for years, but did not know were meditators like myself, have commented that they have never felt that they could speak in psychoanalytic circles about this aspect of who they feel they are, without an anxiety of being thought of as slightly 'wacky' and 'non-psychoanalytic'. So they have kept quiet. For many it has felt odd to keep these two important aspects of who they are separate in their work but not in their private lives, particularly when they are often deeply aware of how significantly their meditation practice helps them to survive, think about and contain the painful turbulent emotions of their patients. This division is slowly being addressed and in the UK there is now a network of those interested in exploring the links between their meditation and clinical practice, in experiential as well as more theoretical ways.[2]

Why has it been so difficult for psychoanalytic thinkers to bring these ideas into the psychoanalytic arena? Several psychoanalytic writers for whom meditation and a spiritual life are clearly important, nevertheless caution about the ways in which meditation can be used defensively or in an idealised way, rather than creatively, presumably responding to the concerns of the profession. Coltart, who has written extensively about what she regards as the 'harmonious, mutually enlightening and potentiating' effects of harnessing psychoanalysis and the practice of Buddhism (Coltart 1996b: 128), writes in the same chapter about:

> ... unfortunate cases where meditation has been poorly taught by an inexperienced amateur to someone whose mental health is by no means sound in the first instance but who is led by enthusiasm or sentiment into a territory he had better been strictly warned off. This kind of breakdown, of which I have seen at least three cases, should provide a strong warning against treating meditation as if it were some sort of alternative health gimmick: there has grown up an unfortunate tendency towards this in the West.
>
> (Coltart 1996b: 135)

And Black whilst advocating his 'case for a contemplative position' writes:

> This picture of a contemplative position also makes room for the reservation that many psychoanalysts feel toward religious ways of thinking, that they can serve as an escape from the real conflicts of the patient's social and biological life. It does so by emphasising that the 'higher' levels of consciousness can indeed be used defensively, to bypass conflict on the lower levels, and if so the result is weakness and incompleteness, sometimes of catastrophic dimensions in the patient's life as a whole.
>
> (Black 2006: 77)

Possibly, the more regularly and seriously people practise meditation, the more aware they become of its full power, rooted as it is in thousands of years of religious and philosophical beliefs and practices. It is not to be taken lightly. And we need to remember that, until Freud and the dawn of this more psychological era (a comparatively recent occurrence and in the main a Western influence), religion and philosophy were two of the main sources of relief for people who were suffering emotional and physical pain. We would be unwise to throw out the baby with the bathwater. There is still much to be learnt from these ideas that have stood the test of time. Sceptics might argue that much of the reason for the survival of religious beliefs is superstition and ignorance. However, it can also be argued that religious beliefs have distilled human values and wisdom over many generations of human existence throughout the world. Psychoanalytic insight and practice is unavailable to the vast majority of people in the world and it is these ancient religious wisdoms and practices which people still turn to in their hour of need. Indeed, it might be argued that the more people in the West meditate and connect with Eastern philosophical traditions, the more they come to appreciate these wisdoms and – in the case of psychoanalytic practitioners who practise meditation – the more these insights start to permeate the personal philosophy that is needed to survive a working life in the profession.

There are many kinds of meditative practice, all seeking, it can be argued, to attain a similar state of mind in the meditator. To quote Coltart, these practices are '. . . designed to clear the mind and open it to self-knowing, truth and understanding; worrying and constant thinking are laid aside, and a kind of empty, alert stillness is aimed for' (Coltart 1993: 113). This is very close to Bion's oft quoted recommendation that when the analyst or therapist enters the consulting room, he or she should try as much as possible to be 'without memory or desire' (Bion 1970).

Additionally, it is helpful to note the use of the idea of 'practice', which is as central to meditation as it is to psychoanalytic work. The word 'practice' indicates a commitment to repeating and learning through experience. The *Oxford English Dictionary* defines 'practice' as 'repeated exercise in an activity requiring the development of a skill' and 'action or execution as opposed to theory'. There is no long-term goal other than to improve at whatever is being practised – be it the piano, football, meditation or psychoanalytic work.

Depending on where and how the meditator is learning to meditate, and who their teacher is, there are also many techniques which help the meditator in her efforts. For example, the breath may be a focus, or the teacher may guide the meditators through a guided meditation or steady walking meditation; mantras, chanting and singing may be used; specific images or feelings may help to draw the mind of the meditator towards stillness. Meditation teachers and groups are central in this process. Meditation is difficult and can be frustrating. Even the greatest spiritual leaders continue to 'practise' – as indeed even the greatest concert pianists also continue to practise. This is a discipline of mind and body that is hard won. Indeed, the calming way in which meditation relates to body *and* mind is now supported by neuroscientific research. The fMRI scans of experienced and inexperienced meditators taken whilst they are meditating show what meditators have known and experienced for generations, that meditation calms the body, brain and mind (Davidson *et al.* 2003; Goleman 2003: 3–27; Lutz *et al.* 2004; Ricard 2007: 186–201).

If the meditator is also a psychotherapist who is trying to help traumatised and distressed patients, the meditative practice can in turn enhance the therapist's ability to regulate the patient's anxiety (through affect attunement as described by Stern (Music 2011: 55–56; Stern 1985), because the capacity to remain calm in the face of the reactive fight–flight anxiety expressed by the patient is enhanced. Gerhardt describes the evidence about the effects of trauma on the brain as resulting from excessive 'corrosive cortisol' levels. Persistently high levels of cortisol in the brains of babies and young children subjected to severe trauma and abuse literally corrode the brain and body and form part of a hormonal feedback loop of reactions between brain and body, overstimulating the body's fight–flight responses as a survival mechanism when faced with trauma (Gerhardt 2004b). It is as if the body's emotional and primitive 'thermostat' regulating the triggering of the fight–flight response becomes set at 'low' so that apparently insignificant experiences trigger major fight–flight responses. At the time of the original trauma, fight–flight responses (which can include freezing, and dissociation, not only physical flight or fight), the body will have been flooded with these hormones. Later, when there is (secondary) triggering of undigested traumatic memories, which need to be thought of as memories-in-feeling as opposed to fully formed thoughts, and which may be external and environmental as well as internal and relational (that is, due to subtle triggers within new relationships), reactive, aggressive and violent behaviour based on bodily experienced primitive 'brain stem' fear ensues (Music 2011a: 92–93; 2009a: 64–67). This is the physical basis of the, at times, extremely violent, sadistic and aggressive behaviour experienced in the consulting room when trying to help this kind of patient.

With traumatised children who have not had the presence of a caring person to help modulate these responses when they were very young, and indeed whose carers or parents may have been the source of the trauma, there is a desperate need for the calming presence of another human being if they are to recover their ordinary developmental pathways. The calmness of meditational states of mind within the therapist can be drawn on to make an additional contribution to the calming effect that the therapist needs to have at times on traumatised and reactive patients, and can be a valuable aspect of the 'presence' of the therapist. It is not that the therapist starts to meditate in the session, but that meditative states of mind are an important part of her usual way of being and true self. It is part of who the therapist is. The inner calmness can also be absorbed in an unconscious to unconscious form of communication where the patient senses this aspect of the therapist's true self, and identifies with it in the same way that other aspects of the person of the therapist are identified with, 'unknowingly'. The clinical example that follows illustrates these possibilities.

It is in these ways that, to quote Coltart, 'The discipline of meditation practice enhances the discipline of one's own contribution to an analytic session which sometimes is, in fact, almost indistinguishable from a form of meditation' (Coltart 1992: 174).

Clinical example

Gail is a patient from whom I have learnt a great deal and have written about elsewhere (Lanyado 2006, 2010). I am grateful to Gail and her family for giving permission for me to write about our work. She was 19 years old when she stopped therapy, having started coming twice weekly when she was 12 years old. As it was important that she weaned herself from the therapy, she decided to move to once weekly work when she went to college aged 16, and then to once monthly consultations for the final year of treatment. I will give an overview of her therapy to show how this illustrates the phases of recovery that I have described above, and then give some more detailed session notes from one of the last sessions before she stopped her once weekly therapy.

Gail's early family history is sad. Her birth mother had learning difficulties and the marital violence between her and Gail's birth father, who was diagnosed with personality disorder, led to the breakdown of their teenage marriage. In addition, both of Gail's birth parents were deaf, but Gail was able to hear normally, which created enormous communication difficulties in this already vulnerable family. Gail was eventually abandoned by her birth mother when she was four years old, following several years of attempts by social workers to support the relationship. She had two foster families over a period of four years before she was adopted at age eight.

For much of the long period of twice weekly therapy, being with Gail was like sitting on the edge of a rumbling volcano. She was highly reactive and likely to 'blow', to erupt into a temper tantrum over tiny mis-attunements on my part to her state of mind. Most of the time I felt I was on red alert during her sessions, felt tense in anticipation of them, and worn out by the end. She frequently needed to escape from the therapy room into the bathroom, as a result of the heightened fight–flight response which I have described.

For a long while, Gail was extremely controlling and manipulative of me. She frequently tried to bully me into giving in to her demands. For example, she often harangued me because I did not give her anything to eat or drink when she came for her session at the end of the school day. Transference interpretations about her experiencing me as a depriving and cruel mother were pointless because she shouted over them or disappeared into the bathroom. I had long given up responding to her in this way but we reached a stage in her therapy where we started to settle into a kind of shared place; she kept control by telling me what role I was to play and what I was to say, and I was able to remain in a non-directive but playful place with her. It was an achievement when these periods of play could last for 10 or 15 minutes at a time, before disrupting for no obvious reason. In this way, islands of more creative experience and playing were starting to emerge in therapy and beginning to coalesce and grow and she was making some progress.

It was at this stage that she started to create *therapeutic transitional experiences* as described above. Here is a small clinical extract.

At the end of a session that had been comparatively playful in this way, Gail asked me as she was leaving the building, 'Monica, why can't I have a drink when I come to see you?' Her plaintive query was completely different from her previous bullying demands and I was immediately alert to the potential for something different to take place between us. Knowing that I was taking the risk that she could explode at my response, I replied, 'You are asking me in such a different way to the way you have asked before, that I'd like to think about it. Can I tell you next session?' Amazingly for someone who usually needed very quick responses to anything she wanted, she agreed to this and left without any further fuss. This was a further indication to me that there was a potential for change to take place, a window of therapeutic opportunity. I decided I would offer her a cold drink which I would have waiting for her in the therapy room at the start of each session, and gave her the choice between juice and milk.

In her next session, I told Gail what I had decided and she chose to have a glass of milk. Milk was her drink of choice for several years, before she switched her preference to a glass of juice. At first, she always drank the milk at the start of the sessions. Then she would simply sip it during sessions. Sometimes, she would be so wrapped up in her play that she wouldn't remember her drink till the end of the session, if at all. I now think of the glass of milk as a therapeutic transitional object that helped her to cope with her anxiety at the start of each session. It helped her to cross the threshold into a transitional space – a space that was alarmingly uncontrollable yet increasingly pleasurable as she started to enjoy playing during her sessions, both on her own and together with me through the play-scripts she spontaneously created. Of course, this also meant that I needed to have her in mind before the session and make sure that there was enough milk available for her drink.

As discussed above, I think of the glass of milk as a therapeutic transitional phenomenon because of the way it was created by Gail and the way in which its importance was accepted by me. I have noted the emergence of new transitional phenomena in the therapy of other patients (Lanyado 2004a). It is in the nature of these adaptations of technique that they are unique to the particular patient. I have not given a glass of milk, or indeed any drink, regularly to a patient before or since. But I have made other highly individualised technical adaptations that I also now think of as belonging to this area of therapeutic transitional experiences that emerge during the therapy of severely deprived and traumatised patients.

While I needed to use all my personal resources to remain as calm as possible in the midst of Gail's storms, there was rarely any peaceful quietness during the sessions that could be even remotely related to anything meditative. In retrospect, I can see that this subtly and slowly started to change after about three years of twice weekly therapy. By this point, Gail could often play for a whole session, with me having a comparatively small role in her play. I was more often able to simply be with her, as she played in a fairly ordinary way for a latency-stage child (although she was now 15 years old) – schools, princesses – always with a twist that expressed her traumatic and neglected past. I was gradually able to become the person that she could feel safe enough to be 'alone in the presence of'.

During the quieter times, I became aware that I was gradually able to be very present for her and not distracted by other thoughts, or feel on the old 'red alert' for her explosions. This state of mind crept up on me over time. I was able to think and share small, simple ideas with her about how her play related to her painful experiences of rejection and neglect in the past. Following a period when I was ill for a few weeks and could not see her, but maintained phone contact, Gail managed to internalise some aspects of her therapy and me in my absence and, when I returned, she was able to tell me how much she had missed me. She had taken a significant developmental step and had grown in response to a difficult external circumstance.

This heralded a much more age-appropriate adolescent phase in her treatment. By now she was 15 years old. Until this time she had mostly played in her sessions in the manner of a latency-age child but following my illness she started to try to reflect on her life, and this was vividly experienced by her decision to bring her 'life-story book' into the therapy room. In the UK, many children who are in the care of the local authorities have a life-story book made for them by foster parents and social workers, complete with photos and details of what happened in their dreadful early lives. These books make grim reading but are important, as they chronicle significant events for the child and are used in many different ways to try to help the child to have a more coherent narrative of his or her life. For 18 months, with her parents' blessing, the life-story book stayed with me and her therapy toys and drawings between sessions, and came out for each session. In this way, she started to explore her painful memories and efforts to make sense of her life, bringing new information into the sessions at times and taking some of the loose leaves of her life-story book home with her at others. This could be seen as another example of a therapeutic transitional experience which bridged her therapy (and me) and her home (and adoptive family), as well as her inner and outer worlds.

Gail spent many very quiet sessions looking intently at the photos in this book, reading what had been written in the book, and occasionally telling me a bit more about her memories. Mostly, I sat quietly with her, saying very little but feeling a great deal. Her glass of milk would be there for her, on the desk that she now worked at, and I would sit next to her.

As her narrative of her life was re-worked and gradually became more coherent, the beginnings of a mourning process emerged and her life started to make a bit more sense to her. The mourning was first experienced as intense sadness and tearfulness in me before it could be experienced in a bearable way within Gail. She gradually became more able to express her love and gratitude, as well as her anger towards her adoptive family. She was even able to find some forgiveness towards her birth mother by recognising her mother's courage in leaving her father to protect herself and her daughter from further injury.

I think it must have been during this phase of her treatment that my presence in the sessions started to have a more meditative aspect to it, although I did not make this connection at the time. It is noteworthy to me now that the arrival of the life-story book in the session also coincided with a time when my meditation practice started to deepen. In the sessions, I was increasingly able simply to sit, to be and then to dwell for longer periods of time with her. During the sessions, these quiet states of mind also seemed to be arising naturally within Gail.

When Gail entered her final year of weekly therapy, she spontaneously started to use the couch in her sessions, facing me and reclining on it in an adolescent, chatty kind of way. Here are some notes from one of her last once weekly sessions, where to my astonishment at the time, a meditative experience took place in the room.

Gail came into the room and went straight to the couch, re-arranging the cushions to make herself comfortable before lying down. I sat opposite to her in what was my usual chair, which resulted in us facing each other. She said 'What? . . .' in an aggressive, challenging way – as if feeling persecuted by my looking at her – a familiar theme. I didn't rise to this and just remained quiet. As if to excuse herself for being 'rude', she said, 'I'm just tired' in a stroppy adolescent-ish way. She then chatted inconsequentially about a broken nail, the dark winter night, how cold it was, the fact that I had the curtains closed and the lights on. She relaxed on the couch, curling up in a loose foetal position in which I couldn't see her face and then became quiet.

After a while I made a comment which was intended to try to help her to talk if she wished to. She told me that she didn't want to talk and then spent the rest of the session – 40 minutes – amazingly still and quiet in this same loose foetal position, but alert and awake. She felt very present and as had so often been my experience when I had been quietly with her in the past, I felt free to think about and experience the ebb and flow of what this extraordinarily still experience with her could be about.

It felt as if she had entered a quiet, un-persecuted space and I was being allowed to follow her into it, feeling separate but intensely 'present'. The space did not feel sad, depressed or angry. Its strongest quality was its intense stillness. At times, it felt as if I was a mother sitting quietly with her baby, not wanting to move in case I disturbed her. But as I became more and more aware of the stillness itself, I was amazed to realise that what I was most aware of was how much the stillness in Gail was like a meditative state.

I found myself thinking of all the different kinds of silence and quietness we had experienced together during her therapy and marvelled at how we had reached this place after all the activity and impulsiveness of the first few years of her therapy. I didn't say any of this to her, not wanting to disrupt the precious state of mind she seemed to be in.

For a while I tried to be as still as she was but realised that I wasn't able to do this despite having meditated in this way for many years. This only served to emphasise to me how extraordinary it was that she was able to stay in this 'place' for as long as she was. As we got closer to the end of the session, I felt that I wanted to say something about what was happening and commented on how different this stillness was from other times we had been quietly together. It seemed to be helping her to feel some peace inside herself, and it seemed to be good for her. Within myself, I realised that what she seemed to be absorbing deeply from me, under the pressure of weekly therapy coming to an end, was that part of me that values these still, meditative states and sees them as being deeply transforming and healing. It was an unconscious identification with a part of me that I had not realised she had somehow perceived.

Without feeling that my words would disrupt the state she was in, I was able to say to her that her ability to reach this stillness was something that would stay with her when she stopped coming to see me each week and that it was a place within her that she could go to when things were hard, that would offer her some peace of mind. It was a link between us and could also be a place of internal refuge to her when she needed it. I didn't refer to the meditative quality of her state of mind as this would have meant little to her, but I did draw her attention to it and describe what she seemed to be experiencing. The session ended, feeling to me like a combination of a therapy session and meditation practice. I told her that we had a few more minutes and at first she jumped up from her position on the couch. However, I said that there was no rush and she could just slowly emerge and get up from the couch when she was ready, which she then did. The sense of stillness remained with her as she left the session.

Whilst I had been very aware of the transformation that had taken place in Gail, it was the contrast between her state of mind in this session and the chaos of her early sessions which stayed with me, and helped me to feel hopeful about her future. During the time of the monthly consultations that followed the end of her weekly therapy, Gail had to face several difficult and distressing life situations. The consultations were very emotional and verbal. It was striking to her parents and to me how sensible, thoughtful, and indeed even how wise she became in the face of these difficulties. Could it have been that this was possible because she had become able to use her capacity to sit, be, and dwell with her problems and her distress in a way that enabled her to hold onto a clear sense of direction and values in her young adult life?

Conclusion

The importance of transitional states of mind in the process of therapeutic change is illustrated by this example, as well as the differing states of mind that the therapist needs to be able to experience in the course of any treatment where change is taking place. Whilst many kinds of cultural activity, such as sports, music and art, are very helpful in calming and focusing the mind and body in the present moment, meditation practice does this directly, using time-honoured techniques to calm and still the mind in ways which can become part of the true self of the therapist. This can become advantageous to patients, particularly when the therapist becomes able to dwell in the present moment, which is so characteristic of transitional experience, for longer periods of time.

This raises the intriguing question of whether certain intense experiences in the present moment might have the power to counteract intense experiences from the past so the past experiences no longer get confused with what is happening now. Separating past and present can be a central therapeutic challenge for traumatised patients. Enabling them to experience the reality of time – that was then, this is now – can be a major therapeutic breakthrough. By learning to be very much in the present, the therapist may be able to create a therapeutic space in which the present moment is fully experienced and the past is truly left where it belongs. It is within this transitional space that change can take place.

Notes

1   Readers wishing to explore thinking about psychoanalysis and religion further are referred to Bomford (2006), Coltart (1992, 1993, 1996a), Cunningham (2006), Epstein (2001, 2006), Frosch (2006), Molino (1999) and Welwood (1983).
2   An annual workshop on psychotherapy and meditation is well established and into its fifth year and a meditation group for psychotherapists meets on a monthly basis.

8 The impact of listening on the listener

Consultation to the helping professions who work with sexually abused young people (2009)

This chapter was first published in the second book in the Independent Psychoanalytic Approaches with Children and Adolescents series Through Assessment to Consultation *(Horne and Lanyado 2009). For a number of years I offered regular consultancy to the staff of a small residential therapeutic community. The problem of how to try to provide a healthier emotional environment which could withstand the onslaught of very disturbed children who could not cope with family life had always interested me. In the 1980s I had worked in a residential school in Scotland, offering intensive and non-intensive psychotherapy for the children, staff training and support, and became fascinated with the staff dynamics and how they affected the care of the children (Lanyado 1988, 1989 and 1993).*

Menzies Lyth's writings helped me to understand more about what was going on, and I was very fortunate many years later, to have the opportunity of regular supervision with her on my consultations to this therapeutic community (Menzies Lyth 1988 and 1989). What I learnt has been enormously helpful in supervising colleagues who work in in-patient, residential and day unit settings, where these intense staff dynamics need to be the subject of constant reflection.

Throughout this book I have emphasised the importance of the therapeutic setting for individual psychotherapy of severely neglected and traumatised children. This chapter addresses the difficulties of residential work in particular, but the central theme is: 'who listens to the listeners' and how are the various professions who work with these children best supported in this very challenging work? The ways in which the very disturbing experiences and behaviour of these children become expressed within the organisational setting and the staff group, are described in some detail. Understanding the group nature of this kind of work is vital.

Many more children need a residential therapeutic setting than receive it. Partly this is the result of the policy decisions about how to care for these children that are discussed in Chapters 1 and 2 of this book. The effect of not investing in good children's home provision for a larger number of children, who then get moved from one foster placement to another throughout their growing up, has meant that only the most difficult cases, if they are lucky, get the funding for the kind of provision described in this chapter. Therapeutic community provision is very labour intensive, and rare, because of the amount of reflection and thoughtfulness that is needed to do the work effectively.

Some people are natural listeners. People like to talk to them and feel heard by them. They are the kinds of people who are suited to working in the 'helping professions'. They are drawn to do the kind of work that others might find anything from not particularly interesting to incredibly demanding and distressing. There are many professional ways of helping other people – teaching, social work, occupational therapy, care work, psychotherapeutic work and so on. And it is probably fair to say that, in all of these professions, being in professionally appropriate and varying degrees of close contact with other people, who are suffering in all kinds of ways, is bound to have an impact on the listener.

Psychoanalytically trained psychotherapists are in a unique position in their under-standing of this impact on the professional, due to detailed attention to and under-standing of the transference–countertransference relationship. As a professional group, we spend a lot of time pondering the impact of one person's emotional life on another and the many forms this kind of communication takes. Indeed, we have refined the process into a particular type of listening – psychoanalytic listening – in which a form of free-flowing attention helps us to focus in on certain kinds of communication as indications of underlying unconscious communications.

This use of ourselves as a means of understanding others, together with the personal analysis or therapy that is central in training, enables us to become more able to stand being close to feelings, communications and experiences which many find intolerable. Most of our colleagues, many of whom work on a day-long basis with the patients we may see at the most for five 50-minute daily sessions in a week, do not have their own therapy to which they can bring all the alarming feelings and responses aroused in them by those they are trying to help. It is inevitable that they will need to protect themselves emotionally in some measure from becoming what is euphemistically called 'too emotionally involved' with those in their care, in order to survive the work on a day-to-day basis.

In this chapter, the focus is on a particular form of consultation to these colleagues which can be offered by child and adolescent psychotherapists. Some are offering work discussion groups to teachers in ordinary schools (Jackson 2002, 2008). Others are offering a combined approach with staff and pupils in ordinary schools as well as specialised settings (Malberg 2008; Maltby 2008; Music and Hall 2008; Sayder 2008). This chapter will discuss the 'impact on the listener' of staff working with children and young people who are at the most disturbed end of the spectrum, and have been severely sexually abused and frequently, repeatedly traumatised and chronically neglected. In these circumstances, an approach which focuses on staff's countertransference responses to children and relationships between staff, together with organisational dynamics, may be necessary for the intensity of the anxieties inherent in the work to be contained adequately.

These are children who have suffered a partial or total breakdown in the caring environment. They have often lost contact with their birth parents as a result of many kinds of severe abuse, neglect or abandonment and have been placed by the child care authorities with foster or adoptive parents, or in a children's home. As well as their inevitable emotionally disturbed behaviour, they are likely to find it extremely difficult to form ordinary loving and trusting relationships with those adults who try to care for them. As a result, they often have to be moved from one foster home to another when their aggressive and disturbed behaviour becomes intolerable for even the most understanding of carers. Adoptions fail for the same reasons. And not surprisingly, these children frequently experience great difficulties in school, which may lead to exclusion from one school after another, quite apart from all the changes of school which are the result of changing foster and adoption placements.

In the UK, often it is not until a child has reached these desperate circumstances of being uncontainable in a family home or ordinary school that the resources of a specialised therapeutic unit will be sought. By this time, the child's emotional condition has often reached a state of such despair and violent breakdown that what would have been a difficult enough task earlier on in the child's life has become close to impossible. There has to be a significant change to an environment in which the child's emotional needs and disturbance are received by a group of well-trained and well-supported adults. The loving care of a single carer, or two carers, in a foster or adoptive home is simply not enough.

Needless to say, the cost of sending a child to this kind of unit is very high, and places in them are scarce. The staff of the unit, both personally and through a transference relationship to the unit as a whole, stand in a kind of loco parentis relationship to the child, particularly in residential units, but also, partially, in specialised day units. The therapeutic task is like trying to replant a failing seedling in a richer and more carefully controlled environment, in the hope that it may yet manage to grow into a reasonably mature plant.

The staff who work in these units are constantly on the receiving end of ferocious, violent and disturbing behaviour and communications, verbal and non-verbal. Whilst the work can be deeply satisfying, it can also be terrifying, potentially emotionally damaging and overwhelming. The countertransference experienced in working with these children needs to be wisely attended to within the day-to-day functioning of the unit if good staff members are to be able to continue doing the work. If this does not happen adequately, the ability to sustain doing the work over time is bound to become compromised with staff becoming unhelpfully personally defended against the awful impact of the children's communications. Unhelpful social defences in the unit's organisational structure are also likely to develop as discussed later in this chapter (Menzies Lyth 1959, 1979, 1988, 1989).

Another possible outcome of the impact of the work is that good and dedicated workers become exhausted and burnt out. Worryingly, I do not think it is an overstatement to say that staff in such units are very much at risk and there can be an alarmingly high casualty rate of good staff who become seriously physically ill or emotionally burnt out, because they have listened so deeply to what those in their care have needed to communicate without the essential safeguard of a reflective space built into their daily working lives.

This chapter discusses the general impact on 'the listener' of what is 'received' in these demanding therapeutic relationships, and more specifically describes the process of consultation to a staff group in a residential unit in which many of the children, as is often the case, have been horribly sexually abused. These are children who have been incestuously abused at a very young age by parental figures and family members. Some have been involved in paedophile rings; their sexual acts have been filmed and have been found on the internet. The perversity of the details of the sexual acts that the children have witnessed and been forced to participate in evokes horror and disbelief that adults can behave in this way with children. Some of the adults responsible for these acts have been imprisoned. Others have been taken to court but there has not been enough legal evidence, despite the often overwhelming evidence from a clinician's point of view. Others have not been prosecuted. Some of the adults have been imprisoned and released having served their sentences. Despite all that has happened, the children often remain ambivalently attached to their abusers in disturbing and perverse ways, unable to form more healthy relationships and attachments.

The sexualised behaviour and sexual experiences of primary school-aged children, who would ordinarily be considered to be in Freud's 'latency' period of sexual development, is particularly disturbing because, even in our highly sexualised society, it is so evidently unacceptable. Adolescents are expected to be intensely sexually aware and active so that the sexual trauma underlying sexually abused young people's behaviour is not so immediately apparent, despite extreme sexual acting out. But the impact on a member of staff of recognising that a seven-year-old boy is deliberately and repeatedly exposing his bottom to her, whilst looking at her in a clearly sexually seductive way, is shocking and needs to remain shocking, however often it happens, if the underlying communication is to be truly received and heard. These are children who have been sexually abused from the start of life and they display and communicate to the therapeutic staff the scars of their experiences whenever they behave in these alarming ways.

Ordinary parental or adult compassionate touch has become so sexualised that, for many of the children in these units, no physical contact with an adult is possible without being experienced by the child as having a strong sexual component. Ordinary physical care – bathtime, bedtime and comforting – is contaminated in the same way. The difficulties of wisely caring for these children, so that gradually they are able to appreciate that not all adults are sexually predatory and that they can be touched and looked after physically and emotionally in a more ordinary way, are enormous and inevitably have a strong impact on the emotional lives of all who work with them. The way in which the staff group works together to help the children as well as to support and understand each other, weaving an interconnecting network of containment – a kind of 'mesh' around the children, will be crucial to the success or failure of the work (Ward and McMahon 1998; Ward *et al.* 2003).

There is a long tradition of therapeutic child care to which psychoanalytic psychotherapists have contributed through offering consultation and clinical supervision to the staff group (Dockar-Drysdale 1963, 1968, 1990; Menzies Lyth 1985; Reeves 2002; Sprince 2002; Wilson 1991, 1999/2009, 2003). Winnicott consulted to Dockar-Drysdale for many years about her work and her application of his ideas to working with children in residential settings at the Mulberry Bush School and the Cotswold Community (Dockar-Drysdale 1990). However it is important to remember that the widespread nature of sexual abuse has only become recognised over the last 30 years. Those writing before the mid-1980s would only rarely have worked with children and young people who had experienced the kinds of abuse with which child and adolescent psychotherapists and therapeutic child care workers are now in daily contact. The ways in which the specific countertransference experience of staff is processed, individually and within staff groups and organisationally, requires particular attention and is described later. Child psychotherapists' direct experience of the deeply disturbing nature of the countertransference when there has been severe sexual abuse enables them to be highly alert to the complex and distressing countertransferential feelings and experiences that staff in special units need help with processing.

Whilst this work is a natural progression from the clinical experience of trying to help these children through individual psychotherapy, it must be emphasised that additional supervision or training is essential in order to undertake the kind of consultation described below. The emphasis is on the staff group, not on discussion of the children themselves. This has echoes of our clinical work with the parents of children referred for psychotherapeutic help – particularly when work with the parents becomes the focus, rather than direct intervention with the child (Bailey 2006). Clinical group supervision and individual supervision, in which children are discussed, may also be led by a child psychotherapist but will take place at another regular time in the staff timetable (Wilson 2003). Wilson describes the essence of this kind of consultation as residing 'in its capacity to contain (Bion 1961) – to receive feelings and observations, to tolerate uncertainty, to allow for reflection and thought and ultimately to empower staff to move forward in their own way' (Wilson 1999/2009: 164).

For reasons of confidentiality – always a particularly difficult issue when effectively writing about colleagues – some of what follows is a composite picture which captures some of the key issues whilst disguising the identity of the colleagues involved. Staff working in these units often feel that they are trying to juggle ten fragile balls in the air, with any one of them coming dangerously close to being dropped and smashed at any given time. Catastrophe always feels alarmingly close. Certainly, my experience of consulting to these staff groups has this quality.

Theoretical tools

There are some ideas which I find particularly helpful in providing a theoretical framework when thinking about this nerve-racking but fascinating work. Before giving an example of the work in which they are embedded, I will enlarge on these ideas so that the example will hopefully make more sense.

Making the implicit explicit

As early as 1959 Menzies Lyth proposed 'that the success and viability of a social institution are intimately connected with the techniques it uses to contain anxiety'. She adds: 'Analogous hypotheses about the individual have long been widely accepted' (Menzies Lyth 1959: 78). Menzies Lyth argued that the nature of the anxiety that needs to be contained will be intimately connected to the 'primary task' of the organisation. The more the organisation is involved with human relationships and the alleviation of suffering, the greater the level of anxiety that it has to contain and process. For example, working with the staff on a children's orthopaedic ward, as Menzies Lyth describes in another classic paper 'The Psychological Welfare of Children Making Long Stays in Hospital' (1982), will entail containing and processing different anxieties from those encountered when working with a management group in manufacturing industry.

Her thesis is that the anxieties raised by the very nature of the primary task, naturally give rise to defences within the individual and within the organisational structure itself. Some of these defences may be essential in order to function – for example, the kind of black humour that can surprisingly be found in the most humane caring environments. However, social defences in organisations can become counterproductive, destructive and deeply resistant to change, just as they can in individuals. In the individual, this can lead to psychological problems. In organisations, this can lead to working environments which are awful to work in, with high staff turnover, stress-related illness and serious physical illness. As a result, some organisations may collapse, or limp along, unable adequately to carry out their primary task in a creative and flexible way.

In work with severely emotionally disturbed children and young people there is also a considerable risk of staff being physically attacked by those they try to care for, because aggression and violence are the children's and young people's established ways of responding to conflict and emotional pain. When staff anxiety is not adequately contained by the organisational structure, a corresponding increase in attacks on staff is one of the distressing outcomes. This anxiety, and the need to attend to the welfare of the staff as well as the welfare of the children, is as fundamental to the consultation process as the need to help parents of children in therapy to survive and grow in the process of being good-enough parents to their children.

Just as in individual work, where there is an underlying principle of trying to bring unconscious anxieties into consciousness so that there is the possibility of facing them, when consulting with a staff group in this way, a very helpful axiom is the need to make what is implicitly being expressed by the group explicit, so that difficult feelings and relationships, and disturbing issues, can be shared in the group and in the room during the consultation (Menzies Lyth 2004). This helps to contain the ever-present propensity to action and not thought-through behaviour by even the most experienced of staff when working with such a troubled client group. As Wilson points out:

In the midst of their everyday ordinary exchanges with children they [staff] deal with a wide variety of children's feelings, many of which are transferred onto them from past experiences. The residence becomes in effect an arena of transference enactment and residential care staff invariably find themselves all too easily perceived inappropriately, for example as depriving, abusive, neglectful or seductive.

(Wilson 1999/2009: 160)

The impact on staff of the perverse experience

Working with groups of severely sexually abused children and young people presents particularly disturbing anxieties which the staff have to learn to bear, think about and process. Anxieties about severe sexual perversity and extreme defences against it are always present in the staff and staff dynamics in organisations trying to help recovery from this kind of trauma.

In *Totem and Taboo* Freud drew attention to the universal abhorrence of sexual abuse and incest and the ways (taboos) in which different societies try to protect children from perverse adult sexuality (Freud 1912–1913). Staff working in these units are not only faced all the time with alarmingly sexualised and inappropriate behaviour in many of the children and young people they work with, but they also know many of the details of, for example, what has happened to a young child who has been incestuously abused by a paedophile ring which included his or her parents. Every sexual taboo and boundary has been repeatedly broken.

This kind of knowledge comes with the child's referral and arrival in the unit. But it also becomes 'known' in the much more powerful form of wordless projections into the staff of the coercion, disgust, horror and terror that the child has experienced. This is particularly likely to happen when sexual abuse has taken place before the child has had a full grasp of language. In addition, many of the children may be disturbingly sexually provocative to staff as a result of their abusive experiences. All forms of communication, particularly non-verbal forms, have to be received, thought about and processed by the individual staff members, as well as by the staff groups. These in turn need to be contained by a well-organised, clear, appropriately managed and structured working environment which provides regular opportunities to talk about and reflect on the impact of the work on the staff.

Some children may become able to make verbal disclosures about the abuse whilst in the unit. But words are woefully inadequate to communicate what needs to be emotionally communicated about their experiences, as adult sexual abuse survivors often testify. And what makes any disclosure authentic is the awful tiny details in what is eventually said, which can only be known from direct experience. Staff members have to be enabled to listen to these terrible communications as openly as possible and are inevitably much affected by them.

In addition, there is now always the anxiety that some member of staff may also be perverse and prey on the youngsters, undetected by colleagues. This is why the preservation of reflective spaces, where staff can think and talk about their experiences with the children, is so vital. However, it is in the very nature of the work that these reflective spaces will be constantly under unconscious and conscious 'attack' and risk of being eroded, due to the kind of attrition which is always present when working with such destructive unconscious and conscious processes. Whenever this starts to happen, it is a warning sign that disturbing communications and feelings are not being processed sufficiently and staff members are being left too much on their own to try to manage the day-to-day impact of the work, rather than doing this as a part of the working group.

To complicate matters further, there are also false allegations about staff, as well as physical attacks on staff, made by the children and young people. These must be followed up according to the procedures of the organisation. Often, bewilderingly for the staff involved, a false allegation or vicious physical attack can come from a child to whom they have been particularly close. Whilst we can understand more about this dynamic through Glasser's thinking about the 'core complex' and Chasseguet-Smirgel's thinking about the 'perverse core', trying to provide sensitive therapeutic care against this backdrop is inevitably fraught with difficulties (Glasser 1979; Chasseguet-Smirgel 1985).

I find Chasseguet-Smirgel's views on sexual perversion particularly relevant when trying to understand the nature of the anxiety that staff in these organisations are trying to find ways of living with, as sanely as possible. Startlingly, in her paper 'Perversion and the Universal Law' she argues that 'there is a "perverse core" within each one of us that is capable of being activated under certain circumstances'. Her paper offers 'an insight into what I see as the wider implications of something that, at first sight, is merely a deviation . . . of sexual behaviour' (Chasseguet-Smirgel 1985: 1).

Whilst her paper is written from the perspective of psychoanalytic work with adult patients, the points that Chasseguet-Smirgel makes about the ways in which all thought, and mental and emotional processes, can become subtly but destructively perverted, eventually leading to a form of chaos in which 'anything goes', are a very accurate description of what life can feel like, when times are difficult, in the kinds of unit described below. This type of intense anxiety can directly be related to the experience of working with sexually abused children. Chaos and a primitive kind of lawlessness, in which no boundaries or distinctions between adults and children are sacrosanct, are always close to the surface – in individual psychotherapy as well as in their everyday lives.

These are children who will think nothing of violently attacking an adult for apparently the most minor of reasons, who denigrate adult experience and knowledge, and have no reason to expect adults to protect them rather than exploit them. The ordinary boundaries between adult responsibility and sexuality and child care have all been broken very early in their lives. In some cases, the basic laws of human nature are mocked and turned 'upside down', bringing chaos in their wake (for a clinical discussion of these issues see Lanyado 2004d). This gives an additional dimension to the impact of the abuse on the child: the very structure of his or her mind and experience of life has been distorted alongside the real sexually abusive experiences that have been suffered. Chasseguet-Smirgel, in discussing these fundamental laws, succinctly writes that 'The bedrock of reality is created by the difference between the sexes and the difference between generations' and emphasises that 'erosion of the double difference between the sexes and the generations is the pervert's objective' (Chasseguet-Smirgel 1985: 2). It is a short step from these statements to an understanding of why psychotic group processes, in Bion's terms, can become predominant in units such as these (Bion 1961). Sanity and reality – knowing 'which way is up', rather than succumbing to perverse thought and logic which attacks and destroys all order and rationality – are easily lost, together with the group's primary task.

All of these anxieties have led to a climate of suspicion (which is in itself at times an extreme social defence against this anxiety), where there can be a managerial and procedural over-zealousness which is deeply traumatising to innocent and dedicated staff. Sometimes the anxiety is contained and processed. At other times, it is on the rampage in the psychotic manner that Bion (1961) describes, making units such as these feel at times very mad places in which to work. There is a frequently expressed anxiety that everything is about to collapse in the manner of the 'nameless dread' that Bion so evocatively portrays. Bion's insights about the psychotic ways in which groups can function have been developed by Menzies Lyth who particularly emphasised this dynamic in an interview she gave towards the end of her life:

> The paper ['The Functioning of Social Systems'] is so shocking that people find it hard to take in. I'm sure it's the same with Bion. The idea that people go about being psychotic all the time is a very dreadful thought that ordinary people can't live with. I mean, even people in the trade can't always live with it . . . What we now appreciate more is that it doesn't matter what institution you go into, it's going to have psychotic defences. Some are better than others.
>
> (Pecotic 2002)

Working with the staff group

These processes are illustrated in the following example. I had regularly consulted to the small senior staff group (five educational and therapeutic child care staff), of a well-respected residential unit for children aged six to eleven, for a number of years at the time of this consultation. On the previous day the unit had received an unexpected but important visitor. Unfortunately, for a number of reasons, both practical and because of ongoing issues in the unit, the staff had not been up to par and this had contributed to the children acting badly in front of the visitor. They had been verbally abusive and physically aggressive to each other and to the staff on duty.

Three of the senior staff (Helen, Dean and Michael) felt that the visitor had experienced a chaotic and highly oppositional children's group and a staff group who had barely been in control of the situation. They knew that whilst there were some mitigating circumstances for the chaos, the unexpected visit and the children's response had revealed the extent to which anxieties were generally not being adequately contained in the unit. Although they had been aware of this to a fair degree prior to the visit, they had not been able to see the severity of the problem until this time.

The sense of 'trying to juggle ten balls' is intense in these units. There can be times when there are not enough referrals and financial pressures necessitate not replacing staff if they leave – only to be followed by new referrals for which there are then not enough experienced staff, at first, on the unit. There can be an unfortunate time lag during which there are serious concerns about understaffing, and overworked staff who can barely manage to contain the children and young people in their care. New children coming to the unit bring a burst of new anxiety and disturbance to whatever precarious emotional balance prevails. New staff, however well experienced, need a period of induction and have to cope with all the anxieties of being a newcomer to the organisational system.

All of these issues have to be thought about alongside the day-to-day therapeutic care of a number of severely disturbed children or young people who can 'blow' violently and self-destructively at any time because of the pain and distress they cannot manage in their internal worlds – and it is this which remains the staff's primary task. This had been the situation for this senior staff group prior to the unexpected visitor.

Somewhat unusually for this well-established senior staff group, they started by allocating blame for what had happened the day before to the junior staff who had been on duty at the time. By doing this, the senior staff were disowning and splitting off their sense of responsibility and feelings of failure by projecting them outside the room, on to another group of people – the junior staff. The fact that the senior staff were actually responsible for managing, supporting and containing the anxiety of this junior staff group did not enter into their thinking at this point as they were unable to face the painful reality of their own responsibility.

On an inter-group dynamic level, the senior staff were now operating as a basic assumption fight/flight group in which blame was allocated to another group who had to be 'taken on' and 'sorted out', in other words 'fought with' (Bion 1961). The senior staff expressed frustration at more junior staff for not internalising all that they, the senior staff, were trying to pass on to them regarding boundaries and containment in the day-to-day care of the young people. To me, this sounded like parents who were at their wits' end over trying to get their offspring to take some responsibility. It was a very clear projection of the senior management team's inability to take responsibility for getting something wrong in their communication with the junior staff. As I was more used to the senior staff group being prepared to accept responsibility, I was rather surprised by the strength of this projection which I suspected was a defence against some unusually severe anxiety.

In their account of what had happened, I also noted a brief reference to what sounded like a disagreement between two of the people in the room over what they, as senior staff on duty at the time, had decided to do to try to contain the situation. They seemed to be trying to avoid dealing with this conflict by putting it outside the room as an inter-group conflict, between the senior and the more junior staff. I pointed out to them that it was easy to blame the more junior staff for not taking responsibility or containing anxieties adequately, but this also applied to this senior staff group, who were responsible for trying to contain their juniors' anxiety. By saying this I was reminding the senior staff of something we often talked about – the value of the many layers of containment, 'Russian doll-like', that contributed to the overall structure and well-being of the unit.

I added that there was also a problem here in the room and that I thought Helen was still feeling angry with Dean about a particular decision they had taken yesterday to try to contain the escalating situation. She agreed that she was angry with him – and that she was also angry with herself for not insisting more that the way she had wanted to deal with the escalating situation was indeed the better way. She felt she had avoided conflict at the time – and indeed might have continued to do this in the group if I hadn't made my comment.

Helen went into some detail about why she thought they had made the wrong decision and how this had not contained the junior staff in a difficult situation. She felt that this has resulted in the junior staff not feeling safe and that this in turn had intensified rather than contained the children's anxieties which were at the root of the behaviour. Dean could listen to this a bit, but the recognition of the conflict between him and Helen was still hard to keep in the room. They both returned to projecting the conflict outside the room, thus creating a potentially unhelpful inter-group dynamic in their minds between themselves, in the room, and the more junior members of staff, outside the room, who were felt to have let the unit down. Helen also knew that Dean was going through a hard time personally and this added to her difficulty in addressing her anger. Underlying this was their profound sense of having let down the children, the junior staff, the unit – and indeed themselves.

One of the other members of the consultation group, John, who had not been present the day before, tried to help Helen and Dean to think a bit about why the senior staff group as a whole was having such difficulty helping the junior staff to internalise the importance of certain basic patterns of care of the young people. Through this, we got a bit closer again to thinking about why the senior group were having such difficulty motivating and containing the junior staff. Something unthinkable was approached again but the 'blame' was still largely put on the junior staff. However, this time Dean commented that another member of staff, Sue, who had also been at the unit the day before, had been unusually quiet in the consultation so far. What did she think about what had happened?

Sue said she was just 'gutted' by what had happened. She had gone home feeling awful. Dean now admitted, so had he. Sue felt that the visitor had seen what they as a senior staff had been unable to see, some poor practice that they should all have picked up much sooner. She keenly felt her responsibility in needing to change this, and in having been party to it creeping up on them as a team. This sounded heartfelt. To myself, I noted that the group's sense of responsibility was re-entering the room, albeit at this stage located mostly within Sue who was expressing the more depressive and reparative feelings, which Helen, Dean and Michael were still finding it too unbearable to stay in touch with more than briefly.

However, Sue's comments were followed by a further refrain from Helen and Dean about how the junior staff were not doing their job properly. All this talk of people outside the room not doing their work properly alerted me to the fact that we, inside the room, were also not doing our work properly. So I said that I felt that the senior staff wanted to shift responsibility to outside this room when it seemed that, right now, all of us in the room (including me) were not doing our job properly. This was an attempt to bring the group back to its primary task – the difficult reality of caring for the children and facilitating the work of the junior staff. The senior staff seemed to be struggling with knowing how to motivate their staff sufficiently and, above all, how to contain the junior staff's anxieties. The role of the consultant to help the group stay 'on task' and not be pulled off task by unconscious group dynamics which take over when anxiety is high, leading to basic assumption group dynamics, is well illustrated by this section of the consultation (Bion 1961).

The response to my comment was a further apparently defensive response from Michael, Helen and Tim protesting about their genuine and serious concerns about a junior staff member's increasingly unwise behaviour with the children. He didn't seem to understand how to hold appropriate boundaries between his professional life and his personal life in his communications with the young people. There was an uncomfortable sexual element to what was either a genuine naivety in the mistakes he was making, or a real unhealthy blurring or even breaking of acceptable boundaries.

It had now become apparent to me that it was this intensified fear of a perverse sexuality being expressed in the unit which was currently particularly disturbing the staff, and which accounted for their unusual defensiveness. The previous ability of the staff group and organisation to contain and work with this ever-present anxiety had been severely challenged by the arrival at the unit of a child who had been abused by a paedophile ring, as well as by a very distressing disclosure of past sadistic sexual abuse by a child who had been in the unit for some time. I commented that I felt that the loosening of boundaries, which seemed to be moving in a potentially sexually perverse direction, painted a picture of the potential for anarchy, complete disintegration and chaos in the unit that the senior staff were finding it intolerable to recognise and try to bear thinking about.

This horrible and frightening feeling was now very alive in the room for all of us. It seemed that we as a group needed genuinely to know about and experience the terror of feeling that an apparently stable structure was descending into chaos and sexual perversity. This was what had been projected into the junior staff the previous day by the young people who felt uncontained and frightened at the best of times. The junior staff, rather than experiencing the supportive and thoughtful containment of the senior staff, had felt the same terror and lack of containment and it was this that had led to the serious acting out of the children. The senior staff had let down the junior staff. Now that the fear of chaos and sexual perversity was so alive in the room, we could start to do the work that was needed to process and contain this anxiety.

This experience in the room was deeply sobering for all of us, but the recognition of this psychic reality enabled senior staff to own responsibility for what had happened and attempt to repair the damage that they felt had occurred because of their difficulty in being sufficiently in touch with the anxiety that their junior staff were feeling. These reparative feelings, which had only resided in Sue, were now very alive in each of the senior staff in the consultation – as well as within a much more helpful working group dynamic. They seemed to rally and find some determination to do better. They knew that they actually had the skills to contain powerful anxieties in the organisation. They now recognised that they had 'been there' before, but they had 'lost it' for a while, and needed to reconnect to their more competent and containing abilities again.

After the consultation, this was in fact what happened and the senior staff, motivating and supporting the junior staff, worked very hard to regain the organisation's balance – which they managed to do for a while until the next eruption of severe anxiety, which knocked them off course again and required further painful working through of the kind that this example illustrates. This is an inevitable part of the ebb and flow of the emotional life of such units. This very demanding work will always feel as if one of the 'ten balls in the air' is about to fall disastrously.

Further thoughts

What can we learn from this 'snapshot' in the midst of a lengthy consultation 'movie'? I hope that the emphasis on bringing what is being expressed 'outside the room' into the room is clear, as is the need determinedly to keep on making what is implicit explicit. It is well known that the difficulty of containing a 'nameless dread' of a chaotic and crazy nature is very alive in any large group dynamic. Large group and inter-group communications can rapidly become quite mad – and this is with comparatively 'sane' adults making up the group. When the group is made up of deeply disturbed and sexually traumatised children and young people and those trying to help them to recover, this frightening dynamic will always be very close to the surface.

Organisations naturally grow their own structures and defences, each in their own rather idiosyncratic way, to try pragmatically to find the best possible ways of living and working with this kind of anxiety. In therapeutic units, these are anxieties that, by the very nature of the work, never go away and, if anything, are reintroduced each time a new child comes into the organisation. This is why it is so important that organisations such as these have external consultants – who are sometimes child and adolescent psychotherapists – to help the staff keep on doing the work.

It can also be seen that part of the consultant's role is to help the staff group keep to their primary task, so that wise reflective thinking about the children's feelings and their impact on the staff can take place. The consultant helps the staff group to recognise when they are caught in primitive, basic assumption, group thinking and behaviour where external and psychic reality can be lost sight of, and thus the primary task of the group is not being attended to. In the example, the staff group found it very difficult to face the reality of their own failure to protect and contain the junior staff's and thus the children's anxieties, and resorted to a fight–flight group dynamic. They also found it very difficult to face the fact that one staff member was possibly behaving in a sexually inappropriate way with the children.

Whilst the staff were unable to face these realities, they were unable to carry out their primary task of helping and protecting the children. Helping the senior staff to face this reality enabled them to talk to the junior member of staff in a thoughtful way – and realise that being rather new to the work, he was simply being naive and needed more careful supervision. They were also able to think creatively about how better to contain the anxieties of the more junior staff, and realised that there had been a lot of slippage in the supervisory structure – the senior staff's responsibility which needed to be rectified. They had recently had many balls in the air. It was the reflective spaces of the organisation that had borne the brunt of this.

The most difficult task in the face of the ever-present fear of psychotic madness, chaos and disintegration in this work is to try to stay sane and not get caught in the undertow of the destructive currents. The external consultant is less prone to this undertow – although far from immune – and continually tries to maintain this saner and more realistic view through the comments she makes to the staff. This enables them to find their way back to the primary task when they have gone off course.

A particularly thorny problem is how much the known personal lives of people in the group should become part of the more public workgroup process. In a group that works closely together – particularly if they have worked together over many years – much is known by one group member about another; but how appropriate or indeed essential is it to bring this into the working group process itself? This is a very difficult question and the balance between what is worked with in the group and what is worked with in more private spaces within the organisation varies enormously according to the philosophy of the organisation as well as the view of the consultant.

Wilson stresses: 'It is of key importance that child psychotherapists are clear in their own minds that they are neither managers nor psychotherapists in this context' (Wilson 1999/2009: 165). Too much of an emphasis on how personal issues and inter-staff relationships impinge on the organisation's work can, at times, take the group far away from their primary task in a way that is 'anti-task'. Too little attention can be rather like behaving as if there is not 'an elephant in the room'. As with the use of interpretation in individual psychotherapy, the unique-ness of the therapeutic dyad, in this instance staff group and consultant, will dictate how much or how little is interpreted, and how. (For a useful discussion of this issue see Maltby 2008.)

For those who wish to do this kind of work, there is expertise available and individual supervision can be a valuable first step in developing appropriate new skills. Another option is to set up small 'workshops' where consultation work can be frankly and confidentially discussed, preferably with a more experienced group leader facilitating the discussion. It can be very alarming and disturbing to become aware of the madness that can lurk within the undercurrents of any organisation, particularly of the kind described above. We are all vulnerable in the midst of this if we do not have the opportunity to share these anxieties, thoughts and experiences with colleagues.

9 Transforming despair to hope in the treatment of extreme trauma

A view from the supervisor's chair (2016)

Retiring from clinical practice but continuing to supervise, give seminars and write has provided an interesting opportunity to think about the work of child psychotherapists from the comfort of the 'supervisor's chair'. Supervisees are often under tremendous pressure from their extremely difficult and needy patients, and within their clinic teams. They greatly need a space in which they can digest and honestly reflect on their work. I am very aware that it is much easier to be in the supervisor's chair than to be facing the, often extraordinary, emotions involved in the therapeutic process. This has prompted me to think about the supervisory process itself, and what it is that child and adolescent psychotherapy supervisees experience within this process that feeds back into the therapeutic process with their patients.

It gradually became clear to me that one of the most valuable aspects of listening to supervisees' accounts of distressing sessions, was that I could help them to see the glimmers of hope that were present in the midst of therapeutic crises. As the previous chapters in this book demonstrate, this work is very personally demanding of the therapist. Supervisees could, at times, feel overwhelmed by the demands of the work and despair about their capacity to help their patients. However I observed with a number of supervisees that when they felt able to spontaneously convey these feelings and thoughts in their supervision session, this despair could become transformed into important turning points in their therapeutic work with the patient. This intrigued me and led to the writing of this paper in 2016, and the writing of this book (Lanyado 2016). I am very grateful to all of my supervisees for the stimulation and learning that working with them has offered to me.

> To hope is to be ready at every moment for that which is not yet born, and yet not become desperate if there is no birth in our lifetime . . . those whose hope is strong see and cherish all signs of life and are ready every moment to help the birth of that which is ready to be born.
> – Fromm, 1968/1970/2010: 22, *The Revolution of Hope*

> The trauma victim may suffer from interpersonal numbing, a giving up of hope for satisfactory human contact which is the destruction of basic trust.
> – Krystal, 1968 cited in van der Kolk, 1987: 154, *Psychological Trauma*

> ... trauma results in a disorder of hope: the capacity of others to provide
> emotional gratification and security is either undervalued or overvalued.
>
> van der Kolk, 1987: 154, *Psychological Trauma*

As a supervisor of clinicians working with severely traumatised children, I have often noticed that there can be a turning point which emerges from times of despair and crisis in the therapeutic process. This paper is an attempt to explore and draw attention to these transformational moments, which are probably much easier to see from the supervisor's perspective than the therapist's. Becoming more aware of these moments, and trusting them as clinical indicators of change taking place, can help therapists to find their 'bearings' in the midst of what is often a distressing and confusing experience in the consulting room.

With the inevitable distress and awfulness of much of these patients' treatments, alongside our psychoanalytic tendency and need to address the negative and destructive aspects of life, it is often hard for the clinician to recognise the early, faint signs of hope and change, particularly when their precursors are shock and despair. But as a supervisor, these transformational moments increasingly stand out for me in the midst of what may otherwise be a chaotic and disturbing session. I now make a point of discussing what may be no more than a clinical hunch of mine at the time – and then waiting as the work proceeds to see if this hunch was justified or not. Whilst in this paper I am exploring an observational experience within the supervisory process, as opposed to conducting a system-atised research project, others have done so: in his fascinating paper Carlberg (1997) has used just this type of clinical experience to carefully and retrospectively research turning points in therapy. It is my contention that we need to become much more aware of these transformational moments of hope so that we can facilitate their growth into as much recovery from trauma as is possible, for to quote Fromm again: 'Hope is the psychic concomitant of life and growth' (Fromm 1968/1970/2010: 25).

Genuine hope is quite different from manic and other defensive forms of hope, and different also from denial. As van der Kolk and Krystal imply in the above quotes, hope is associated with 'satisfactory human contact' (Krystal 1968 cited in van der Kolk 1987: 154) and experiencing 'the capacity of others to provide emotional gratification' (van der Kolk 1987: 154), presumably including the need for intimacy and authentic relatedness. The kind of hope that I am discussing in this paper follows a time of despair in the therapeutic process. This can also be a time of intimacy and authentic relatedness, when there is an intense sense of the patient and therapist having reached 'rock bottom' in an open and honest way. This is communicated in the therapeutic process itself, and then in the supervisory process which follows the session.

In a broader context, the recovery of hope after trauma is associated with positive emotional growth and positive internal and external change. Hope is the strength of life re-asserting itself after a period of bleak 'interpersonal numbing'. We have much to learn about the strength of this 'rhythm of life' from observing the sheer irrepressibility of life after seeming utter devastation; for example the ability of vegetation to return to the landscape after forest fires, or indeed the first green shoots of spring after the dark and cold of winter.

A view from the supervisor's chair

For many years now, I have been in the interesting and privileged position of offering clinical supervision to psychotherapists working with severely traumatised and neglected children and teenagers. This provides a thought-provoking, intimate and stimulating 'bird's eye view' of many treatments and patient–therapist couples. I have gradually realised that this experience is rather like a 'live/natural' research project, generating observations, ideas and hypotheses within me about the psychoanalytic therapeutic process, which draw on the clinical material that is brought to the supervisory session.

When the supervisory relationship is working well, it plays a significant role in trying to disentangle aspects of the therapists' countertransference within the safe and protected space of supervision. For example, I have learnt to listen carefully for unusual gaps and holes in the clinical accounts; for times when the supervisee has found it really difficult to write up the notes or has needed extra time to recover from a difficult session. I listen to the emotions expressed by the therapist about the patient and try to encourage the supervisee to examine these feelings within the supervision space, whilst respecting that some of these emotions may be private and need to be examined elsewhere.

Within an established supervisory relationship, it becomes possible to think honestly about difficult feelings that the therapist experiences during the session that are on the edge of consciousness and very much the stuff of inchoate emotional communication – *both* within the patient–therapist relationship *and* within the therapist–supervisor relationship. When these feelings become alive within the supervision process, this can in turn benefit the patient because what was previously so hard to acknowledge and think about, has now been thought about by the therapist together with the supervisor, within the safe and contained confines of supervision. At times such as these, the supervisor helps the therapist to 'hold' difficult and disturbing experiences, and this enables the therapist, in turn, to hold the difficult and disturbing experiences being expressed by the patient. This combination of experience and reflection within the supervision session can then become part of the conscious awareness of the supervisee when he or she returns to the clinical situation. Whilst this is helpful to the supervisee, it is also helpful to the supervisor. To draw on the evocative title of Patrick Casement's classic book about 'internal supervision', *On Learning from the Patient*, when I am listening to supervisees' accounts of their work, I am 'learning from the supervisee' (Casement 1985).

Whilst psychoanalytic theory and practice has to address the most destructive aspects of what lies within every one of us, it also relies on the inherent powers of recovery within the individual. Recovery, particularly when potentiated from within the therapeutic relationship, can bring about extraordinary internal transformation. Then the painful and horrific events and relationships that have brought terrible suffering into a traumatised patient's life have not been eradicated, but have been transformed to varying degrees, into more symbolic forms, enabling a new life narrative to emerge. Unconscious enactments and destructive repetitions of the traumatic events lessen and become more consciously recognised. New emotional development and growth that may have come to a halt following the trauma now becomes possible.

Michael Parsons captures the essence of this transformative process. He writes:

> Whatever the analyst's orientation, it is the essential *humanity* of the *psychoanalytic* process that helps the human being on the couch to think it might be possible to change. And the specifically *psychoanalytic* quality of the *human* process that the analyst offers is what provides patients with the means to change.
>
> (Parsons 2014: 204, italics in original)

In their ground breaking paper *Non-interpretive mechanisms in psychoanalytic therapy: the 'something more' than interpretation*, Stern and his colleagues within the Boston Process of Change Group developed a new language and theory for researching what it is that brings about change in the therapeutic relationship (Stern *et al.* 1998). This carefully researched paper identifies what the authors term 'moments of meeting' which take place within the 'shared implicit relationship' *between* the patient and therapist, and they understand these as the 'something more' than interpretation that brings deep change in therapy. I am building on Stern and his colleagues' ideas in what follows, and suggesting that one of the consequences of moments of meeting in therapy and in supervision, is 'moments of hope' that change is possible, even in the aftermath of severe trauma and despair.

As a profession, child and adolescent psychotherapists tend to be caring and thoughtful people even before undertaking the training. Training analysis and supervision build on these personal strengths during training and after. But we can become worn down, and even burnt out and physically ill because of the demands of the work and the deep ways in which we need to make use of our 'Self' in order to help the patient. We can lose sight of the importance of hope, and indeed of faith in the analytic process itself. We can doubt whether the psychoanalytic process is helpful or suitable for certain cases – and of course at times it may not be.

However maybe we also risk becoming accommodated to our own strengths, not seeing the positive qualities that we take with us into the consulting room, qualities which I would argue are a significant part of the solid core of us, the 'presence' of the therapist, which our patients perceive as potentially helping them to become less troubled and unhappy (Lanyado 2004a). The impact on the therapist who is trying to be as open as possible to so many highly disturbing and distressing communications is profoundly challenging and upsetting, and at times also corrosive. The process of trying to communicate with and to understand such patients can leave the therapist in a pretty desperate state, very much in need of what Sterba (1934) quoted in Casement (1985) calls 'an island of contemplation'. It is these most troubling cases that are often taken to supervision.

Ogden writes that the 'psychoanalytic supervisory relationship is ... an indispensable medium through which psychoanalytic knowledge is passed from one generation of psychoanalysts to the next' (Ogden 2009: 31). I want to explore and build on some of Ogden's ideas about supervision, through addressing what happens when the shock waves of traumatic experience come alive within the supervisory process. In addition to the psychoanalytic knowledge that Ogden refers to, emotions that relate to the therapist's countertransference experience with the patient are re-experienced and begin to be processed during supervision. The countertransference experience is, in effect, the link between the patient, therapist and supervisor. Again, Ogden has interesting ideas about this, thinking about the process as follows:

> The analyst does not bring the analysand to the supervisory session: rather (with the help of the supervisor) the analyst 'dreams up' the patient in the supervisory session . . . – 'dreaming up the patient' – in the supervisory setting represents the combined effort of the analyst and the supervisor to bring to life in the supervisions what is true to the analyst's experience of what is occurring at a conscious, preconscious and unconscious level in the analytic relationship.
>
> (Ogden 2009: 34)

This idea of what is co-created within the supervision – 'dreaming up the patient' – is very resonant with Winnicottian theories about how psychotherapy takes place in the transitional space *between* the therapist and the patient, as a result of their relatedness, and indeed also builds on these concepts. Vastardis and Phillips develop these notions about supervision further again in their paper about their shared experience of their supervision process, as supervisor and supervisee (Vastardis and Phillips 2012).

With this in mind, 'supervision' almost feels like a misnomer for the process that takes place in the 'supervisory setting'. The *Concise Oxford Dictionary* describes 'supervision' as to 'superintend, oversee the execution of (a task etc), or actions or work of a person' (Clarendon Press 1990). There are very directive, managerial connotations in this definition, which do not sit comfortably with what Ogden is describing as 'dreaming up the patient' or indeed what Winnicott is describing in *Playing and Reality* when thinking about 'where' psychotherapy takes place – that is, the unique in-between, paradoxical, transitional space of the relationship between patient and therapist, or therapist and supervisor (Winnicott 1971).

Putting together these two sets of ideas about the shock waves of trauma and the supervisory process, where does the notion of 'transforming despair to hope' fit in? Whilst as a supervisor I am in the privileged position of not having to face the tremendously difficult sessions my supervisees are facing daily, it is nevertheless my job to listen with every bit of my being to what they tell me about their work.

Gradually out of the complexity of all that happens within the supervisory session, I have come to feel that a very important part of my function is to notice and to nurture the potential for genuine moments of hope which can, quite paradoxically, emerge from moments of dark despair in the therapeutic process. Not surprisingly, these moments may often not be registered by the therapists who find themselves in the midst of the very helplessness I am hearing about. As part of the patient–psychotherapist couple, this experience can be very intense at times. I am not talking about empty reassurance from myself to the therapist, but about being alert to the potential for early signs of *positive* change and hope in the therapeutic process, which can emerge just as things are looking and feeling so dark. These early signs need the therapist's attention and thoughtfulness, but not necessarily the therapist's words through interpretation to the patient. It is a fragile process which has more to do with holding one's breath so as not to disturb it, rather than with trumpeting its arrival.

Of course, the therapist also has to be alert to *negative* change in the patient and particularly with severely traumatised patients, to be aware of the undertow of the unconscious pressure to repeat traumatic experiences in the present. It would be foolish to seem to assert that all despair can ultimately lead to hope. Sadly, some terrible situations do go from bad to worse, and as therapists we have to face realistically these situations in which psychotherapy cannot be of help to the child or family.

In particular, as the examples later in this paper demonstrate, when there has been extreme trauma, and the therapist describes a shocking experience in the therapy session, the shock wave of the trauma may be experienced in a particular way by the supervisor through a moment-of-meeting within the supervision session, when discussing the clinical material. Just like a tsunami that sweeps over the landscape leaving terrible destruction, the shock waves of trauma can decimate the ability to think, and the therapist can briefly experience a sense of disintegration and collapse of all boundaries, which puts him or her in deep contact with the experience of the traumatised patient. These experiences often need to be discussed in supervision, but this can be a revealing, emotional and intense experience within the supervisory relationship itself. When this happens, it can feel as if the therapist/supervisor is 'pierced' by the projections, in a way that confirms that what is being communicated has authentically been comprehended by the other (Horne 2009 and personal communication, Heimann 1950). The powerful authenticity of what I have come to think of as 'moments of meeting' within the supervisory relationship, can help to deepen the whole quality of that relationship. They are moments of change and of hope in the supervisory relationship and, as I illustrate in the two examples later in this paper, they can lead to turning points and transformational moments in the patient therapist relationship.

Shock waves and defences

Whilst Parsons' and Ogden's ideas are tremendously helpful, they are nevertheless writing about work with adult patients, in the main seen in private practice.

Psychotherapeutic work with children is very different. Due to the sadly ever-shrinking availability of child psychotherapy clinical time within the public sector, it is often only the most severe cases that get to the top of the waiting list and are offered psychotherapy. This group of patients is often highly traumatised and neglected with very complex problems involving a network of professionals as well as foster and adoptive parents. It is increasingly rare to see 'ordinary' neurotic patients from intact families. Plus, the work is taking place within the box-ticking, computerised and over-procedurised culture we now live within, factors which seem to gobble up valuable clinical time and skills and diminish the containing function of the multi-disciplinary clinic team.

It is precisely because external reality, both past and present, is so complex that it must be carefully thought about and absorbed by the therapist if the child's distress and predicament is to be fully understood. It is also why, in my view, case 'management' concerning these complex external realities must be discussed within supervision, alongside concentrated psychoanalytic listening to the child's communications from the internal world, communications that may, of course, take many forms. The traumatised child's vulnerability, pain and helplessness are dreadful and it can take quite a while before the fullness of this really gets through to the therapist. When it does, deep feelings are stirred in the therapist which need to be explored within the supervisory process. The epicenter of the shock wave is in the child patient. The adults and other children in the child's world are made very aware of this by the child's distressed, disturbing and violent behaviour. Foster and adoptive parents, residential care staff, teachers, doctors, siblings, foster siblings and classmates all experience these shock waves in some form – for example as verbal and physical aggression, distressing and distressed communications, manic and highly reactive behaviour.

The therapist experiences the shock waves in a different way and is trained to try to listen psychoanalytically and to receive with body and soul all that is being communicated. In everyday life and relationships with others, despite the best will in the world, the behaviour and emotional communication coming from the child may simply become unmanageable and as a result people need to defend themselves from what is projected into them by the child. Then there is no possibility of the child's communication being received, let alone processed in any way by another human being. The child remains shut out and isolated from 'satisfactory human contact' (as in the opening quote from Krystal 1968: 154). And, even though it is the therapist's job to receive the communications as fully as he or she can, there are often times when it is all too much for the therapist as well. During training, and at other times in the therapist's professional life, it will be possible for him or her to take these overwhelming experiences to their own analyst to express, explore and digest. But much of the time these difficulties will be taken to supervision or colleagues in the clinic team. If this does not happen, there is the risk of the therapist becoming less and less open to the child's communications of trauma and more and more defended against them. These are the times when hope can shut down. It is part of the supervisor's work to try to fully experience the impact of the shock wave as communicated by the supervisee, and then to stand back and try to think about the experience. This can help the supervisee to remain as open as possible to what is being communicated by the patient; more receptive, less defended and more contained as a result of supervision, particularly at a time of crisis.

Frances Tustin, writing about her work with children in autistic states of mind, reminds us of the importance of maintaining hope. She writes:

> As I see it, in everything that we do, we need to come down on the side of life and hope.
>
> (Tustin 1986: 294)

This can be very hard to achieve in practice and it is precisely this that I wish to explore through the examples that follow. I have various questions in mind: does a moment-of-meeting in supervision, translate into moments of meeting in the therapy itself? And to enlarge on this question: are transformational moments of meeting between the patient and therapist also intrinsically moments of hope which can be further recognised and nurtured by the supervisory process itself? Are these turning points in supervision then translated into further turning points in the therapy as a part of a newly established benign circle of development and growth? Are they the counterpart of what the philosopher Buber evocatively refers to as 'I Thou' meetings (Buber 1937) which are, to quote Michael Parsons again, 'the essential humanity of the psychoanalytic process' (Parsons 2014)?

In the two examples from supervision which follow, only a very brief case history will be given, and facts that do not affect the essence of the case material have been altered in order to protect the patient's and the supervisee's confidentiality. Both supervisees and their colleagues involved with the patient have given their permission for our supervisions to be used to demonstrate the *processes* I am focusing on in this paper and I am grateful to them for this. By focusing on the processes, I hope that it is possible to avoid getting too involved in the case material itself and instead focus on what is happening in the supervisory relationship.

An additional factor to have in mind is that within our profession, we have a number of different ways of thinking about and working psychotherapeutically, which is naturally reflected within the supervisory process as well. I see these differences as representing different paths towards the same end – improving the well-being and mental state of our patients. They are different ways of making human contact. The theoretical ideas which have helped me to think about this work come from an independent tradition, and draw heavily on Winnicottian ideas about the maturational processes and the facilitating environment, and the importance of transitional experiences and playing (Winnicott 1965, 1971).

The first example is about hope in the consulting room; the second about hope in the professional network.

Example 1. Hope in the consulting room

Brief history: Tina was born to a mother diagnosed with mental health problems. There were a number of foster placements as mother was often unable to look after Tina. Eventually a kinship carer was identified but unfortunately, after a few months, it emerged that a close friend of his who had regular contact with Tina, had been charged with a sexual offence against children. It was possible that this person had abused Tina but this was never proven, however Tina did at times behave in very sexualised and boundary-less ways. When Tina was four she was adopted. She started psychotherapy when she was six and a half because her violent outbursts were often unmanageable and unfathomable to her adoptive parents. Her parents were seen regularly at the clinic, and there were regular reviews with the psychotherapist.

Clinical extract: The clinical extract below is from when Tina had been in therapy for about one year. There had been very little overtly sexualised clinical material until a few weeks before this session, and the transference relationship was conflicted but could include brief and valuable times of intimacy. This suggested that the 'core complex' of longing for and dreading intimacy that Glasser describes, was beginning to soften (Glasser 1998). Tina was still very traumatised and various small triggers could cause panics when she would try to hide in the room, clearly in terror. She could also suddenly attack her therapist in shocking ways and had scratched her, broken her glasses, and tried to strangle her. Despite this there was a real fondness and good communication between them as well as a slowly growing capacity for intimacy.

The following material came after a few sessions in which the therapist started to wonder to herself whether Tina could be beginning to try to share her conscious memories of being sexually abused. This became explicit in a shocking way in this session. The clinical excerpt comes roughly half way through the session and came after Tina had already tried to approach the memories several times through her play, but had run out of the room or diverted to other play because, in her words, she 'needed a break'. The play she was finding it so hard to keep going with, was about some little 'piggies' who were in a bath. I quote from the therapist's session notes:

> *She goes back to the piggies. I wonder if she can show me what happens next. They are in the bath and the tiger cub comes in. I comment that there is a lot I am not sure about but I wonder if*

> *something is happening to the piggies. She walks along the window sill to the couch and lies down facing me. She pulls up her skirt around her waist and bending her knees lets them fall open so that her knickers are exposed. She fingers these and looks at me. I feel shocked. I say that I think she is showing me something about the piggies and their knickers and their private area. Perhaps someone did something to them that they didn't like. I am speaking very gently but feel as if the next part of the session is a bit of a blur.*

The supervisory session and process: The supervisory relationship was well established and we had often wondered when more explicit sexual material would emerge in the session. So it was not as if the therapist was unprepared for what happened in the session. However, it was nevertheless deeply shocking and upsetting for the therapist who not only found the rest of the session to be a 'bit of a blur', but was clearly upset during our supervision about the impact this material had on her. She had found it very hard to put the patient out of her mind in the time between the session and the supervision. The 'shock wave' had really got through to her and rolled on into our supervisory session.

I am very grateful to this supervisee for our discussions whilst I was preparing this paper. We talked about what happened during this supervision (for which we both had our supervision notes) as one that had stood out in my mind and in hers, as a powerful experience and what could be described as a 'moment-of-meeting' in supervision. The supervisee felt that the supervision helped her to be in touch with her own feelings of terrible helplessness as she listened to and watched her patient. The supervision helped us to relate this to the child's terrible feelings of helplessness at the time of the suspected abuse, as well as her utter aloneness. Possibly when the child became able to share her experience so rawly with her therapist, and with such an impact, the communication was received fully and forcefully by her therapist, and so was communicated powerfully in turn during the supervision. This is the 'piercing' experience to which Horne refers (personal communication 2015). I also find Ogden's idea of 'dreaming up the patient' very helpful here – Tina seemed vividly present in the supervision room at this point – although Ogden extends his thinking and his approach to supervising a good way beyond this (Ogden 2009).

I had the advantage of being one step removed from the shocking experience that the supervisee brought to supervision, and was able to think about what had happened, as well as to draw on my experience of similar cases. But essentially the work of finely understanding and appreciating the child's traumatic emotional state was appreciated within our supervisory relationship, through the moment-of-meeting that was experienced between the supervisee and myself. What then rolled on from the supervision into the treatment was co-created by the two of us, and then the two of them – therapist and patient. Importantly, as if to confirm the significance of the communications between patient, therapist and supervisor around this experience in the consulting room, the supervisions that followed this one indicated that Tina was increasingly able to trust her therapist and to dare to get closer to her. There was a new feeling of hope in the treatment for the therapist and child, as well as for her adoptive parents and within the supervisory process.

During the supervision itself, we were also able to note the supervisee's defences coming to the fore – her sense of being 'in a blur' possibly connecting to a mild dissociative state which blurred the impact of what she was listening to and witnessing. The 'blur' possibly also gave some indication of the defences the child might have used at the time of the traumatic experience, which may very well have included dissociation. We were able to think about the value of these defences at the time of trauma taking place – but also the need for these defences to soften so that less extreme defences could gradually come into play, over time. This applied both to the patient and to the therapist in her efforts to really listen to and receive what the patient was communicating.

Searles quoted in Odgen (2009) refers to this process:

> . . . The (conscious and unconscious) processes at work currently in the *relationship between* patient and therapist are often reflected in the (conscious and unconscious) *relationship between* therapist and supervisor . . .
>
> (Searles 1955: 159, italics in original)

Ogden also refers to this process, describing the connection between the analytic process and the supervisory process as being like two facets of a single set of conscious and unconscious relationships, internal and external, involving the supervisor, supervisee and patient (Ogden 2009).

In response to what I had written above about this experience in supervision, the supervisee added some further thoughts. In particular she felt it was very helpful that she did not feel alone in the clinical experience, which she linked to Marianne Parsons' thoughts about helplessness in the absence of a protective other (Marianne Parsons 2009). The supervisee felt that within the context of the supervisory relationship, I was her 'protective other' helping her to hold the strong feelings of helplessness that had been evoked, which in turn enabled her to help her patient. The supervisee also felt that she carried a heavy responsibility to respond wisely to the clinical material, respecting confidentiality whilst needing to think about whether any action was required on her part. She felt that talking about the session was like 'lifting a burden' which put her in touch with thoughts about the burden of secrecy that children experiencing abuse often carry. She described that

> . . . supervision felt like a transitional space between maintaining confidentiality and transparency or disclosure, a protected space that didn't need to be one thing or the other . . . Sharing this I think was crucial in helping me not to rebound with an intrusive 'need to know'. . . and the shockwaves could be absorbed by you as well.

Example 2. Hope in the network

Another function of the supervision of psychotherapists who are working with severely traumatised children, is to try to help them to function positively within the network of professionals and parents/foster parents/adoptive parents. Together, this group of adults need to provide the best possible internal and external facilitating emotional environment within which the child or adolescent patient can try to root and grow, develop and recover. Indeed, when this network is not able to work together in a reasonably constructive way, aware of how easily the group dynamics in this professional group can be affected by the difficulties of the case, the patient–therapist couple may not be sufficiently contained and the psychoanalytic psychotherapy may be ill advised. When this happens, the network is unconsciously much more likely to act out the conflicts of the child patient and become full of defences and splits, rather than to contain and manage them (Menzies Lyth 1979). Here follows another example from the supervision of a child in the first few months of therapy.

Brief history: The patient was an 8-year-old girl, growing up within a violent inner city area in the north of England. Her mother, whilst still in many ways a part of this culture, authentically wanted better for her daughter Stella, and, having sought help from CAMHS, made such a strong and trusting relationship with the parent worker, that the parent worker felt that it was worth trying to see if psychotherapy could help Stella. Possibly the influence of their nurturing church community had (to quote the supervisee) contributed to 'the hopeful qualities' in the mother and child. Mother bought Stella reliably for her sessions and made good use of her own weekly sessions. Because of the problems of abuse and violence in the extended family and local culture, there was considerable doubt in my mind about whether the mother and daughter would be able to change if they remained within the social environment they currently lived in, but the parent worker felt that the mother had a very strong commitment to trying to change and really wanted help. The multi-disciplinary team at the clinic was very used to working with families like this and the family were not known to social services.

Clinical material: From the start of treatment this supervisee, who had many years of clinical experience, was clear that Stella took her way outside her comfort zone and that her countertransference experience was very hard to manage in a tolerant and non-retaliatory way. Stella was aggressively controlling and contemptuous of her in ways that really got under her skin and made her feel humiliated and ridiculous. Stella intruded into her personal space in ways she found disturbing and deeply disrespectful. However, Stella always came to therapy (to quote the therapist) '. . . with "hopeful intent", stuck to therapy from the very first day, and did not flee from it'. At times Stella would completely refuse to leave the room at the end of the session, managing on one memorable occasion to extend the session by 20 minutes. In addition, Stella sometimes soiled herself during the sessions which was particularly difficult to manage when she was also displaying herself in sexually provocative ways. All of this in a little girl who dressed like a seductive woman.

The supervisee brought up a session that she had been unable to write up. As already indicated, I find this is often a pointer to undigestible aspects of the transference relationship. However, because of this, we do not have detailed process notes, though I did take my own notes during the supervision that I have checked out since with the supervisee for accuracy.

> From the start of the session Stella was loud, aggressive and verbally abusive to the therapist, who felt she could not be heard, and had no voice. Stella had possibly wet her pants a bit before she even got into the room and must have displayed herself so that the therapist could see that her pants and tights were a bit wet. Then, to the therapist's horror, she started to strip off in a highly seductive way and the therapist felt panicked by what she was doing. Whilst noting her panicky feelings, the therapist said very firmly to Stella that she should not remove her clothes. Stella stopped, but then started to wail loudly for several minutes saying 'It's all your fault!', in a manic almost 'possessed' way. The therapist felt shocked and drawn into what she called 'an unbounaried space'. It was as if when the therapist did not admire her or become seduced by her, Stella was thrown into a completely desolate, rejected and abandoned place. By this point in the session Stella didn't seem to recognise who the therapist was and had become completely out of control. The supervisee felt it was as if she was with someone who was mad.

Supervisory process: Whilst feeling very sad for Stella and whatever she had experienced and was enacting, the supervisee also felt very angry with her unrelenting, extreme denigration of her. We were able to discuss the impact of Stella's powerful projections of panic, shock and helplessness into the therapist and her feeling that she was unable to defend herself from her onslaught. We were also able to think about how angry this experienced therapist felt with Stella's extreme contemptuousness of her and I was aware throughout the supervision that she was really struggling with her anger and wish to retaliate, but finding it very hard to talk about this. This supervisee and I had not been working together for very long and were still establishing the supervisory relationship. Whilst we discussed the clinical material, I found myself wondering whether she might feel ashamed to expose the full extent of her angry feelings and wondered if I could help her to say more. So I was relieved when, at the very end of the supervision, I think after I had prompted her by asking what she would really have liked to say to Stella, she spontaneously and angrily replied 'I wanted to say "Don't waste my time!"' This was in response to her sense of hopelessness and futility in trying to help a patient who was so determinedly contemptuous of her. She explained to me that she felt that there were many other children on the clinic's waiting list who could make much better use of her time and the clinic was under enormous pressure because of the long waiting list for treatment.

In response to her comments, I recall I said something like: 'Now I think we are getting somewhere. What you have just said is really important'. In truth I was not entirely sure in what way it was important, but I did know that the supervisee's spontaneity and honesty were a great relief and broke a tension. In retrospect, I think this was a moment of despair as well as a moment-of-meeting in the supervision, where the supervisee expressed her own hopelessness about her ability to help the patient. Expressing these feelings was a considerable risk for her so early on in the supervisory relationship, as she was exposing feelings to me that made her feel vulnerable and somewhat ashamed. But this was also, paradoxically, a turning point in her countertransference response to Stella and helped her to find a way forward in the therapy. Possibly the issues of honesty and truth, which were inevitably significant issues for this child from a gang culture background, were played out and faced in the supervision when the supervisee was able to say what she really felt. In addition, it is possible that exposing her own raw feelings, in the way that Stella had when she enacted being sexually seductive and then feeling horribly rejected, helped the therapist to understand Stella's dilemmas better.

When the supervisee read an earlier draft of this paper, she added that she had remembered that when Stella started to remove her top, her head may have got stuck in it, or she may even have wanted to cover her eyes. She now found herself wondering whether at the time Stella may have dimly felt a sense of shame in what she was doing, which was in the therapist's words 'an indicator of something Stella herself was not comfortable with at some level, and maybe in that lies the hope for change'. Again, it is interesting to note how the supervisee's feelings of shame, that I had wondered about during the main part of the supervision, may also have been a reflection of Stella's feelings of shame about her sexually seductive behaviour. All of this of course is much easier to detect in hindsight than whilst the events unfolded.

The supervisee's ability to express these feelings, led to a discussion with the parent worker about the suitability of the case for psychotherapy, which in turn lead to the case being discussed in the multi-disciplinary team meeting and then to it being discussed in a regular meeting between senior CAMHS clinicians and Social Services. From this point onwards, the supervisee's anxiety became more contained, and she felt less helpless and overwhelmed. Indeed, she felt empowered by the fact that by managing to voice her concerns to the parent worker, she had prompted appropriate action in the professionals' network.

Interestingly in the meanwhile, and somewhat to the supervisee's surprise, the extreme sexual seductiveness within the sessions did not return and Stella started to show more respect for the boundaries that the therapist was trying to establish. However she remained extremely contemptuous and denigrating of the therapist. Nevertheless, it was also slowly possible for the therapist to gradually recognise the defensive function of her awful behaviour as reflecting Stella's extreme fear of being alone in a room with an adult whom she automatically assumed would be abusive. This helped the therapist to tolerate Stella's behaviour a little bit more. The therapist's natural ability to keep ordinary parental boundaries firmly and in a matter of fact way was a very helpful experience for Stella and she started to have calmer times in the sessions and to co-operate over using the toilet and changing her clothing when she had wet or soiled herself. At times she started to play more like an ordinary little girl and she clearly began to feel safer in the room. She also started to be able to leave the sessions on time and was able to accept interpretations about an increased sense of being safe in the room with her therapist. These were surprisingly rapid and genuine changes – which confirmed the parent-worker's initial conviction that this was a mother and daughter who were very open to change. The changes helped the therapist to feel more hopeful that she might be able to help Stella after all. Stella was not 'wasting her time' and the network of professionals were able to do helpful supportive safeguarding work around the family.

Impressively, six weeks after the shocking session described above, the supervisee was able to say that she was much less annoyed by Stella and was feeling more relaxed and less on her guard when with her. This was despite her soiling having become more regular during the sessions. Stella was clearly a very troubled little girl, and at times a troubled soiling baby, but she was now able to trust her therapist more, and to allow her therapist to take a parental role when necessary in the sessions. The seductive behaviour had almost disappeared, and when I asked the therapist how she felt about Stella now, once more to her surprise, she realised that she felt that she liked her, felt protective of her and that the psychotherapy was established and moving on.

Transforming despair to hope

In the context of this paper, how can we understand the change from the supervisee feeling utterly despairing about her ability to help Stella, and her feeling some weeks later that she was now able to be more relaxed with her – as indeed she clearly was with the therapist – and that maybe this child was not wasting her therapy time after all? The buffering of the shock waves of the counter-transference experience within the supervisory space is similar to the previous example. This enabled the supervisee to make good use of her counter-transference and to see behind her patient's desperate defences.

Maybe the moment of hope arises when someone who desperately needs help dares to cry out to someone who is prepared to try to give that help. Stella's mother had made what sounded like an unusually powerful connection with the parent worker, who had been able to hear her cry for help. However terrible the traumatic experiences may be, if someone is able to listen to and hear that cry, there is, paradoxically, a moment of hope, trust and meeting with another human being, which can become a turning point.

The supervisee, by expressing her true feelings about this patient in supervision, also then felt empowered and less helpless, and was able to engage me in helping her with a very worrying case, as well as becoming able to engage the whole professional network in an appropriate way so that they could do whatever was possible to help Stella and her mother. Via this route, hope was expressed in the network, which could then properly start to work as effectively as it could to protect and help Stella and her mother. This can be understood as the 'primary task' of this group of adults so that they can then become focused on the needs of the child, in the way that Menzies Lyth describes in which the capacity to attend to the primary task is understood as being a core aspect of the health of any organisation or group (Menzies Lyth 1979).

I am left wondering whether there is something about the kind of crisis that can arise in the patient–therapist couple when trauma shock waves flow that requires a different kind of containment to the containment of other feelings – such as emptiness, loneliness and anger. Is it particularly difficult for the therapist, on his or her own, to process shock waves, which by their very nature will present themselves as a shock rather than as an ache? In some respects, it is when the patient and the therapist have touched the depths of despair during a crisis that they potentially become able to see the dawn of hope. This is different from the steadfastness in the countertransference that is needed to keep on bearing – to use the examples above – emptiness, loneliness and anger in the counter-transference.

Any crisis also contains the seeds of a turning point for the better, or of course the worse. It might be that both supervisees, by bringing the crisis so clearly to supervision, were able to avoid becoming more defended to their patient's communications because they engaged in the supervisory process so fully, and as a result were able to use the crisis as a positive turning point in the therapy.

Within the supervisory process, something similar is going on when there is a moment-of-meeting, such as those described in my examples. The supervisee in each instance, whilst expressing very different feelings, was reaching out for help and I was trying to respond. These moments are intrinsically moments of hope – hope that through 'satisfactory human contact' something might change –

something that antidotes the 'disorder of hope' that is such a dire consequence of traumatic experience.

Fromm notes that one of the outcomes of the shattering of hope can be a 'hardening of the heart' of the individual. However he also notes that:

> Not so rarely, a miracle happens and a thaw begins. It may simply be that they meet a person in whose concern and interest they believe, and new dimensions of feeling open. If they are lucky, they unfreeze completely and the seeds of hope that seem to have been destroyed altogether come to life.
>
> (Fromm 1968/1970/2010: 33)

Appendix
Publications

1985 'Surviving trauma – dilemmas in the psychotherapy of traumatized children'. *British Journal of Psychotherapy* 2(1): 55–62, and *Bulletin of the British Association of Psychotherapists*.

'Divorce: a child's eye view'. In *In the Best Interests of the Child?* Report published by the Scottish Family Conciliation Service.

1986 'The child in the family today – the effect of parental attitudes and problems on children' in *Children in Today's Society*. Report on the Scottish Children's Panel Summer School.

1987 'A-symbolic and symbolic play: developmental perspectives in the treatment of disturbed children'. *Journal of Child Psychotherapy* 13(2): 33–44.

1988 'Working with anxiety in a residential special primary school'. *Maladjustment and Therapeutic Education* 6(1): 36–48.

1989 'United we stand . . .? Stress in residential work with disturbed children'. *Maladjustment and Therapeutic Education* 7(3): 136–146.

'Variations on a theme of transference and counter-transference'. *Journal of Child Psychotherapy* 15(2): 85–102.

1991 'Putting theory into practice: working with perversion and chaos in the analytic process'. *Journal of Child Psychotherapy* 17(1): 25–40.

'On creating a psychotherapeutic space'. *Journal of Social Work Practice* 5(1): 31–40.

1993 'Stress – an occupational hazard of working with disturbed children'. *Educational Therapy and Therapeutic Teaching* 1(2): 23–38.

1994 '"In the beginning" – Observations of newborn babies and their families'. *Journal of the British Association of Psychotherapists* 26: 3–21.

Review of *Pregnancy. The Inside Story* by Joan Raphael-Leff. *International Journal of Psycho-Analysis* 75(4): 127–131.

Hodges, J., Lanyado, M., and Andreou, C. 'Sexuality and violence: preliminary clinical hypotheses from the psychotherapeutic assessments in a research programme on young sexual offenders'. *Journal of Child Psychotherapy* 20(3): 283–308.

1995   Lanyado, M., Hodges, J., Bentovim, A., Andreou, C., and Williams, B. 'Understanding boys who sexually abuse other children: a clinical illustration'. *Psychoanalytic Psychotherapy* 9(3): 231–242.

Review of *Treating Survivors of Satanist Abuse* by Valerie Sinason (ed.). *Journal of Child Psychotherapy* 21(1): 127–131.

Review of *Francis Tustin. Makers of Modern Psychotherapy* by Sheila Spensley. *Psychoanalytic Psychotherapy* 9(3).

1996   'Winnicott's Children: the holding environment and therapeutic communication in brief and non-intensive work'. *Journal of Child Psychotherapy* 22(3): 423–443.

1997   'Memories in the making: the experience of moving from fostering to adoption for a five year old boy'. *Journal of the British Association of Psychotherapists* December: 3–18.

Review of *Postpartum Depression and Child Development* by L. Murray and P. J. Cooper (eds). *Infant Observation* 2(1).

Hodges, J., Williams, B., Andreou, C., Lanyado, M., Bentovim, A., and Skuse, D. 'Children who sexually abuse other children'. In The Right Honourable Justice Wall (ed.). *Rooted Sorrows: Psychoanalytic Perspectives on Child Protection, Assessment, Therapy and Treatment.* Bristol: Family Law, Jordan Publishing: 120–129.

Skuse, D., Bentovim, A., Hodges, J., Stevenson, J., Andreou, C., Lanyado, M., Williams, B., New, M., and McMillan, D. *The Influence of Early Experience of Sexual Abuse on the Formation of Sexual Preferences During Adolescence.* Report commissioned by the Department of Health. Behavioural Sciences Unit, Institute of Child Health, London.

1998   Skuse, D., Bentovim, A., Hodges, J., Stevenson, J., Andreou, C., Lanyado, M., New, M., Williams, B., and McMillan, D. 'Risk factors for development of sexually abusive behaviour in sexually victimised adolescent boys: cross sectional study'. *British Medical Journal* 317: 175.

1999   'Holding and letting go: some thoughts about the process of ending therapy' (1999 and 2001). *Journal of Child Psychotherapy* 25(3): 357–378 and *Kinderanalyse* 2/2001: 357–378.

'"It's just an ordinary pain": thoughts on joy and heartache in puberty and early adolescence'. Chap. 9 in D. Hindle and M. Smith (eds). *Personality Development: A Psychoanalytic Perspective.* London: Routledge: 92–115.

Lanyado, M., and Horne, A. (eds). *The Handbook of Child and Adolescent Psychotherapy. Psychoanalytic Approaches.* London: Routledge. Italian translation published in 2003, Czech translation published 2004.

Horne, A., and Lanyado, M. 'Introduction'. Chap. 1 in ibid. 1–16.

Lanyado, M., and Horne, A., 'The therapeutic relationship and process'. Chap. 5 in ibid. 56–72.

'Brief psychotherapy and therapeutic consultations: how much therapy is good enough?' Chap. 16 in ibid. 233–246.

'The treatment of traumatisation in children'. Chap. 19 in ibid. 275–291.

Edwards, E., and Lanyado, M., 'Autism: clinical and theoretical issues'. Chap. 27 in ibid. 429–444.

Review of *The Language of Winnicott. A Dictionary of Winnicott's Use of Words* by J. Abrams. *Journal of Child Psychotherapy* 25(1).

Review of *A History of Child Psychoanalysis* by C. Geissman and P. Geissman. *Clinical Child Psychology and Psychiatry* 4(4): 612–614.

2000 'Fenomeni transizionali e cambiamento psichico: Riflessioni sul ruolo del transfert e della relazione "attuale" nel passagio dall affidamento all adozione'. ('Transitional phenomena and psychic change: the role of transference and the new relationship as seen in the therapy of children moving from fostering to adoption') Richard e Piggle. *Studi psicoanalitici del bambino e dell adolescente.* 8(3): 283–293.

2001 'Daring to try again: the hope and pain of forming new attachments'. *Therapeutic Communities* 22(1): 5–18.

'The symbolism of the story of Lot and his wife: the function of the "present relationship" and non-interpretative aspects of the therapeutic relationship in facilitating change'. *Journal of Child Psychotherapy* 27(1): 19–33.

Letter to the Editors: 'Transition and change: a response to commentaries on The symbolism of the story of Lot and his wife'. *Journal of Child Psychotherapy* 27(2): 226–230.

2002 'Creating transitions in the lives of children suffering from "multiple traumatic loss"'. In L. Caldwell (ed.). *The Elusive Child.* London: Karnac: 93–112.

2003 'The emotional tasks of moving from fostering to adoption: transitions, attachment, separation and loss'. *Clinical Child Psychology and Psychiatry* (Special Edition on Fostering and Adoption) 8(3): 337–349.

'The roots of mental health: emotional development and the caring Environment'. Chap. 4 in J. Pooley, A. Ward, K. Kasinski, and A. Worthington (eds). *Therapeutic Communities for Children and Young People.* London: Jessica Kingsley: 65–81.

Review of *Being Alive: Building on the Work of Anne Alvarez.* Judith Edwards (ed.). *YoungMinds Magazine* 63 (Mar/Apr 2003).

2004   *The Presence of the Therapist. Treating Childhood Trauma.* London: Brunner-Routledge. Finnish translation.

'Psychoterapie deti v dobe prechodu z pestounske pece do adopce: technicke otazky.' *Revue Psychoanalyticka Psychoterapie* V(1): 23–34.

2006   Lanyado, M., and Horne, A. (eds). *A Question of Technique.* Independent Psychoanalytic Approaches with Children and Adolescents Series. London: Routledge.

Lanyado, M., and Horne, A., (eds). 'The context'. Chap. 1 in ibid. 1–9.

'The playful presence of the therapist: "antidoting" defences in the therapy of a late adopted adolescent patient'. Chap. 8 in ibid. 130–148.

'Doing "something else": the value of therapeutic communication when offering consultations and brief psychotherapy'. Chap. 12 in ibid. 203–223.

Lanyado, M. and Horne, A. 'Conclusion: where independent minds meet'. Chap. 14 in ibid. 239–238.

'Clinical commentary'. *Journal of Child Psychotherapy* 33(1): 94–107.

'Psykoterapeutyrket – balansen mellan arbete och privatliv' (interview about the balance of personal and professional lives of psychotherapists), interview and translation by Britta Blomberg for *Mellanrummet* No. 15: 97–110.

2007   'Speelse aanwezigheid van de therapeut: "tegengif" voor de defensies van een geadopteerde adolescente in therapie'. In Nicole Vleigen and Lieve Van Lier (eds). *Een Spel Voor Twee Spelers.* Leuven/Leusden: Acco.

2008   'Session with Peter and discussion'. *Mellanrummet* No. 18.

'Playing out not acting out: the development of the capacity to play in the therapy of children who are "in transition" from fostering to adoption'. Chap. 9 in D. Hindle and G. Shulman (eds). *The Emotional Experience of Adoption. A Psychoanalytic Perspective.* London and New York: Routledge.

Corner, L., Hinshelwood, B., Agulnik, P., Flynn, D., Motz, A., Welldon, E., Nuemann, J. E., and Lanyado, M. 'Tribute to Isabel Menzies Lyth 1917–2008'. *British Journal of Psychotherapy* 24(4).

'Preface' in E. Cleve. *A Big One and A Little One is Gone*. London: Karnac: xv–xvii.

'"Dwelling in the present moment": An exploration of the resonances between transitional experiences and meditative states'. *Psychoanalytic Perspectives* 5(2): 69–85.

2009   Horne, A. and Lanyado, M. (eds). *Through Assessment to Consultation*. Independent Psychoanalytic Approaches with Children and Adolescents Series. London and New York: Routledge.

Horne, A., and Lanyado, M. 'Introduction: "appropriate to the occasion"'. Chap. 1 in ibid. 1–7.

'The impact of listening on the listener: consultation to the helping professions who work with sexually abused young people'. Chap. 11 in ibid. 141–156.

Lanyado, M., and Horne, A. (eds). *The Handbook of Child and Adolescent Psychotherapy: Psychoanalytic Approaches*, 2nd edn. London and New York: Routledge. Translated into Japanese 2013.

Horne, A., and Lanyado, M. 'Introduction'. Chap. 1 in ibid. 1–12.

Lanyado, M., and Horne, A. 'The therapeutic setting and process'. Chap. 10 in ibid. 157–174.

'Brief psychotherapy and therapeutic consultations: how much therapy is "good-enough"'. Chap. 12 in ibid. 191–205.

'Psychotherapy with severely traumatized children and adolescents: "Far beyond words"'. Chap. 20 in ibid. 300–315.

2010   'Psychoterapie deti v dobe prechodu z pestounske pece do adopce'. *Revue Psychoanalytcicka Psychoterapie* X(111): 28–41.

'Transformation through play: living with the traumas of the past'. Chap. 1 in K.V. Mortensen and L. Grunbaum (eds). *Play and Power*. London: Karnac.

'Avslutningar – overgang och forandring' (interview about endings in psychotherapy), interview and translation by Britta Blomberg for *Mellanrummet* No. 23: 93–104.

2012   Horne, A., and Lanyado, M. (eds). *Winnicott's Children*. Independent Psychoanalytic Approaches with Children and Adolescents Series. Hove, UK and New York: Routledge. Published in German 2016, Frankfurt a. M.: Brandes and Apsel.

Horne, A. and Lanyado, M. 'Introduction'. In ibid. xxiii.

'What is therapeutic about communication?'. Chap. 2 in ibid. 25–40.

'Transition and change: an exploration of the resonances between transitional phenomena and meditative states'. Chap. 8 in ibid. 123–139.

2014   'The value of meditative states of mind in the therapist'. Chap. 11 in M. Bazzano (ed.). *After Mindfulness.* Basingstoke, UK: Palgrave Macmillan: 148–162.

'The presence of the therapist'. Chap. 5 in M. Pozzi (ed.). *The Buddha and the Baby.* London: Karnac: 53–65.

Foreword in K. Cullen, L. Bondi, J. Fewell, E. Francis, and M. Ludlum (eds). *Making Spaces: Putting Psychoanalytic Thinking to Work.* London: Karnac.

Clinical commentary. *Journal of Child Psychotherapy* 40(2): 214–217.

2015   Horne, A., and Lanyado, M. (eds). *An Independent Mind: Collected Papers of Juliet Hopkins.* Independent Approaches with Children and Adolescents Series. Hove, UK and New York: Routledge.

'Trauma and child psychotherapy: introduction'. In ibid. 1–3.

'Integrating and exploring Winnicott: introduction'. In ibid. 119–121.

2016   'Transforming despair to hope in the treatment of extreme trauma: a view from the supervisor's chair'. *Journal of Child Psychotherapy* 42(2): 107–121.

2017   'Putting down roots: the significance of technical adaptations in the therapeutic process with fostered and adopted patients'. *Journal of Child Psychotherapy.*

References

Abram, J. (1996) *The Language of Winnicott. A Dictionary of Winnicott's Use of Words.* London: Karnac.

Ainsworth, M. (1982) 'Attachment: retrospect and prospect'. In C. M. Parkes and J. Stevenson-Hinde (eds). *The Place of Attachment in Human Behaviour.* London: Tavistock.

Ainsworth, M. D., Behar, M. C., Waters, E., and Wall, S. (1978) *Patterns of Attachment: Assessed in the Strange Situation and at Home.* Hillsdale, NJ: Lawrence Erlbaum.

Alvarez, A. (1992) 'Child sexual abuse. The need to remember and the need to forget'. Chap. 12 in A. Alvarez. *Live Company. Psychoanalytic Psychotherapy with Autistic, Borderline, Deprived and Abused Children.* London and New York: Tavistock/Routledge.

Alvarez, A. (2000) 'Moral imperatives in work with borderline children: the grammar of wishes and the grammar of needs'. In J. Symington (ed.). *Imprisoned Pain and its Transformation: A Festschrift for H. Sidney Klein.* London: Karnac: 5–20.

Alvarez, A. (2012) *The Thinking Heart. Three Levels of Psychoanalytic Therapy with Disturbed Children.* London and New York: Routledge.

Anthony, A. (2009) 'Baby P: born into a nightmare of abuse, violence and despair, he never stood a chance'. *The Observer*, 16 August 2009.

Attenborough, D. (2011) *Frozen Planet.* BBC Television Documentary Series.

Attenborough, D. (2016) *Planet Earth II.* BBC Television Documentary Series.

Bacciagaluppi, M. (2012a) *Paradigms in Psychoanalysis. An Integration.* London: Karnac.

Bacciagaluppi, M. (2012b) 'Trauma'. Chap. 5 in *Paradigms in Psychoanalysis. An Integration.* London: Karnac: 77–117.

Bailey, T. (2006) 'There's no such thing as an adolescent'. Chap. 11 in M. Lanyado and A. Horne (eds). *A Question of Technique.* Independent Psychoanalytic Approaches with Children and Adolescent Series. London and New York: Routledge: 180–199.

Balint, M. (1968) *The Basic Fault.* London: Tavistock.

Baradon, T. (2010) 'Epilogue – "Ghosts and angels in the nursery": windows of opportunity and remaining vulnerability'. Chap. 13 in T. Baradon (ed.). *Relational Trauma in Infancy. Psychoanalytic, Attachment and Neuropsychological Contributions to Parent–Infant Psychotherapy.* London and New York: Routledge: 209–219.

Barnes, J. (2013) *Levels of Life.* London: Jonathan Cape.

Bartram, P. (2003) 'Some oedipal problems in work with adopted children and their parents'. *Journal of Child Psychotherapy* 29(1): 21–36.

Batty, D. (2004) 'Timeline: the history of child protection' in *The Guardian*, 23 April 2004.

Bazzano, M. (2014) *After Mindfulness.* Basingstoke, UK: Palgrave Macmillan.

Bion, W. R. (1961) *Experiences in Groups.* London: Tavistock.

Bion, W. R. (1962) *Learning from Experience*. London: Heinemann.

Bion, W. R. (1970) *Attention and Interpretation*. London: Tavistock.

Bion, W. R. (1980) *Bion in New York and São Paulo*. Strath Tay, UK: Clunie Press.

Black, D. M. (ed.) (2006) *Psychoanalysis and Religion in the 21st Century: Competitors or Collaborators?* London: Routledge.

Black, D. M. (2011) *Why Things Matter: The Place of Values in Science, Psychoanalysis and Religion*. London and New York: Routledge.

Bomford, R. (2006) 'A simple question?' In D. M. Black (ed.). *Psychoanalysis and Religion in the 21st Century: Competitors or Collaborators?* London: Routledge.

Bollas, C. (1995) *Cracking Up*. London and New York: Routledge.

Boston, M., and Szur, R. (eds) (1983) *Psychotherapy with Severely Deprived Children*. London: Routledge and Kegan Paul.

Boswell, S., and Cudmore, L. (2017) 'Understanding the "blind spot" when children move from foster care to adoption'. *Journal of Child Psychotherapy* 43(2).

Bowcott, O. (2017) 'We need to rethink adoption in the social media age, says senior judge'. www.theguardian.com/society/2017/mar/09/we-need-to-rethink-adoption-in-the-social-media-age-says-senior-judge. 9 March.

Bowlby, J. (1944) 'Forty-four juvenile thieves: their characters and home life'. *International Journal of Psychoanalysis* 25: 1–57.

Bowlby, J. (1951) *Maternal care and Mental Health*. World Health Organisation, Monograph Series No. 2.

Bowlby, J. (1953) *Child Care and the Growth of Love*. Harmondsworth, UK: Penguin.

Bowlby, J. (1969) *Attachment and Loss* (Vol. 1). London: Hogarth Press and the Institute of Psychoanalysis.

Bowlby, J. (1973) *Attachment and Loss* (Vol. 2). London: Hogarth Press and the Institute of Psychoanalysis.

Bowlby, J. (1979) *The Making and Breaking of Affectional Bonds*. London and New York: Tavistock Publications and Routledge.

Bowlby, J. (1980) *Attachment and Loss* (Vol. 3). London: Hogarth Press and the Institute of Psychoanalysis.

Bowlby, J. (1988a) *A Secure Base. Clinical Applications of Attachment Theory*. London: Routledge.

Bowlby, J. (1988b) 'The origins of attachment theory'. Chap. 2 in *A Secure Base. Clinical Applications of Attachment Theory*. London: Routledge: 20–38.

Bowlby, J. (1988c) 'On knowing what you are not supposed to know and feeling what you are not supposed to feel'. Chap. 6 in *A Secure Base. Clinical Applications of Attachment Theory*. London: Routledge: 99–118.

Buber, M. (1937) *I and Thou*. London: Continuum.

Caldwell, L., and Joyce, A. (eds) (2011) *Reading Winnicott*. New Library of Psychoanalysis, Teaching Series. London and New York: Routledge.

Canham, H. (2003) 'The relevance of the Oedipus myth to fostered and adopted children'. *Journal of Child Psychotherapy* 29(1): 5–19.

Canham, H. (2004) 'Spitting, kicking and stripping: technical difficulties encountered in the treatment of deprived children'. *Journal of Child Psychotherapy* 30(1): 143–154.

Cant, D. (2005) '"Only connect" – a sexually abused girl's re-discovery of memory and meaning as she works towards the transition from a therapeutic community to a foster home'. *Journal of Child Psychotherapy* 31(1): 6–23.

Cant, D. (2008) 'The Birthday Boys: issues of time and timing in the tale of two therapies with two adolescent boys'. *Journal of Child Psychotherapy* 34(2): 207–221.

Carlberg, G. (1997) 'Laughter opens the door: turning points in child psychotherapy'. *Journal of Child Psychotherapy* 23(3): 331–349.

Casement, P. (1985) *On Learning from the Patient*. London and New York: Tavistock Publications.

Casement, P. (2002) *Learning from our Mistakes: Beyond Dogma in Psychoanalysis and Psychotherapy*. Hove, UK: Brunner-Routledge.

Cassidy, J., and Shaver P. R. (eds) (1999) *Handbook of Attachment. Theory, Research and Clinical Applications*. London and New York: Guilford Press.

Chasseguet-Smirgel, J. (1985) 'Perversion and the universal law'. Chap. 1 in J. Chasseguet-Smirgel. *Creativity and Perversion*. London: Free Association Books.

Cleve, E. (2002) *A Big One and a Little One is Gone. Crisis Therapy with a Two Year Old Boy*. London: Karnac.

Coltart, N. (1992) *Slouching towards Bethlehem . . . And Further Psychoanalytic Explanations*. London and New York: Free Association Press and Guilford Press.

Coltart, N. (1993) *How to Survive as a Psychotherapist*. London: Sheldon Press.

Coltart, N. (1996a) 'Endings'. Chap. 9 in N. Coltart *The Baby and the Bathwater*. London: Karnac: 141–154.

Coltart, N. (1996b) 'Buddhism and psychoanalysis revisited'. Chap. 6 in N. Coltart *The Baby and the Bathwater*. London: Karnac: 125–140.

Concise Oxford Dictionary (1990) Oxford: Clarendon Press.

Cregeen, S. (2017) 'A place within the heart: finding a home with parental objects'. *Journal of Child Psychotherapy* 43(2), 159–174.

Cunningham, M. (2006) 'Vedanta and psychoanalysis'. In D. M. Black (ed.). *Psychoanalysis and Religion in the 21st Century: Competitors or Collaborators?* London: Routledge.

Davidson, R. J., Kabat-Zinn, J., Schumacher, J., Rosenkranz, M., Muller, D., Santorelli, S. F., Urbanowski, F., Harrington, A., Bonus, K., and Sheridan, J. F. (2003) 'Alterations in brain and immune function produced by mindfulness meditation'. *Psychosomatic Medicine* (65): 564–570.

Daws, D. (1999) 'Brief psychotherapy with infants and their parents'. Chap. 18 in M. Lanyado and A. Horne (eds). *The Handbook of Child and Adolescent Psychotherapy. Psychoanalytic Approaches*. 1st edn. London and New York: Routledge: 261–272.

Daws, D., and de Rementeria, A. (2015) *Finding Your Way to your Baby. The Emotional Life of Parents and Infants*. London and New York: Routledge.

Delap, L. (2015) Policy Papers. Child welfare, child protection and sexual abuse, 1918–1990. *History and Policy* 30 July 2015.

Diamond, J. (2015) 'Reflections on the evolution of the Mulberry Bush School and Organisation 1948–2015'. July 2015. www.goodenoughcaring.com

Dickens, C. (1837) *Oliver Twist*.

Didion, J. (2005) *The Year of Magical Thinking*. London: Fourth Estate.

Dockar-Drysdale, B. (1963) *Consultation in Child Care*. London: Longman.

Dockar-Drysdale, B. (1968) *Therapy in Child Care*. London: Longman.

Dockar-Drysdale, B. (1990) *The Provision of Primary Experience: Winnicottian Work with Children and Adolescents*. London: Free Association Books.

Dowling, D. (2006) '"The capacity to be alone": rediscovering Winnicott and his relevance to parent–infant psychotherapy'. Chap. 4 in M. Lanyado and A. Horne (eds). *A Question of Technique*. Independent Psychoanalytic Approaches with Children and Adolescents Series. Hove, UK and New York: Routledge: 63–80.

Dowling, D. (2009) 'Thinking aloud: a child psychotherapist assessing families for court'. Chap. 3 in A. Horne and M. Lanyado (eds). *Through Assessment to Consultation*.

Independent Psychoanalytic Approaches with Children and Adolescents Series. London and New York: Routledge: 9–25.

Dowling, D. (2012) 'Hate in the counter-transference: Winnicott's contribution to our understanding of hatred in our work as child psychotherapists'. Chap. 5 in A. Horne and M. Lanyado (eds). *Winnicott's Children.* Independent Psychoanalytic Approaches with Children and Adolescent Series. Hove, UK and New York: Routledge: 77–87.

Edgecombe, R. (2000) *Anna Freud: A View of Development, Disturbance and Therapeutic Technique.* London: Routledge.

Edwards, J. (2000) 'On being dropped and picked up: adopted children and their internal objects'. *Journal of Child Psychotherapy* 26(3): 349–369.

Eigen, M. (2008) 'Primary aloneness'. *Psychoanalytic Perspectives* 5(2): 63–68.

Epstein, M. (1995) *Thoughts without a Thinker.* New York: Basic Books.

Epstein, M. (2001) *Going on Being: Buddhism and the Way of Change, a Positive Psychology for the West.* New York: Broadway Books.

Epstein, M. (2006) 'The structure of no structure: Winnicott's concept of unintegration and the Buddhist notion of no-self'. In D. M. Black (ed.). *Psychoanalysis and Religion in the 21st Century: Competitors or Collaborators?* London: Routledge.

Fraiberg, S., Adelson, E., and Shapiro, V. (1980) 'Ghosts in the nursery: a psychoanalytic approach'. In S. Fraiberg (ed.). *Clinical Studies in Infant Mental Health. The First Year of Life.* London: Tavistock: 164–196.

Fransman, T. (2002) Personal Communication.

Freud, S. (1905) *Jokes and their Relation to the Unconscious,* Volume 8 of *The Standard Edition of the Complete Psychological Works of Sigmund Freud* (1956–1974). London: Hogarth Press and Institute of Psycho-Analysis.

Freud, S. (1913) *Totem and Taboo,* Volume 12 of *The Standard Edition of the Complete Psychological Works of Sigmund Freud* (1956–1974). London: Hogarth Press and Institute of Psycho-Analysis: 121–144.

Freud, S. (1914) *Remembering, Repeating and Working Through,* Volume 12 of *The Standard Edition of the Complete Psychological Works of Sigmund Freud* (1956–1974). London: Hogarth Press and Institute of Psycho-Analysis: 145–156.

Freud, S. (1917) *Mourning and Melancholia,* Volume 14 of *The Standard Edition of the Complete Psychological Works of Sigmund Freud* (1956–1974). London: Hogarth Press and Institute of Psycho-Analysis: 243–258.

Freud, S. and Breuer, J. (1895) *Studies on Hysteria,* Volume 2 of *The Standard Edition of the Complete Psychological Works of Sigmund Freud* (1956–1974). London: Hogarth Press and Institute of Psycho-Analysis.

Freud, A., and Burlingham, D. (1944) *Infants without Families: The Case for and against Residential Nurseries.* New York: International Universities Press.

Fromm, E. (1968/1970/2010) *The Revolution of Hope: Toward a Humanised Technology.* New York: Harper and Row (1968 and 1970), and New York: American Mental Health Foundation (2010).

Frosch, S. (2006) 'Psychoanalysis and Judaism'. In D. M. Black (ed.). *Psychoanalysis and Religion in the 21st Century: Competitors or Collaborators?* London: Routledge.

Furman, E. (1974) *A Child's Parent Dies: Studies in Childhood Bereavement.* New Haven, CT: Yale University Press.

Gerhardt, S. (2004a) *Why Love Matters. How Affection Shapes a Baby's Brain.* Hove, UK and New York: Brunner-Routledge.

Gerhardt, S. (2004b) 'Corrosive cortisol'. Chap. 3 in *Why Love Matters. How Affection Shapes a Baby's Brain.* Hove, UK and New York: Brunner-Routledge.

Gerhardt, S. (2004c) 'Building a brain'. Chap. 2 in *Why Love Matters. How Affection Shapes a Baby's Brain.* Hove, UK and New York: Brunner-Routledge.

Gibbs, I. (2006) 'A question of balance: working with the looked after child and his network'. Chap. 7 in M. Lanyado and A. Horne (eds). *A Question of Technique.* Hove, UK: Routledge: 115–129.

Glasser, M. (1979) 'Some aspects of the role of aggression in the perversions'. In I. Rosen (ed.). *Sexual Deviation,* 2nd edn. Oxford: Oxford University Press.

Glasser, M. (1998) 'On violence: a preliminary communication'. *International Journal of Psychoanalysis* 79(5): 887–902.

Goleman, D. (2003) *Destructive Emotions and How We Can Overcome Them: A Dialogue with The Dalai Lama Narrated by Daniel Goleman.* London: Bloomsbury.

Green, V. (1998) '"Donald": the treatment of a five year old boy with an experience of early loss'. Chap. 6 in A. Hurry (ed.). *Psychoanalysis and Developmental Therapy.* Psychoanalytic Monographs No 3. London: Karnac: 136–152.

Green, V. (2013) 'Grief in two guises: "Mourning and melancholia" revisited'. *Journal of Child Psychotherapy* 39(1): 76–89.

Hanh, T. N. (2005) *Being Peace.* Berkeley, CA: Parallax Press.

Helfer, R. E., and Kempe, C. H. (1968) *The Battered Child.* Chicago, IL and London: University of Chicago Press.

Henry, G. (1974) 'Doubly deprived'. *Journal of Child Psychotherapy* 4(2): 29–43.

Heimann, P. (1950) 'On counter-transference'. *International Journal of Psycho-Analysis* 31: 81–84.

Hesse, E., and Main, M. (1999) 'Second generation effects of trauma in non-maltreating parents: dissociated, frightening and threatening parental behaviour'. *Psychological Enquiry* 19: 481–540.

Hindle, D. (2000) 'The merman: recovering from early abuse and loss'. *Journal of Child Psychotherapy* 26(3): 369–391.

Hindle, D., and Shulman, G. (eds) (2008) *The Emotional Experience of Adoption. A Psychoanalytic Perspective.* Abingdon, UK and New York: Routledge.

Holmes, J. (1993) *John Bowlby and Attachment Theory. Makers of Modern Psychotherapy.* London and New York: Routledge.

Holmes, J. (2001a) 'Endings in psychotherapy'. Chap. 12 in J. Holmes. *The Search for the Secure Base. Attachment Theory and Psychotherapy.* Hove, UK and Philadelphia, PA: Brunner-Routledge: 130–143.

Holmes, J. (2001b) 'Attachment and the storied self'. Chap. 7 in J. Holmes. *The Search for the Secure Base. Attachment Theory and Psychotherapy.* Hove, UK and Philadelphia, PA: Brunner-Routledge: 65–79.

Holmes, J. (2001c) 'Attachment and narrative in psychotherapy'. Chap. 8 in J. Holmes. *The Search for the Secure Base. Attachment Theory and Psychotherapy.* Hove, UK and Philadelphia, PA: Brunner-Routledge: 80–94.

Hopkins, J. (1990/2015) 'The observed infant of attachment theory'. Chap. 4 in A. Horne and M. Lanyado (eds) *An Independent Mind. Collected Papers of Juliet Hopkins.* Hove, UK and New York: Routledge: 53–63.

Hopkins, J. (1994/2015) 'Infant-parent psychotherapy. Selma Fraiberg's contribution to understanding the past in the present'. Chap. 8 in A. Horne and M. Lanyado (eds). *An Independent Mind. Collected Papers of Juliet Hopkins.* Hove, UK and New York: Routledge: 97–106.

Hopkins, J. (1999/2015) 'Narcissistic illusions in late adolescence: defensive Kleinian retreats or Winnicottian opportunities?' *Psychoanalytic Inquiry* 19: 229–242; and

Chap. 12 in A. Horne and M. Lanyado (eds). *An Independent Mind. Collected Papers of Juliet Hopkins*. Hove, UK and New York: Routledge: 141–153.

Hopkins, J. (2000/2015) 'Overcoming a child's resistance to late adoption. How one new attachment can facilitate another'. *Journal of Child Psychotherapy* 26: 335–347; and Chap. 7 in A. Horne and M. Lanyado (eds). *An Independent Mind. Collected Papers of Juliet Hopkins*. London and New York: Routledge: 84–93.

Horne, A. (2001) 'Brief communications from the edge: psychotherapy with challenging adolescents'. *Journal of Child Psychotherapy* 27(1): 3–18.

Horne, A. (2003) 'Oedipal aspirations and phallic fears: on fetishism in childhood and young adulthood'. *Journal of Child Psychotherapy* 29(1): 37–52.

Horne, A. (2006) 'Interesting things to say – and why'. Chap. 13 in M. Lanyado and A. Horne (eds). *A Question of Technique*. Hove, UK and New York: Routledge: 224–238.

Horne, A. (2009) 'From intimacy to acting out: assessment and consultation about a dangerous child'. Chap. 9 in A. Horne and M. Lanyado (eds). *Through Assessment to Consultation*. Independent Psychoanalytic Approaches to Children and Adolescent Series. London and New York: Routledge: 110–124.

Horne, A. (2012) 'On delinquency'. Chap. 12 in A. Horne and M. Lanyado (eds). *Winnicott's Children*. Independent Psychoanalytic Approaches with Children and Adolescents Series. London and New York: Routledge: 186–202.

Horne, A. (2015) Conversation with Anne Horne, 15 May.

Horne, A., and Lanyado, M. (eds) (2009) *Through Assessment to Consultation*. Independent Psychoanalytic Approaches with Children and Adolescents Series. London and New York: Routledge.

Horne, A., and Lanyado, M. (eds) (2012) *Winnicott's Children*. Independent Psychoanalytic Approaches with Children and Adolescents Series. London and New York: Routledge.

Horne, A., and Lanyado, M. (eds) (2015) *An Independent Mind. Collected Papers of Juliet Hopkins*. Independent Psychoanalytic Approaches with Children and Adolescents Series. Hove, UK and New York: Routledge.

Hugo, V. (1862/1994) *Les Misérables*. K. Carabine (ed.). Ware, UK: Wordsworth Editions; translated by C. E. Wilbour.

Hunter, M. (2001) *Psychotherapy with Children in Care. Lost and Found*. Hove, UK and Philadelphia, PA: Brunner-Routledge.

Hurry, A. (1998) 'Psychoanalysis and developmental therapy'. Chap. 2 in A. Hurry (ed.). *Psychoanalysis and Developmental Therapy*. London: Karnac: 32–73.

Ironside, L. (2002) 'Living in a storm: an examination of the impact of deprivation and abuse on the psychotherapeutic process and the implications for clinical practice'. Unpublished PhD thesis: University of East London and Tavistock Clinic Library.

Ironside, L. (2004) 'Living a provisional existence: thinking about foster carers and the emotional containment of children placed in their care'. *Adoption and Fostering* 28(4): 39–49.

Ironside, L. (2009) 'Working with foster carers'. Chap. 22 in M. Lanyado and A. Horne (eds). *The Handbook of Child and Adolescent Psychotherapy. Psychoanalytic Approaches*, 2nd edn. Hove, UK and New York: Routledge: 328–338.

Jackson, E. (2002) 'Mental health in schools: what about the staff? Thinking about the impact of work discussion groups for staff in school settings'. *Journal of Child Psychotherapy* 28(2): 129–146.

Jackson, E. (2008) 'The development of work discussion groups in educational settings'. *Journal of Child Psychotherapy* 34(1): 62–82.

Jones, A. (2010) 'The traumatic sequelae of pathological defensive processes in parent–infant relationships'. Chap. 5 in T. Baradon (ed.). *Relational Trauma in Infancy. Psychoanalytic, Attachment and Neuropsychological Contributions to Parent–Infant Psychotherapy*. London and New York: Routledge: 75–87.

Joyce, A. (2010) 'Infantile psychosomatic integrity and maternal trauma'. Chap. 4 in T. Baradon (ed.). *Relational Trauma in Infancy. Psychoanalytic, Attachment and Neuropsychological Contributions to Parent-Infant Psychotherapy*. London and New York: Routledge: 62–74.

Kasinski, K. (2003) 'The roots of the work: definitions, origins and influences'. Chap. 3 in A. Ward, K. Kasinski, J. Pooley, and A. Worthington (eds). *Therapeutic Communities for Children and Young People*. London and New York: Jessica Kingsley: 43–64.

Kempe, C. H., Silverman, F. N., Steele, B. F., Droegemueller, W., and Silver H. K. (1962) 'The battered child syndrome'. *Journal of the American Medical Association* 181(1): 17–24.

Kempe, C. H. (1977) 'Sexual abuse, another hidden paediatric problem'. C. Anderson Aldrich Lecture. *Paediatrics* 62(3): 382–389.

Kennedy, M., Kreppner, J., Knights, N., Kumsta, R., Maugham, B., Golm, D., Rutter, M., Schlotz, W., and Sonuga-Barke, E. (2016) 'Early severe institutional deprivation is associated with a persistent variant of adult attention-deficit/hyperactivity disorder. Clinical presentation, developmental continuities and life circumstances in the English and Romanian Adoption Study'. *Journal of Child Psychology and Psychiatry* 57(10): 1113–1125.

Kenrick, J. (2000) '"Be a kid": the traumatic impact of repeated separations on children who are fostered and adopted'. *Journal of Child Psychotherapy* 26(3): 393–412.

Krystal, H. (1968) *Massive Psychic Trauma*. New York: International Universities Press.

Lanyado, M. (1985) 'Surviving trauma – dilemmas in the psychotherapy of traumatised children'. *British Journal of Psychotherapy* 2(1); and *Bulletin of the British Association of Psychotherapists* July: 50–62.

Lanyado, M. (1988) 'Working with anxiety in a residential special primary school'. *Maladjustment and Therapeutic Education* 6(1): 36–48.

Lanyado, M. (1989) 'United we stand . . .? Stress in residential work with disturbed children'. *Maladjustment and Therapeutic Education* 7(3): 136–146.

Lanyado, M. (1993) 'Stress – an occupational hazard of working with disturbed children'. *Educational Therapy and Therapeutic Teaching* 1(2): 23–38.

Lanyado, M. (2001) 'The symbolism of the story of Lot and his wife: the function of the "present relationship" and non-interpretative aspects of the therapeutic relationship in facilitating change'. *Journal of Child Psychotherapy* 27(1): 19–33.

Lanyado, M. (2002) 'Creating transitions in the lives of children suffering from "multiple traumatic loss"'. Chap. 5 in L. Caldwell (ed.). *The Elusive Child*. London: Karnac: 93–112.

Lanyado, M. (2003) 'The emotional tasks of moving from fostering to adoption: transitions, attachment, separation and loss'. *Clinical Psychology and Psychiatry* (Special Edition on Fostering and Adoption) 8(3): 337–349.

Lanyado, M. (2004a) *The Presence of the Therapist*. Hove, UK: Brunner-Routledge.

Lanyado, M. (2004b) 'Holding and letting go: some thoughts about ending therapy'. Chap. 8 in *The Presence of the Therapist. Treating Childhood Trauma*. London and New York: Brunner-Routledge: 117–130.

Lanyado, M. (2004c) 'The presence of the therapist and the process of therapeutic change'. Chap. 1 in *The Presence of the Therapist. Treating Childhood Trauma*. London and New York: Brunner-Routledge: 3–14.

Lanyado, M. (2004d) 'Struggling with perversion and chaos in the therapeutic process: the need for the patient to "know" the therapist'. Chap. 4 in *The Presence of the Therapist. Treating Childhood Trauma*. London and New York: Brunner-Routledge: 57–72.

Lanyado, M. (2006) 'The playful presence of the therapist: "anti-doting" defences in the therapy of a late adopted adolescent patient'. Chap. 8 in M. Lanyado and A. Horne (eds). *A Question of Technique*. London and New York: Routledge: 13–148.

Lanyado, M. (2008a) 'Dwelling in the present moment'. An exploration of the resonances between transitional experiences and meditative states'. *Psychoanalytic Perspectives* 5(2): 69–85.

Lanyado, M. (2008b) 'Playing out not acting out: the development of the capacity to play in the therapy of children who are "in transition" from fostering to adoption'. Chap. 9 in D. Hindle and G. Shulman (eds). *The Emotional Experience of Adoption. A Psychoanalytic Perspective*. London and New York: Routledge: 155–167.

Lanyado, M. (2009) 'The impact of listening on the listener. Consultation to the helping professions who work with sexually abused young people'. In A. Horne and M. Lanyado (eds). *Through Assessment to Consultation*. London and New York: Routledge: 141–156.

Lanyado, M. (2010) 'Transformation through play: living with the traumas of the past'. Chap. 1 in K. V. Mortensen and L. Grunbaum (eds). *Play and Power*. European Federation of Psychoanalytic Psychotherapists (EFPP) Book Series. London: Karnac Books: 1–20.

Lanyado, M. (2012) 'Transition and change: An exploration of the resonances between transitional and meditative states of mind and their roles in the therapeutic process'. Chap. 8 in A. Horne and M. Lanyado (eds). *Winnicott's Children*. London and New York: Routledge: 123–140.

Lanyado, M. (2014) 'The value of meditative states of mind in the therapist'. In M. Bazzano (ed.). *After Mindfulness*. Basingstoke, UK: Palgrave Macmillan: 148–162.

Lanyado, M. (2016) 'Transforming despair to hope in the treatment of extreme trauma: a view from the supervisor's chair'. *Journal of Child Psychotherapy* 42(2): 107–121.

Lanyado, M. (2017) 'Putting down roots: the significance of technical adaptations in the therapeutic process with fostered and adopted children'. *Journal of Child Psychotherapy* 43(2): 208–222.

Lanyado, M., and Horne, A. (2006) *A Question of Technique*. Independent Psychoanalytic Approaches with Children and Adolescents Series. London and New York: Routledge.

Leach, P. (2016) *When Parents Part: How Mothers and Fathers Can Help Their Children Deal with Separation and Divorce*. New York: Vintage Books.

Lewis, C. S. (1961) *A Grief Observed*. London: Faber and Faber.

Lutz, A., Greischar, L. L., Rawlings, N. B., Ricard, M., and Davidson, R. J. (2004) 'Long-term meditators self-induce high amplitude gamma synchrony during mental practice'. *Proceedings of the National Academy of Sciences of the United States of America* 101: 46.

Main, M. (1995) 'Recent studies in attachment: overview with selected implications for clinical work'. In S. Goldberg, R. Muir and J. Kerr (eds). *Attachment Theory: Social, Developmental and Clinical Perspectives*. Hillsdale, NY: Analytic Press.

Main, M., and Solomon, J. (1986) 'Discovery of an insecure-disorganised/disorientated attachment pattern'. Chap. 6 in T. B. Brazelton and H. Yogman (eds). *Affective Development in Infancy*. Norwood, NJ: Ablex.

Main, M., Kaplan, K., and Cassidy, J. (1985) 'Security in infancy, childhood and adulthood. A move to the level of representation'. In I. Bretherton and E. Waters (eds). *Growing Points of Attachment Theory and Research* (Monograph 50 of the Society for Research in Child Development.) Chicago, IL: University of Chicago Press: 66–104.

Malberg, N. T. (2008) 'Refusing to be excluded: finding ways of integrating psychotherapeutic modalities to the emerging needs of a pupil referral unit'. *Journal of Child Psychotherapy* 34(1): 101–110.

Maltby, J. (2008) 'Consultation in schools: helping staff and pupils with unresolved loss and mourning'. *Journal of Child Psychotherapy* 34(1): 83–100.

Mathers, S., Hardy, G., Clancy, C., Dixon, J., and Harding, C. (2016) *Starting Out Right: Early Education and Looked After Children.* Nuffield Foundation, Oxford: University of Oxford and Family and Childcare Trust.

McDougall, J. (1989) *Theatres of the Body. A Psychoanalytic Approach to Psychosomatic Illness.* London: Free Association Books.

McGilchrist, I. (2009) *The Master and his Emissary. The Divided Brain and the Making of the Western World.* New Haven, CT, and London: Yale University Press.

Melzak, S. (1992) 'Secrecy, privacy, survival, repressive regimes and growing up'. *Bulletin of Anna Freud Clinic* 15: 205–224; and www.freedomfromtorture.org website.

Melzak, S. (2005) 'Using storytelling in psychotherapeutic group work with young refugees'. *Group Analysis* 38(2): 293–306; and www.freedomfromtorture.org website.

Melzak, S. (2017a) 'Building seven bridges with young asylum seekers living in exile in the UK (Part 1)'. *Psychodynamic Practice* 23(3): 235–248.

Melzak, S. (2017b) Personal communication.

Menzies Lyth, I. (1959) 'The functioning of social systems as a defence against anxiety'. In I. Menzies Lyth (eds). *Containing Anxiety in Institutions: Selected Essays* (Vol. 1). London: Free Association Books.

Menzies Lyth, I. (1979) 'Staff support systems: task and anti-task in adolescent institutions'. In I. Menzies Lyth (eds). *Containing Anxiety in Institutions: Selected Essays* (Vol. 1). London: Free Association Books.

Menzies Lyth, I. (1982) 'The psychological welfare of children making long stays in hospital: the art of the possible'. In I. Menzies Lyth (eds). *Containing Anxiety in Institutions: Selected Essays* (Vol. 1). London: Free Association Books.

Menzies Lyth, I. (1985) 'The development of the self in children in institutions'. In I. Menzies Lyth (eds). *Containing Anxiety in Institutions: Selected Essays* (Vol. 1). London: Free Association Books.

Menzies Lyth, I. (1988) *Containing Anxieties in Institutions: Selected Essays* (Vol. 1). London: Free Association Books.

Menzies Lyth, I. (1989) *The Dynamics of the Social. Selected Essays* (Vol. 2). London: Free Association Books.

Menzies Lyth, I. (2004) Personal communication.

Midgley, N. (ed.) (2013) 'The Hampstead war nurseries'. Chap. 5 in *Reading Anna Freud.* New Library of Psychoanalysis. Hove, UK and New York: Routledge: 69–82.

Midgley, N., Anderson, J., Grainger, E., Nesic-Vuckovic, T., and Urwin, C. (2009) *Child Psychotherapy and Research. New Approaches, Emerging Findings.* Hove, UK and New York: Routledge.

Molino, A. (ed.) (1999) *The Couch and the Tree. Dialogues in Psychoanalysis and Buddhism.* London: Constable.

Music, G., and Hall, B. (2008) 'From scapegoating to thinking and finding a home: delivering therapeutic work in schools'. *Journal of Child Psychotherapy* 34(1): 43–61.

Music, G. (2009a) 'The contribution of neuroscience'. In M. Lanyado and A. Horne (eds). *The Handbook of Child and Adolescent Psychotherapy: Psychoanalytic Approaches*, 2nd edn. Hove, UK: Routledge.

Music, G. (2009b) 'Neglecting neglect: some thoughts about children who have lacked good input, and are "undrawn" and "unenjoyed" '. *Journal of Child Psychotherapy* 35(2): 142–156.

Music, G. (2011a) 'Biology and the brain'. Chap. 8 in *Nurturing Natures. Attachment and Children's Emotional, Sociocultural and Brain Development*. Hove, UK and New York: Psychology Press: 83–95.

Music, G. (2011b) 'Trauma, neglect and their effects'. Chap. 17 in *Nurturing Natures. Attachment and Children's Emotional, Sociocultural and Brain Development*. Hove, UK and New York: Psychology Press: 202–210.

Ogden, T. H. (1999) *Reverie and Interpretation: Sensing Something Human*. London: Karnac.

Ogden, T. H. (2009) 'On Psychoanalytic Supervision'. Chap. 3 in *Rediscovering Psychoanalysis: Thinking and Dreaming, Learning and Forgetting*. New Library of Psychoanalysis Series. London and New York: Routledge: 31–49.

Onions, C. (2009) 'Parent-Infant psychotherapy'. Chap. 14 in M. Lanyado and A. Horne (eds). *The Handbook of Child and Adolescent Psychotherapy. Psychoanalytic Approaches*, 2nd edn. London and New York: Routledge: 220–234.

Onions, C., and Browner, J. (2012) 'Spaces for growth. Where milieu therapy and psychotherapy meet'. Chap. 9 in A. Horne and M. Lanyado (eds). *Winnicott's Children*. Independent Psychoanalytic Approaches with Children and Adolescents Series. London and New York: Routledge: 143–156.

Ottoway, C., and Selwyn, J. (2016) *'No-one told us it was going to be like this'. Compassion Fatigue and Foster Carers*. Bristol, UK: University of Bristol.

Papadopoulos, R.K. (2002) *Therapeutic Care for Refugees. No Place like Home*. London: Karnac.

Parkes, C. M. (1972) 'The cost of commitment'. Chap. 1 in C. M. Parkes (ed.). *Bereavement: Studies of Grief in Adult Life*. Harmondsworth, UK: Pelican Books.

Parsons, M. (2000) 'Vocation and martial art'. In *The Dove that Returns, the Dove that Vanishes*. New Library of Psychoanalysis. London: Routledge.

Parsons, M. (2006) 'Ways of transformation'. In D. M. Black (ed.). *Psychoanalysis and Religion in the 21st Century: Competitors or Collaborators?* New Library of Psychoanalysis. London: Routledge.

Parsons, M. (2009) 'The roots of violence: theory and implications for technique with children and adolescents'. Chap. 24 in M. Lanyado and A. Horne (eds). *The Handbook of Child and Adolescent Psychotherapy*, 2nd edn. London and New York: Routledge: 361–380.

Parsons, M. (2014) 'Listening out, listening in, looking out looking in'. Chap. 8 in *Living Psychoanalysis*. London and New York: Routledge: 113–136.

Parsons, M. (2014) 'An independent theory of technique'. Chap. 12 in *Living Psychoanalysis*. London and New York: Routledge: 184–204.

Pecotic, B. (2002) Interview with Isabel Menzies Lyth. *Organisational and Social Dynamics* 2(1): 2–44.

Phillips, A. (1988) *Winnicott*. Fontana Modern Masters Series. London: Fontana Press.

Pozzi Monzo, M. (2014) *The Buddha and the Baby. Psychotherapy and Meditation in Working with Children and Adults*. London: Karnac.

Raphael. B. (1984) *The Anatomy of Bereavement: Handbook for the Caring Professions*. New York: Jason Aronson.

Reeves, C. (2002) 'A necessary conjunction: Dockar-Drysdale and Winnicott'. *Journal of Child Psychotherapy* 28(1): 3–27.

Ricard, M. (2007) *Happiness*. London: Atlantic Books.

Robertson, J. (1953) *A Two Year Old Goes to Hospital* (16-mm film, 40 minute and 30 minute versions in English and French). Ipswich, UK: Concord Video and Film Council.

Robertson, J., and Robertson, J. (1989) *Separation and the Very Young*. London: Free Association Books.

Robinson, F., Luyten, P., and Midgley, N. (2017) 'Child psychotherapy with looked after and adopted children: A UK national survey of the profession'. *Journal of Child Psychotherapy* 43(2): 1–20.

Rose, M. (1990) *Healing Hurt Minds: The Peper Harow Experience*. London: Tavistock/ Routledge.

Rubin, J. B. (2006) 'Psychoanalysis and spirituality'. In D. M. Black (ed.). *Psychoanalysis and Religion in the 21st Century: Competitors or Collaborators?* New Library of Psychoanalysis. London: Routledge.

Ryz, P., and Wilson G. (1999) 'Endings as gain'. *Journal of Child Psychotherapy* 25(3): 379–403.

Sayder, S. (2008) 'Joining up with "not us" staff to run adolescent groups in schools'. *Journal of Child Psychotherapy*, 34(1): 111–126.

Schachter, J., Martin, G. C., Gundle, M. J., and O'Neill, M. K. (1997) 'Clinical experience with post-termination meetings'. *International Journal of Psycho-Analysis* 78(6): 1183–1198.

Schore, A. (2003) *Affect Disregulation and Disorders of the Self*. New York: Norton.

Solomon, J., and George, C. (eds) (1999) *Attachment Disorganisation*. London and New York: Guilford Press.

Searles, H. (1955) 'The informational value of the supervisor's emotional experiences'. In *Collected papers on Schizophrenia and Related Subjects* (1965). New York: International Universities Press: 157–176.

Selwyn, J., Wijedasa, D., and Meakins, S. (2014) 'Beyond the adoption order: challenges, interventions and adoption disruption'. Bristol, UK: University of Bristol.

Simmonds, J. (2008) 'Developing a curiosity about adoption'. In D. Hindle and G. Shulman (eds). *The Emotional Experience of Adoption: a Psychoanalytic Perspective*. Abingdon, UK: Routledge.

Simmonds, J. (2009) 'Adoption: developmental perspectives within an ethical, legal and policy framework'. In G. Schofield and J. Simmonds (eds). *The Child Placement Handbook*. London: BAAF.

Simmonds, J. (2013) 'The making and breaking of relationships: organizational and clinical questions in establishing a family life for looked after children?'. In M. Tarrent Sweeney and A. Vetere (eds). *Mental Health Services for Vulnerable Children and Young People*. London: Routledge.

Sloan Donachy, G. (2017) 'The caregiving relationships under stress: foster parents' experience of loss of sense of self'. *Journal of Child Psychotherapy* 43(2): 223–242.

Solnit, R. (2016) *Hope in the Dark. Untold Histories. Wild Possibilities*. Edinburgh, UK: Cannongate Books.

Solomon, J., and George, C. (1999) *Attachment Disorganisation*. New York: Guilford Press.

Sprince, J. (2002) 'Developing containment: psychoanalytic consultancy to a therapeutic community for traumatised children'. *Journal of Child Psychotherapy* 28(2): 147–161.

Sterba, R. (1934) 'The fate of the ego in analytic therapy'. *International Journal of Psycho-Analysis* 15: 117–126.

Stern, D. (1985) *The Interpersonal World of the Infant: A View from Psychoanalysis and Developmental Psychology*. New York: Basic Books.

Stern, D., Sander, L., Nahum, J., Harrison A., Lyons-Ruth, K., Morgan A., Bruschweiler-Stern, N., and Tronick, E. (1998) 'Non-interpretive mechanisms in psychoanalytic therapy: the "something more" than interpretation'. *International Journal of Psycho-Analysis* 79: 903–921.

Sternberg, J. (2005) *Infant Observation at the Heart of Training.* London: Karnac.

Sternberg, J. (2006) 'Not simply "doing": thoughts from the literature on technique'. Chap. 3 in M. Lanyado and A. Horne (eds). *A Question of Technique.* Independent Psychoanalytic Approaches with Children and Adolescents Series. Hove, UK and New York: Routledge: 34–59.

Sternberg, J. (2016) 'A child psychotherapist's way of engaging in assessments for the courts'. *Journal of Child Psychotherapy* 42(3), 328–340.

Sylva, K., Melhuish, E., Sammons P., Siraj-Blatchford, I., and Taggart, B. (eds) (2010) *Early Childhood Matters: Evidence from the effective pre-school and primary school project.* London: Routledge.

Symington, N. (1994) *Emotion and Spirit: Questioning the Claims of Psychoanalysis and Religion.* London: Karnac.

Tronick, E. Z. (2003) 'Of course all relationships are unique: how co-creative processes generate unique mother–infant and parent–therapist relationships and change other relationships'. *Psychoanalytic Inquiry* 23(3): 473–491.

Tustin, F. (1986) *Autistic Barriers in Neurotic Patients.* London: Karnac.

Tustin, F. (1994) 'The perpetuation of an error'. *Journal of Child Psychotherapy* 20(1): 3–23.

Van der Kolk, B. A. (1987) *Psychological Trauma.* Washington, DC: American Psychiatric Press.

Van Ijzendoorn, M. H., and Sagi, A. (1999) 'Cross-cultural patterns of attachment. Universal and contextual dimensions'. Chap. 31 in J. Cassidy and P. R. Shaver (eds). *Handbook of Attachment. Theory, Research and Clinical Applications.* London and New York: Guilford Press: 713–734.

Vastardis M., and Phillips, G. (2012) 'On psychoanalytic supervision: avoiding omniscience, encouraging play'. Chap. 7 in A. Horne and M. Lanyado (eds). *Winnicott's Children.* Independent Psychoanalytic Approaches with Children and Adolescents Series. London and New York: Routledge: 105–122.

Viorst, J. (1986/1998) *Necessary Losses.* New York: Fireside Books.

Wallerstein, J., and Lewis, J. M. (2004) 'The unexpected legacy of divorce: Report of a 25-year study'. *Psychoanalytic Psychology* 21(3): 353–370.

Wallerstein, J., and Resnikoff, D. (1997) 'Parental divorce and developmental progressions: An enquiry into their relationship'. *International Journal of Psycho-Analysis* 78: 135–154.

Ward, A. (2003) 'Using everyday life: opportunity-led work'. Chap. 7 in A. Ward, K. Kasinski, J. Pooley, and A. Worthington (eds). *Therapeutic Communities for Children and Young People.* London and New York: Jessica Kingsley: 119–132.

Ward, A., Kasinski, K., Pooley, J., and Worthington, A. (2003) *Therapeutic Communities for Children and Young People.* London and New York: Jessica Kingsley.

Ward, A., and McMahon, L. (eds) (1998) *Intuition Is Not Enough. Matching Learning with Practice in Therapeutic Child Care.* London and New York: Routledge.

Welwood, J. (ed.) (1983) *Awakening the Heart. East/West Approaches to Psychotherapy and the Healing Relationship.* Boulder, CO, and London: New Science Library, Shambala.

Wilson, P. (1991) 'Review of "Consultation in Residential Care"'. *Journal of Child Psychotherapy* 18(1).

Wilson, P. (1999/2009) 'Consultation in residential care'. Chap. 18 in M. Lanyado and A. Horne (eds). *The Handbook of Child and Adolescent Psychotherapy. Psychoanalytic Approaches*, 2nd edn. London and New York: Routledge: 276–284.

Wilson, P. (2003) 'Consultation and supervision'. Chap. 14 in A. Ward, K. Kasinski, J. Pooley and A. Worthington (eds). *Therapeutic Communities for Children and Young People*. London and New York: Jessica Kingsley: 220–232.

Wilson, P. (2009) 'Delinquency'. Chap. 26 in M. Lanyado and A. Horne (eds). *The Handbook of Child and Adolescent Psychotherapy. Psychoanalytic Approaches*, 2nd edn. London and New York: Routledge: 406–422.

Winnicott, D. W. (1947/1949) 'Hate in the counter-transference'. Chap. 3 in L. Caldwell and A. Joyce (eds) (2011) *Reading Winnicott*. New Library of Psychoanalysis. London and New York: Routledge: 70–82. Online Collected Works of D. W. Winnicott www.oxfordclinicalpsych.com 3:2:1.

Winnicott, D.W. (1949) 'Mind and its relation to the psyche-soma'. Chap. 19 in D. W. Winnicott (1958) *Collected Papers. Through Paediatrics to Psycho-Analysis*. London: Tavistock Publications. Online Collected Works of D. W. Winnicott www.oxford clinicalpsych.com 3:4:20.

Winnicott, D. W. (1956) 'Primary maternal preoccupation'. Chap. 24 in D. W. Winnicott (1958) *Collected Papers. Through Paediatrics to Psycho-Analysis* (1958). London: Tavistock Publications: 300–305. Collected Works. Online Collected Works of D. W. Winnicott www.oxfordclinicalpsych.com 5:2:16.

Winnicott, D. W. (1958) 'The capacity to be alone'. Chap. 2 in D. W. Winnicott (1965) *The Maturational Processes and the Facilitating Environment*. London: Hogarth Press and Institute of Psychoanalysis: 29–36. Online Collected Works of D. W. Winnicott www.oxfordclinicalpsych.com 5:3:20.

Winnicott, D. W. (1960) 'The theory of the parent-infant relationship'. Chap. 7 in L. Caldwell and A. Joyce (eds) (2011) *Reading Winnicott*. New Library of Psychoanalysis. London and New York: Routledge: 147–181. Online Collected Works of D. W. Winnicott www.oxfordclinicalpsych.com 6:1:20.

Winnicott, D. W. (1964) *The Child the Family and the Outside World*. Harmondsworth, UK: Penguin Books.

Winnicott, D. W. (1965) *The Maturational Processes and the Facilitating Environment*, London: Hogarth Press.

Winnicott, D. W. (1971a) *Playing and Reality*. London: Tavistock; reprinted 1974. Harmondsworth, UK: Pelican.

Winnicott, D. W. (1971b/1953) 'Transitional objects and transitional phenomena'. Chap. 1 in D. W. Winnicott (1971a) *Playing and Reality*. London: Tavistock: 1–30; reprinted 1974. Harmondsworth, UK: Pelican. Online Collected Works of D. W. Winnicott www. oxfordclinicalpsych.com 3:6:6.

Winnicott, D. W. (1971c) 'The place where we live'. Chap. 8 in D. W. Winnicott (1971a). *Playing and Reality*. London: Tavistock: 122–129; reprinted 1974. Harmondsworth, UK: Pelican. Online Collected Works of D. W. Winnicott www.oxfordclinicalpsych.com 8:2:1.

Winnicott, D. W. (1971d/1967) 'Playing: a theoretical statement'. Chap. 3 in D. W. Winnicott (1971a). *Playing and Reality*. London: Tavistock; reprinted 1974, Harmondsworth, UK: Penguin: 44–61. Online Collected Works of D. W. Winnicott www.oxfordclinicalpsych.com 8:2:15.

Index

For Product Safety Concerns and Information please contact our EU
representative GPSR@taylorandfrancis.com
Taylor & Francis Verlag GmbH, Kaufingerstraße 24, 80331 München, Germany

www.ingramcontent.com/pod-product-compliance
Lightning Source LLC
Chambersburg PA
CBHW070426270326
41926CB00014B/2962